"*Technology-Based Training* provides a practical and highly useful perspective on how to tackle the world of learning and technology. Enjoy and learn!"

—*Elliott Masie,*
The Masie Institute

"*Technology-Based Training* is a must-read for anyone thinking about moving toward web delivery as a technology solution for performance improvement. Kruse and Keil build an easy-to-understand case for moving toward web-based training and also provide a great base of knowledge for designers of training."

—*Barbara Stebbins,*
supervisor of design, Ford

"Kevin Kruse has been there and done that with technology-based training. He knows what to anticipate and consider in the design of effective programs, and he knows how to help people to get the results they want."

—*Todd Macalister, president,*
Charles River Instructional Systems

"*Technology-Based Training* comes at the best time for our industry. We are all searching for ways to fully utilize the recent advances in technology to improve performance. Kruse and Keil take you step by step through the whole process."

—*Jim DeMaioribus, director, sales training,*
Ortho-McNeil Pharmaceuticals

"A model of clarity and common sense. Kruse and Keil debug and demystify the development of technology-based training, while giving the sector its due respect as a new potent global industry."

—*Kieran J. McBrien, CEO,*
Transware Ltd.

"Finally! A book that brings grounding to the promising, multibillion dollar on-line training market. A must-read for anyone serious about entering this market."

—*Shanti Mittra, investment manager,*
Primus Venture Partners

"Whether you are in the midst of a project or just thinking about one, *Technology-Based Training* is an invaluable resource book to keep by your side. The examples, case studies, and plain English style explain everything you need to know to make TBT work for you."

—*Mohit Bhargava, principal,*
Aptech Worldwide Inc.

"A little art, a little science—and a wealth of ideas for the designer and the learning professional."

—*Virginia Bandremer,*
organization effectiveness consultant

Technology-Based Training

Technology-Based Training

THE ART AND SCIENCE OF DESIGN, DEVELOPMENT, AND DELIVERY

Kevin Kruse
Jason Keil

San Francisco

ISBN: 0-7879-4626-5

Library of Congress Cataloging-in-Publication Data
Kruse, Kevin.
    Technology-based training : the art and science of design,
development, and delivery / Kevin Kruse, Jason Keil.
       p.   cm.
    Includes bibliographical references and index.
    ISBN 0-7879-4626-5
    1. Employees—Training of—Computer-assisted instruction.
2. Computer-assisted instruction. 3. Occupational training
—Computer-assisted instruction. I. Keil, Jason. II. Title.
HF5549.5.T7K72 1999
658.3'12404—dc21   99-44485

Printed in the United States of America

Published by

Jossey-Bass
Pfeiffer
350 Sansome Street, 5th Floor
San Francisco, California 94104-1342
(415) 433-1740; Fax (415) 433-0499
(800) 274-4434; Fax (800) 569-0443

Visit our website at: www.pfeiffer.com

Acquiring Editor: Matthew Holt
Director of Development: Kathleen Dolan Davies
Developmental Editor: Susan Rachmeler
Senior Production Editor: Pamela Berkman
Cover Design: Tom Morgan/Blue Design

Printing   10   9   8   7   6   5   4   3   2   1

 This book is printed on acid-free, recycled stock that meets or exceeds the minimum GPO and EPA requirements for recycled paper.

CONTENTS

FOREWORD

This is a truly exciting time for learning and training professionals. The role of technology in our society, in our organizations, and in our views of learning is creating a unique moment of innovation, experimentation, and excitement.

Every week, several new products or services are announced in the learning and training field. Major technology departments have integrated the concept of knowledge transfer and management into the core of their offerings and plans. And words about the importance of learning and workforce skills are now heard on the lips of CEOs and other senior executives.

Driving this excitement (or even frenzy) are several core business needs:

- Organizations must develop ways of delivering learning and skills to the workforce on a continuous rapid basis. As our organizations operate on "Internet time," where cycles are measured in hours and days rather than months or years, the delivery models and methods for training must keep pace.

- Organizations must develop ways of creating a huge collection of learning assets, at a faster authoring rate and with a lower cost per module. As consumers, we are being spoiled by the vastness of the Internet and are demanding similar quantity of learning choice at work.

- Organizations must develop ways of distributing information, skills, and attitudes to the widest part of the enterprise, increasingly scattered across the globe.

- Organizations must develop ways of blending the power of the classroom with the potential of technology to extend and enrich face-to-face learning situations.

Most of this is good news for the developer or buyer of learning resources. Our choices and resources are expanding, and the learning function is getting a new charge of respect. However, all of this activity can also be confusing and disabling. Our colleagues are asking important questions to guide them in starting their work in the digital age of learning:

- How do we get started? What are the first steps in implementing a learning technology pilot or project in our organization?

- How is learning and training different when it is delivered from a computer screen rather than by an instructor and a flipchart?

- How do we apply good instructional design models to learning technology, while allowing learners greater choice in the application of scope and sequence?

- How do we cope with the ever changing and improving technology? Can we make wise learning investments when everything is changing continuously?

- If we build it, will they come? How do we market learning programs in ways that will capture the attention and interest of our workforce?

These issues are the core of the agenda for the learning and training community in the next several years. We need to draw upon what we have learned over thousands of years about how adults transfer knowledge and skills. We need to apply and adapt good instructional design theory and practice to the world of learning technology. And we need to study emerging perspectives on how people are adding technology to their lives. A tall and exciting set of marching orders for our field.

In my twenty-five years of experience in the training world, I have seen many trends and fads come and go. The learning technology opportunity is much more than a trend. It is a fundamental shift in how our society handles information and knowledge. Future generations will compare this moment to the introduction of the printing press. And we are in the first years of this revolution, where experimentation, reflection, and even a few failures are core to the innovation process. I would humbly urge my colleagues to consider these thoughts as they help invent the future:

- *Try what you are selling!* It is critical that we develop our own tastes and preferences in the learning technology world. I am amazed when I meet developers and designers who have never taken a course delivered over the Web, yet are creating products they assume others will like.

- *Pilot, test, beta and feedback!* Label your first several projects as pilots or experiments. This changes the way in which the learner and even your boss views the efforts. In a pilot, I focus and provide feedback on what could make the learning better. Once it is packaged as a "done deal," we hear more comments about what it is not. We should also avoid locking into one approach or design before testing several models.

- *Don't forget what we know!* Sometimes technology can seduce us into thinking that a cool spinning logo will make a learning program more effective. Not! Remember that the training process continues to be about mapping the needs of a learner to master a set of information that will make them better at performing a work task. Don't lose the training dialogue in the midst of a technology fascination.

- *Collaborate as you invent!* The MASIE Center found that over 92 percent of large- and medium-size organizations are building new training programs with some form of technology-based delivery. Turn to your training and learning colleagues in other organizations as peers for collaboration and discovery. Dare to share even your flops; they will reciprocate with theirs. Invention happens when we can leverage the wisdom of multiple organizations and individuals.

Technology-Based Training provides a practical and highly useful perspective on how to tackle the world of learning and technology. Enjoy and learn!

Sarasota Springs, New York
August 1999

Elliott Masie

Elliott Masie is president of The MASIE Center, an international think tank focused on learning and technology. He is the author of *TechLearn Trends,* a free weekly newsletter on changes in the world of knowledge transfer. His web site is http://www.masie.com

To my wife, Beth—thank you for your patience and support while this book stole away so many nights and weekends. I love you.

—*Kevin Kruse*

To my father for making me who I am, to my mother for making me want to write, to my brother and sisters for making me laugh, and to Jenny for making me love her.

—*Jason Keil*

ACKNOWLEDGMENTS

All books require a tremendous team effort, and this one was no different. While only two names adorn the cover and receive the glory, there are many individuals whose contributions were just as critical to the success of this project.

Trish Krotowski organized our thoughts, turned ramblings into prose, and provided tremendous moral support throughout the process. Trish, thanks for teaching us how to tame "the beast."

We'd like to thank Jennifer Sapala for her excellent work creating the illustrations, screen images, and various cover designs under impossible deadlines.

Carlos Fernandez, Steve Krichten, and Lynn Cain created the companion CD-ROM and Web site. Their work brings to life the full dynamism and creativity of technology-based training, which cannot be truly known through this black and white text.

Lynn Cain also provided invaluable production assistance, organization, and scheduling support. Thanks for being the gatekeeper and saying no to all those who wanted meetings on "book days."

Thanks to everyone who reviewed early sections of the book, with special acknowledgment to Brendan Watson for his detailed feedback on each and every chapter.

We are especially grateful to our editors at Jossey-Bass/Pfeiffer, Matt Holt and Susan Rachmeler, for giving us this opportunity and adding the polish to our manuscript.

Most important, we are indebted to the TBT professionals at Raymond Karsan Associates, the most dedicated TBT team on the planet, who work daily to turn the abstract ideas in this book into concrete solutions for our clients. Thank you, Jennifer Barilla, Joel Basa, Adam Bauser, Mike Boudreau, Lynn Cain, Wendy Collins, Carlos Fernandez, Andy Howe, Sanghun Kim, Steve Krichten, Amy Madia, Joe Martin, Todd Matthiessen, Chris Maynard, R.J. Melia, April Murray, Carol Robotti, Jen Sapala, Stephen Scarpulla, Dave Schmoyer, Christine Shugg, Andrew Szemiot, Andrea Tucci, Brendan Watson, Jon Wilson, and Navarrow Wright.

Acknowledgments

Introduction

The pace of change in the world of technology has truly become breathless. People now talk about Internet years the same way they talk about dog years—at least seven to one human year. As always, these changes bring both new challenges and exciting opportunities. The application of technology for learning has moved way beyond the early adopters and is now a core component of most organizations' strategies for developing human assets.

The goal of this book is to teach you how to design, develop, and manage technology-based training (TBT) programs that will get measurable results for your organization. This book does *not* teach you the specific tasks related to scripting, creating media, or programming. Rather, it provides you with the fundamental principles behind quality instruction, interface design, project management, vendor relations, and program evaluation.

WHO SHOULD READ THIS BOOK

Technology-Based Training was written for anyone who wants to learn how to develop, manage, or sell effective CD-ROM and Web-based training programs. The book provides training managers, instructors, instructional designers, consultants, and developers with guidelines, worksheets, and tools for ensuring that their programs achieve actual business results. Information technology professionals will also gain insights into the world of training and development and will learn how to support the performance goals of the organization. Finally, this book provides a crash course for senior executives who want to understand if TBT is a sound investment for their organization.

WHAT THE BOOK COVERS

This book is organized into three parts. Part One, "Designing Effective Technology-Based Training," presents the elements of programs that are effective and engaging and that get measurable business results. Chapter One introduces the basic concepts of TBT, including a myriad of terms and acronyms. Chapter Two addresses the fundamental first question, Should this program be developed on CD-ROM or as Web-based training? Chapter Three provides an overview of the systematic project development process that ensures on-time, on-budget, high-quality development. Chapter Four presents the key principles of adult learning theory, along with specific examples of how these concepts are applied to TBT script development. Chapter Five covers user interface design principles that apply specifically to the field of TBT.

Part Two, "Managing Technology-Based Training," builds on the theoretical aspects of Part One and walks through the business aspects of TBT. Chapter Six explains the importance of measuring the financial impact of your training programs and presents a step-by-step methodology for calculating the return on the investment. Chapter Seven, written especially for training managers, covers vendor selection as well as vendor management. Chapter Eight explains the needs of senior management and how to internally promote TBT investments in a manner that addresses these needs.

Part Three, "Case Studies," shows how the abstract concepts reviewed in Parts One and Two have been applied in real-world TBT projects. Chapter Nine presents a CD-ROM–based project undertaken with a major pharmaceutical company. Chapter Ten reviews a CD-ROM–based instructional software simulation developed for a beverage company. Chapter Eleven walks through a low-bandwidth Web-based training product that covers interviewing skills. Chapter Twelve covers a high-bandwidth Web-based training program developed for a major airline.

The appendixes provide a variety of tools and additional resources that can immediately be used on the job, including a model request for proposal (RFP), a model proposal response, worksheets for calculating financial returns, and lists of additional resources for ongoing education.

HOW TO USE THE ACCOMPANYING CD-ROM AND WEB SITE

Many of the job aids, templates, worksheets, Web sites, and samples introduced in this book can be accessed via the accompanying CD-ROM or on the complementary Web site. The CD-ROM contains:

- *Job aids.* These aids include checklists and questionnaires that will help you evaluate interfaces, select vendors, and more.
- *Slide shows.* PowerPoint presentations are included that provide detailed information about the features and benefits of Web-based training and the principles of instructional design. They can be used to educate your peers or to build a business case with senior executives.
- *Web-based training demos.* Even if you don't have Internet access, use your Web browser to access these Web-based training tutorials. Examples include an overview of clinical pharmacology, and instructions on how to conduct job interviews.
- *Sample documents.* Use these templates to generate an RFP, design document, or script.
- *Web links.* Use your Web browser to access this page of bookmarked Internet Web sites related to the field of technology-based training.

The following minimum specifications are required for accessing the included documents, demos, and Web sites:

- 486 or Pentium processor–based personal computer
- Microsoft Windows 95 or Windows NT 3.51 or later
- Minimum RAM: 32 MB or higher
- 4X speed CD-ROM drive or faster
- SoundBlaster-compatible audio card with speakers
- 800 × 600 screen resolution with 256 colors or higher
- Netscape Navigator 4.0 or MS Internet Explorer 4.0 or higher Web browser

- Microsoft Word version 6.0 for Windows 95 or later
- Microsoft PowerPoint version 4.0 for Windows 95 or later

To access the Internet, a 28.8 baud modem or faster connection is required.

For additional instructions on accessing the files, view the README text file on the CD-ROM.

When customizing documents, be sure to save them to your desktop or hard drive, rather than to the CD-ROM. Open the document and use the "Save As" command to rename the file to make sure you create an editable file.

To obtain ongoing information and tools, to communicate with other training professionals, and to contact the authors directly, connect to the Internet and use your Web browser to link up with the Technology-Based Training Supersite at <www.tbtsupersite.com>.

part one

Designing Effective Technology-Based Training

Overview of Technology-Based Training

Don't look up before you've finished reading this paragraph because the world as you know it may have changed. It certainly feels that way these days, doesn't it? The world of business and the world of technology are changing at a breakneck pace. For training professionals, the impact of these changes is compounded—and sometimes overwhelming. This book seeks to give training professionals who are unfamiliar with technology-based training (TBT) a tool for wading through the myths and misconceptions surrounding TBT. It is intended to help you determine if TBT can solve some of your business challenges and guide you in selecting TBT that suits your needs.

Although training has evolved significantly over the last thirty years, it is technology, the much more volatile part of TBT, that makes this subject area so exciting and so potentially frightening. But don't worry. Training is the focus and root of the term *technology-based training* and by anchoring yourself to the fundamentals of effective training you can keep from getting lost in the sometimes stormy sea of bits, bytes, and bandwidth. Trust your instincts about what is and what isn't good training. Remember that the bottom line in TBT, as with so many things in life, isn't the package but the contents. Feel free to look up now, but if the world has changed while you were reading, don't say I didn't warn you.

What You Will Learn in This Chapter

- How TBT is defined

- Terms related to TBT

- The most commonly used classifications of TBT programs

- The role of interactivity in good TBT products

- Some of the advantages and disadvantages of TBT

- The roles and responsibilities of TBT team members

- What tools are needed to develop TBT

WHAT IS TECHNOLOGY-BASED TRAINING?

TBT can be a confusing topic in part because of the alphabet soup of acronyms, technology-related buzzwords, overlapping definitions, variety of delivery options, and converging histories of the two disciplines of technology and training. In the current marketplace, what most people really mean when they use the term *technology-based training* (and its multiple synonyms) is multimedia CD-ROM and Web-based training. Training products that take these forms are the particular focus of this book.

Defining Technology-Based Training

TBT is really nothing more than using technology to deliver training and educational materials.

Technology-based training is the all-inclusive term for training delivered by a number of means. In the past, these have included the use of mainframe computers, floppy diskettes, multimedia CD-ROMs, and interactive videodisks. Most recently, Internet and Intranet delivery have become preferred delivery options.

Intellectual Heritage of Technology-Based Training

Psychological theories of learning, particularly of adult learning, come to bear on TBT. Good instruction, administered in the form of TBT or through traditional methods, should be based on established theories of learning.

To paraphrase Robert Gagné, a seminal thinker in the field of instructional design, instruction is the set of events that initiate learning in an individual.

Teaching is similarly defined as the set of events that may have a direct effect on an individual's learning. Instruction may include events generated by a page of print, a lecture, a picture, a television program, objects on a computer screen, animation, or physical objects assembled in a way to facilitate learning.

A discussion of what learning is, is significantly stickier than a discussion of what instruction is. An overly simplified definition of learning that will serve my purpose here is *the acquisition of desired traits, knowledge, and skills, and the ability to utilize them.*

Notice that none of our definitions of instruction, teaching, and learning make any reference to a teacher. Instead, they focus on the interaction between the learner and the set of events that influence learning. Thus we have come upon one of the tenets on which TBT is founded: instruction, teaching, and learning do not necessarily require a teacher.

Exponential Growth in Use of TBT

Intuition can largely guide you to what can and cannot be trained with TBT. It is safe to assert that a computer will never be able to teach one human being how to love another. But it will be limiting if we assume too many restrictions on what can be accomplished by TBT. Can a computer product aid in teaching managers how to deal empathetically with their employees? That is just what Raymond Karsan Associates' Management Results, discussed in Chapter Eleven, and similar soft-skills training programs are doing. By comparison, *Training* magazine estimates that by the year 2000 fully 50 percent of all of corporate training interventions will be delivered via CD-ROM or corporate Intranets (Lakewood Publications, 1998). As computer systems proliferate and more importantly, as trainers realize the potential of TBT, expenditures on TBT will continue to increase.

The projected 100 percent annual growth rate in TBT (International Data Group, 1998) is being driven by increases in the availability of network bandwidth, the decreasing price of multimedia computers, and the development of more services and products from vendors. This trend will have a huge impact on the way organizations look at professional training and education. Businesses will be faced with the pressure of transforming from being places where employees come to work and produce to being environments in which employees learn and grow. Perhaps nobody's life will be changed more than the training managers and instructors of today's workforce. Keeping up with new technology, managing new vendor relationships, tracking bigger budgets, and providing more accountability to senior executives are but some of the new challenges to face.

Terms Associated with TBT

Understanding what is and what isn't TBT can be confusing due to the wealth of terms that exist to define the same thing. Some people prefer the phrase *learning to training* ("dogs are trained, people learn") and use the term *technology-based learning* (TBL) instead of technology-based training. In business, where most companies have training departments rather than learning departments, the term *technology-based training* is most frequently encountered. For that reason, and as a matter of personal preference, this is the term that will be used throughout the book.

Other commonly used terms include *computer-based training* (CBT), *computer-based learning* (CBL), *computer-based instruction* (CBI), *computer-based education* (CBE), *Web-based training* (WBT), *Internet-based training* (IBT), *Intranet-based training* (also IBT), *browser-based training* (BBT), and any number of others (see Figure 1.1). Some of these, such as WBT, can be seen as specific subsections of TBT while others, notably computer-based training, are less specific. Other confusion arises from technical definitions that differ from their

Figure 1.1
Synonyms for TBT

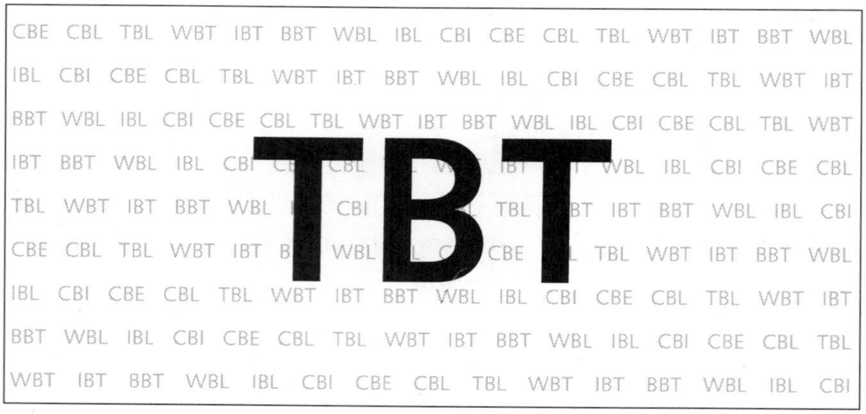

popular use. For example, the terms CBT, CBI, and CBL are sometimes used generically to refer to all types of TBT but are generally used to describe older disk-based training.

A term beginning with the word *computer* frequently but not always refers to interactive tutorials distributed on floppy diskettes. The term *multimedia training* is usually used to describe training delivered via CD-ROM. This rule of thumb is complicated by the fact that advances in Internet technology now make it possible for network-based training to deliver audio and video elements as well.

Distance learning, another commonly used term, accurately describes many types of TBT, but it is most often used to describe interactive satellite videoconferences and the use of the Internet/Intranet by live instructors to facilitate a training class.

To further complicate matters, some theorists divide TBT into three distinct branches: computer-aided instruction (CAI), computer-managed instruction (CMI), and computer-supported learning resources (CSLR) (see Figure 1.2). The first term, CAI, encompasses the portion of a given TBT product that provides the instruction, such as the tutorials, simulations, and exercises. The second term, CMI, refers to the testing, record keeping, and study guidance functions of a TBT product. The last term, CSLR, encompasses the communication, database, and

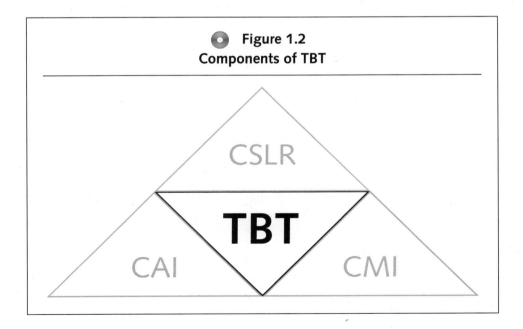

Figure 1.2
Components of TBT

CSLR

TBT

CAI   CMI

performance support aspects of TBT. Although these distinctions can prove useful in academic research and discussion, it is enough for most of us to know that they exist and that they all refer to parts of the greater whole, TBT.

Types of TBT

Just as there are many names for TBT itself, there are many names for *types* of TBT. For an analogy, consider how you might categorize a movie. Is it a blockbuster or an independent film, a psychological thriller or a comedy, a family film or an adult film, a short film or a long film, a good film or a bad film? Similarly, TBT products are often segmented according to some sampling of their characteristics. It is good to remember that each TBT product is unique and its value is determined solely on the basis of its ability to be used by an audience to learn materials relevant to their needs. That being said, classifications can be made. Three types of classification are prevalent: by delivery method, by mode of instruction, and by level of interactivity. The first of these, delivery method, will be discussed in Chapter Two. For now, let's focus on the other two.

MODES OF TECHNOLOGY-BASED TRAINING

A number of fundamental modes of training or instructional models make up the backbone of valid and valuable training. Although any of these can be used as a guide no matter what type of technology is chosen, the specific strengths and weaknesses of each particular training mode should be considered in order to maximize learner benefits.

Tutorials

Tutorials are one of the most ancient and commonly used modes of training. A good tutorial, based on the ones administered by Socrates millennia ago, engages the learner in a dialogue, requiring some form of interaction before moving from one area of instruction to another. Many tutorials basically consist of a linear presentation of content. When implemented poorly, a tutorial can become what is derisively referred to as an *electronic page-turner,* or *scroller.* This type of program presents content directly without giving the learner any opportunity to interact other than to call for the next screen. When implemented properly, using the classic principles of instructional systems design, guided tutorials can be engaging and effective. The key to useful tutorials in TBT are interactions that establish pace, clarify content, and instill confidence.

Branching can greatly enhance the effectiveness of a tutorial, allowing it to operate in the way a skilled teacher does. A question posed following an instructional moment can determine whether the student has mastered the content. If mastery is not achieved, one branch is followed and another approach is provided to eliminate confusion. Only after mastery is achieved is the branch containing the next piece of information followed. Figures 1.3, 1.4, and 1.5 illustrate the differences between a linear structure, a simple branching structure, and a complex branching structure. Note how many additional screens need to be created when a complex branching is used in place of linear presentation of content.

Simulations

Realism is the key to successful simulations, but not every element of a simulation has to be realistic in order for it to be instructionally valid. Although hearing a telephone ring in the background of an office simulation adds to the depth of the user's experience, being able to answer that phone and talk with a customer adds value to the user's learning experience. Simulations are often used to recreate lifelike job situations.

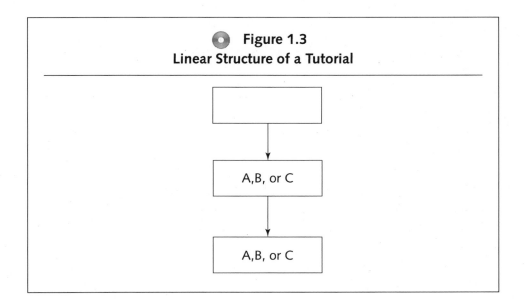

**Figure 1.3
Linear Structure of a Tutorial**

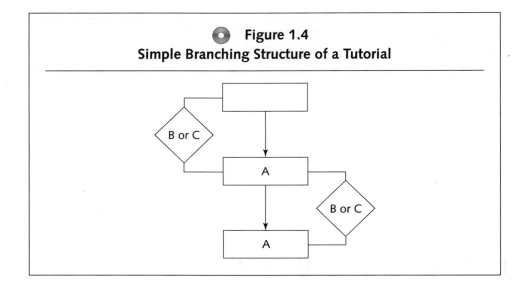

Figure 1.4
Simple Branching Structure of a Tutorial

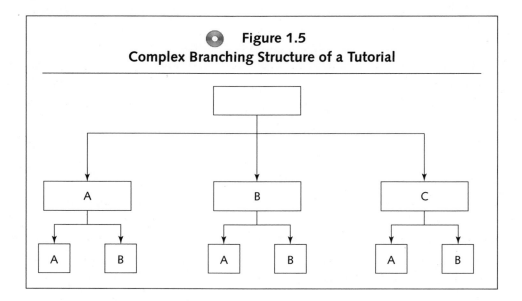

Figure 1.5
Complex Branching Structure of a Tutorial

The best example of a simulation is the complex flight simulator employed by pilots. More commonly encountered simulations are the scenarios deployed in training classrooms as role-playing exercises.

Current technology enables students to interact with on-screen participants in nonlinear, discovery-learning-based scenarios. Within discovery-learning scenarios, learners navigate through realistic settings and learn as they explore instead of accessing content via menu structures. Sales calls, customer-service scenarios, computer repairs, surgery, and the full responsibility of running a business can all be simulated. Simulations of software functionality are particularly prolific and learner benefits have been well documented. Cutting-edge programs now exist that use virtual reality to enable students wearing goggles and sensor gloves to be immersed in a digitally created environment. The challenge to the trainer is to isolate the elements of a situation that can be controlled and that must be mastered by the learner in reality and then to put the learner in control of these elements in the simulation. All the realism in the world cannot make a simulation a valuable learning tool without the elements of guidance, remediation, and feedback.

Drill-and-practice exercises can be considered particular types of simulation or they can be considered modes of training entirely separate from simulation. A typical drill-and-practice exercise simulates one or more of the features of a system and requires the learner to practice operations repeatedly on only these features.

True simulations and simulation-based drill-and-practice exercises have in common the ability to reveal a learner's actions and reactions in a realistic, protected environment where time and distance are collapsed. In sales-call simulations, such as the one illustrated in Figure 1.6, learners can try out various sales approaches without the jeopardy of awkward social situations.

Electronic Performance Support Systems

Performance support systems (EPSSs) are created to give individuals the tools they need to perform a required task when they need it. In a way, a EPSS is the opposite of a tutorial. Whereas a tutorial instructs a learner and then requires that the learner perform, a EPSS requires the learner to determine when he or she needs assistance and then to ask for the required guidance. The most ubiquitous example of an EPSS is the help feature built into Microsoft's Office applications. A simple example of a non-TBT performance support tool is an inventory checklist created for a grocery clerk.

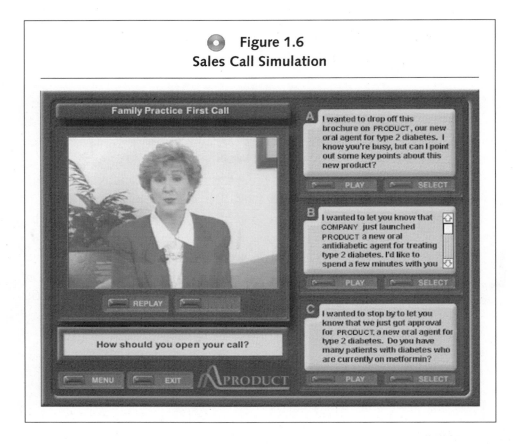

Figure 1.6
Sales Call Simulation

When learning is measured by the ability to exhibit a behavior or set of behaviors competently and consistently, as much TBT is, the focus on training is shifted to a focus on performance. If the goal of a training initiative is to improve performance on the job, many would argue that training is not going to be effective. These proponents of EPSSs urge that no tutorial or testing elements should be included, that training should give way to assistance.

A growing consensus in the industry is that TBT should include imbedded support systems that provide instant guidance at the time and place of need. With the advent of WBT and the emergence of the hyperlink paradigm, the convergence of TBT and EPSSs is almost complete. Web-based tutorials can be completed independently as learning exercises by new users and still be delivered as just-in-time chunks of information and interactive tools at the desktop. Figure 1.7 illustrates a

Figure 1.7
Electronic Performance Support Tool from a Raymond Karsan Associates' Management Results Training Product

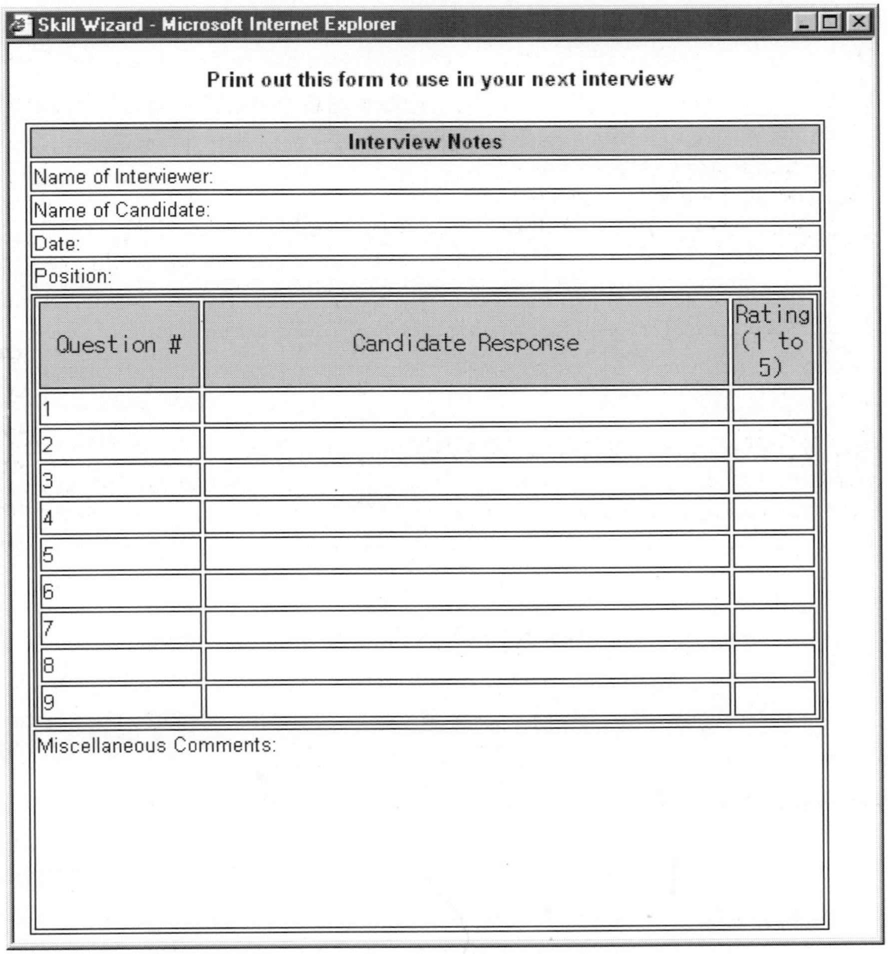

Skill Wizard - Microsoft Internet Explorer _ ☐ ✕

Print out this form to use in your next interview

Interview Notes		
Name of Interviewer:		
Name of Candidate:		
Date:		
Position:		

Question #	Candidate Response	Rating (1 to 5)
1		
2		
3		
4		
5		
6		
7		
8		
9		

Miscellaneous Comments:

performance support tool imbedded in Raymond Karsan Associates' Management Results training product.

The challenge of creating useful EPSSs obviously consists of determining what tools are needed by a population and providing those tools. In the context of TBT, the further challenge is to create systems that allow an individual who needs a tool to recognize that such a tool exists and then be able to use that tool.

Instructional Games

The inclusion of games has often been a hitch in getting management to agree to TBT initiatives. Many learning theories contend, however, that games are essential to the learning exhibited by children and can be usefully extended into the realm of adult learning. Games can have great value, possibly greater value than any other mode of instruction, in reducing learner tension and increasing learner engagement. The reluctance toward employing games to teach is becoming less apparent as supervisors are educated in learning theory and as many who have experience in gaming for educational purpose move into management roles.

Games in the style of TV game shows have long been used in the classroom to provide a fun and effective method for reinforcement and self-assessment. Instructional games that use the latest computer technologies are equally effective. Games can run the gamut from simple speed-and-accuracy typing exercises to complex business simulators in which a student might run an entire factory. Instructional games can also replicate classic, arcade, and game show styles such as tic-tac-toe, auto racing, and *Jeopardy*. An instructional game that mimics the arcade game *Asteroids* is illustrated in Figure 1.8. During the game, learners must answer questions in order to blast oncoming asteroids. Though the game is similar to a standard multiple choice exercise, the theme adds to the learner's engagement.

The defining characteristic of instructional games is a set of goals or a competitor to provide motivation in addition to the learning. For maximum success, the motivational element of the game should run parallel to the overall motivation for the training. The game's instructional value should be aligned with the objectives of the overall course. There is little merit to using games as a reward for completing learning objectives exterior to the games themselves.

Tests, Record Keeping, and Guidance

Automated assessments are another commonly used facet of TBT. When companies first adopt TBT initiatives, testing and record-keeping systems are often

Figure 1.8
Instructional Game Based on Asteroids Arcade Game

accepted earlier than programs that integrate multiple training modes, due to their ease of implementation and their quickly recognizable returns.

On-line tests can be used for self-assessment purposes or they can be computer graded and the results reported to central administration. The explosion of enterprise-wide networks now provides the power to assess thousands of individuals and track their progress against specific job competencies throughout their life within an organization. Technological systems that eliminate the clerical duties of a student progressing through a long course of study make TBT attractive to the learner. Similarly, the ability of TBT to enable supervisors to monitor progress makes it attractive to an organization. Figure 1.9 illustrates a feature of an oncology training program that tracks for its user what areas of the hospital he or she has and has not already "visited."

The latest and most sophisticated technology-based tests are tightly linked to learning objectives, which in turn can help create a completely personalized

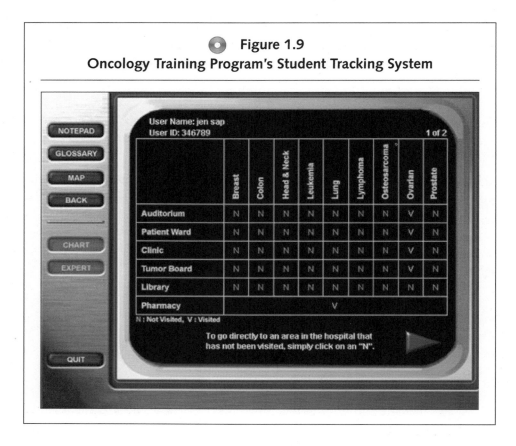

Figure 1.9
Oncology Training Program's Student Tracking System

	Breast	Colon	Head & Neck	Leukemia	Lung	Lymphoma	Osteosarcoma	Ovarian	Prostate
Auditorium	N	N	N	N	N	N	N	V	N
Patient Ward	N	N	N	N	N	N	N	V	N
Clinic	N	N	N	N	N	N	N	V	N
Tumor Board	N	N	N	N	N	N	N	V	N
Library	N	N	N	N	N	N	N	N	N
Pharmacy					V				

User Name: jen sap
User ID: 346789
1 of 2

N : Not Visited, V : Visited

To go directly to an area in the hospital that
has not been visited, simply click on an "N".

NOTEPAD
GLOSSARY
MAP
BACK
CHART
EXPERT
QUIT

curriculum. A TBT program with a prescription generator can base an individualized course of study on the areas in which the learner has shown the least strength.

Combining the Modes

Maximum learner benefit can be achieved by combining several training modes in one project. Truthfully, the merit of each mode varies with the training goals, and some modes are ill-suited to meet some needs. For example, a complex virtual-reality simulation of a classroom created to teach arithmetic is a gross misapplication of technology. That is not to say that TBT cannot improve simple training; on the contrary, technologically mediated drill-and-practice exercises and testing might benefit a learner, especially someone who is not succeeding with traditional methods. Generally, complex learning objectives are best achieved when learners are presented content using a combination of modes.

INTERACTIVITY

Interactivity, most basically defined, is the exchange of information between two distinct entities. In the context of TBT, interactivity is the ability of a technology to gather information regarding the needs of a learner and then shape and provide instruction specifically suited to meeting those needs. Defining interactivity too strictly can limit its creative application. A sample of interactivity types would undoubtedly include multiple-choice questions, hyperlinks, branching structures, and matching exercises.

Why Interactivity Is Important

Boldly and bluntly put, interactivity is what entirely differentiates TBT from its alternatives. This is not to say that TBT is the only method of instruction that provides interactivity. On the contrary, the student-teacher dynamic is the ideal example of beneficial interactivity. TBT has the ultimate promise of providing a similar dynamic to each learner whenever, wherever, and with whatever privacy is requested.

Beneficial interactivity is the defining characteristic of intelligently created TBT. But interactivity should be included only where it adds to learning potential, not to fill quotas or provide window dressing.

ADVANTAGES AND LIMITATIONS OF TBT

The vast movement toward TBT is clearly motivated by the many benefits it offers. Regardless of how much TBT is praised and innovated, computers will never completely eliminate human instructors and other forms of educational delivery. What is important to know is exactly what TBT advantages exist and when these outweigh the limitations of the medium.

Features Unique to TBT

Like no other training form, TBT promises to provide a single experience that accommodates the three distinct learning styles of auditory learners, visual learners, and kinesthetic learners. Auditory learners comprehend and remember material most effectively when they hear it; visual learners comprehend and remember material most effectively when they see it; kinesthetic learners comprehend and remember material most effectively when they physically interact with it. Other unique opportunities created by the advent and development of TBT are more efficient training of a globally dispersed audience and reduced publishing and distribution costs as WBT becomes a standard.

TBT also offers individualized instruction, which print media cannot provide and which instructor-led courses allow for clumsily and at great cost. In conjunction with assessing needs, TBT can also target specific needs. And by using learning-style tests, TBT can locate and target individual learning preferences.

Additionally, TBT is self-paced. Advanced learners are allowed to speed through or bypass instruction that is redundant while novices may slow down their progress, thus eliminating frustration with themselves, their fellow learners, and the course.

In these ways, TBT is effective for learners with a maximum range of learning styles, preferences, and needs.

Collaborative Learning

All collaborative learning theory contends that human interaction is a vital ingredient of human learning. It is particularly crucial to consider this when designing TBT, realizing the potential the medium has to isolate learners. By including bulletin board services, threaded discussions, chats, e-mail, and conferencing, this potential drawback is reduced.

Advantages to the Trainer or Organization

This book covers the advantages and disadvantages to organizations and learners that can be realized through TBT. Some of the most outstanding advantages to the trainer or organization are as follows:

- *Reduced overall cost* is the single most influential factor in adopting TBT. The elimination of costs associated with instructors' salaries, meeting-room rentals, and student travel, lodging, and meals is directly quantifiable. The reduction of employees' time spent away from the job may be the most positive offshoot.

- *Learning times are reduced* an average of 40 to 60 percent, as found by Brandon Hall (1997, p. 108).

- *Increased retention* of information and its application to the job averages an increase of 25 percent over traditional methods, according to an independent study by J. D. Fletcher (*Multimedia Review,* Spring 1991, pp. 33–42).

- *Consistent delivery* of content that would be diluted by filtering through instructors is possible with TBT.

- *Expert knowledge* is communicated, but more importantly captured, with TBT.

- *Proof of completion and certification,* essential elements of training initiatives, can be automated.

Advantages to the Learner

Along with increased retention, reduced learning time, and the rest of the aforementioned benefits, particular advantages of TBT for students include the following:

- *On-demand availability* allows students to complete training conveniently during off-hours or from home.

- *Self-pacing* for slow or quick learners reduces stress and increases satisfaction.

- *Interactivity* engages users, pushing them rather than pulling them through training.

- *Confidence* that refresher or quick reference materials are available reduces the burden of responsibility of mastery.

Disadvantages to the Trainer or Organization

TBT is not, however, the be-all and end-all to every training need. It does have limitations, among them the following:

- The *up-front investment* required of a TBT solution is larger than for traditional approaches due to development costs. Budgets and cash flows will need to be negotiated.

- *Technology issues* that play a role include whether the existing technology infrastructure can accomplish the training goals, whether additional technology expenditures can be justified, and whether compatibility of all software and hardware can be achieved. *and bandwidth*

- *Inappropriate subject matters* for TBT do exist, though they are few. Even the acquisition of skills that involve complex physical-motor or emotional components (for example, juggling or mediation) can be augmented with TBT.

Disadvantages to the Learner

The reasons that TBT may not excel over other approaches to training include the following:

- The *technology issues* of learners are most commonly technophobia and unavailability of required technologies.

- *Portability* of training has become a strength of TBT with the proliferation of network-linking points and laptop and notebook computers, but it does not rival that of print media.

- Reduced social and cultural interaction can be a drawback. However, the impersonality, lack of communication mechanisms such as body language, and elimination of peer-to-peer learning that are part of this potential disadvantage are lessening with advances in communications technologies.

THE PROJECT TEAM: ROLES AND RESPONSIBILITIES

Creating effective TBT in today's marketplace is becoming an increasingly difficult prospect for one person to carry out alone. First, creating TBT is complex; it requires a wealth of talents. Most *authoring systems,* the primary tools employed to create TBT products, claim—some rightly and some inaccurately—that they can be mastered by a novice. One person certainly can create an effective TBT product, but the myriad responsibilities and specialties required are more efficiently divided among members of a team.

Regardless of how much division of labor is applied, each team member will likely play more than one role. Only in the most monolithic software development houses are the duties so divided that no team member has more than one area of expertise and no tasks are shared. The extreme cases in which one "producer" juggles all the responsibility—from instructional design to art design and creation to programming—result in an inferior product, an extended development schedule, a burnt-out employee, or some combination thereof.

In cases of contracted TBT development, the client may be asked by the vendor to play certain and various roles. The vendor conversely will be asked, required, or possibly demanded to assume a set of roles and responsibilities.

Development teams are notoriously eclectic bunches. The team members can vary widely between those who are self-taught and those with academic credentials, such as degrees in instructional design, psychology, programming, art, and other areas of study.

The following roles, responsibilities, and attributes are provided as a jumping-off point only. An in-house production may combine the roles of client-sponsor and vendor. A small project may see many of these roles collapsed into one or two positions. A large undertaking will probably require that many of these duties, particularly graphic art and programming, be assigned to groups of interdependent collaborators. The critical question to consider is whether the requisite talents and personnel exist within an organization to develop their own TBT or if outsourcing is the most appropriate path.

Client-Sponsor

The sponsor of a TBT project, often a training manager or director of training, acts on behalf of his or her organization to ensure that the product that gets created reduces cost, increases productivity, or in some other way adds value. Ultimate responsibility for the success or failure of a project rests with this person because she or he usually supervises the overall team or selects and manages an outside vendor. Along with or in place of a project manager, this role encompasses the acquisition of a budget for program development, final approval power, schedule creation, and revision. When a client-vendor relationship is established, the client negotiates with peers internally, such as the information technology department, student population, and senior executives, to make sure that the TBT initiative is appropriately implemented.

It is helpful for a sponsor to have prior experience in project management and a training background. He or she must have a good understanding of business need, student population, and internal political issues. Other desirable attributes of a client-sponsor are the following:

- Capacity to organize a team effort
- Scrutiny in selecting team members or a vendor
- Willingness to explore radical solutions
- Ability to secure and manage budgets

Project Manager

The project manager is the person who ultimately guarantees on-time, on-budget delivery of a TBT solution. He or she is responsible to the client-sponsor for the quality of the finished product. The management and coaching of all other team members is left to the project manager, who serves as a single point of contact among disparate team members, and in the case of an outsourced project, between team members and the client. The project manager guides the approval process, including obtaining feedback from evaluations, implementing revisions, and drafting progress reports.

Good organization skills, time management, and the ability to juggle multiple tasks are all prerequisites of an effective project manager. Other positive attributes include the following:

- Experience in multiple backgrounds (jack-of-all-trades)
- Basic understanding of technical, design, and media issues
- Knowledge of the fundamentals of instructional design
- Mastery of financial fundamentals
- Proficiency using scheduling, productivity, and communication tools, including GANTT charts, spreadsheets, and conferencing technologies

Subject Matter Expert

The subject matter expert, or SME, contributes the core content and original materials and is available for information acquisition through formal or informal interviews. She or he provides access to source materials and reference items such as books, articles, videotapes, and static art. In the client-vendor model, the client assigns this person as one who can give guided tours of facilities, explain processes, create flow diagrams, provide sample dialogue, and shape simulated settings. It is the responsibility of the SME to review for accuracy the design documents, scripts, and final deliverable.

A master of the selected content area should fill this role. For example, if selling skills are being taught, the SME may be a company's top-selling representative. Someone with years of experience and high peer evaluations would be selected to shape instruction on management techniques. In the case of software training, the SME would probably be someone who had a role in the design of the software or someone certified as an expert. For a TBT to be beneficial, the SME must

- Be committed to the project
- Understand the amount of time required
- Be able to communicate to outsiders without using jargon

Instructional Designer

A typical instructional designer has a background in liberal arts, frequently including a master's degree or doctorate in instructional design, psychology, education, or multimedia technology. This team member must be very analytical, have good communication skills, and be very organized. A successful instructional designer works quickly in a fast-changing environment.

It is the instructional designer's responsibility to conduct high-level analysis of performance goals, audience, training needs, and technology limitations. In concert with the sponsor, project manager, and SME, the instructional designer creates the design document, specifies learning objectives, selects interactive exercises, and creates evaluation questions. In the early design phases, this person may have to create script and screen templates and will often be the lead scriptwriter. Additionally, the instructional designer supervises the formative and summative evaluations. Borrowing an analogy from movies, the project manager is the producer, the instructional designer is the director.

The best instructional designers

- Have a basic understanding of technology in order to know what is or is not possible given certain technological realities
- Appreciate and apply a breadth of adult learning theories
- Quickly and accurately recognize performance and knowledge gaps

Writer

Working after the instructional designer has created an outline, the writer creates and revises the script that actually dictates the words, images, and video and audio elements that are presented to the audience. The writer works with the artists and programmers to ensure that what is envisioned can actually be implemented within the time, budget, and technology constraints. It is the writer's responsibility to apply navigation directions to the scripts; to add notes indicating any special functions, links, or other software behaviors; and to create alternate items if necessary.

A prior knowledge of the content or topic being trained is helpful but not necessary. An effective writer has

- Good communication skills
- A writing style that is concise, direct, and engaging
- Creativity to increase learner engagement

Graphic Artist

From the blueprints created by the instructional designer and writer, the graphic artist creates screen layouts; interface items such as buttons, windows, and menus; and graphics and animations necessary to the program. The work could include original illustrations and cartoons, simple flow diagrams, manipulated stock photography, and images obtained with a digital camera. In addition to two-dimensional work, there may exist a need for three-dimensional images and animation, particularly when immersive metaphors and simulations are desired.

Although bachelor's degrees from art school are common, many graphic artists are self-taught. Multimedia artists need

- Creativity tempered with an understanding of the intended audience, client culture, and learning preferences
- Understanding of human computer factors and interface design
- Ability and willingness to adapt to a dynamic set of standards and tools

Programmer

Using the script as a guide, the programmer is expected to assemble different elements (text, audio, video, graphics, and animation) into a coherent whole. He develops the rapid prototype, the programmed working model, on which the final product is based. The programmer is called on to debug a program following alpha and beta tests, to create databases, and to construct reporting mechanisms used for student tracking.

Like graphic artists, programmers may have specialized degrees or be self-taught. Multimedia development is usually accomplished using not advanced languages but rather Hypertext Markup Language (HTML) or authoring systems, programs that facilitate TBT creation. A multimedia programmer should have

- An analytical, methodical approach to work
- Ingenuity in the creation of reusable objects and engines
- Ability to code optimally and choose the right tool based on the technologies available to the audience

Audio and Video Producers

Other specialists oversee the preproduction, production, and postproduction of video and audio elements. Preproduction includes the selection and preparation of shooting locations and the set up of equipment; production encompasses the creation of raw audio and video content; and postproduction primarily refers to the editing and refinement of content to a desired duration and quality.

Industry experience is particularly desired for these team members. More often than not, the audio-video crew is contracted.

Quality Reviewers

Quality review is most frequently assigned to various team members with other roles and supplemented by outsider talent for thoroughness. Copyeditors particularly excel in this role. Those with attention to detail, a good eye, technology knowledge, and a drive to do out-of-the-ordinary things with software are invaluable resources.

The quality reviewers work internally during development, alpha, and beta stages; they check the program for general quality and bugs; and they create change reports. Quality personnel inspect

- Functionality under various operational conditions to confirm the software's compliance with expectations
- Content in the program to make sure it matches the content in the script or text-based document

- Logic and inconsistent behavior throughout the application
- Performance and proper operation of the product on a variety of systems with assorted hardware configurations, as well as operating systems, concurrently running software, and installed peripheral devices
- Accessibility and usability of the product, the intuitive nature of the user interface, the look and feel of the program, on-screen dialogues and prompts, user-error forgiveness, and context-sensitive help

Administrators

Administrators facilitate communication, track expenditures, and assist in reproduction and distribution of materials, among other duties. Increases in the size of teams and projects contribute to the need for oversight by administrative personnel.

TOOLS NEEDED TO CREATE TBT

Each craftsman selected to be part of a project team applies a tool or set of tools to accomplish his or her duties. Here is an overview of some of the equipment and software choices available to would-be TBT developers. Because of the fast pace of changing technology, a team needs to consider almost daily the tools it uses to make sure that they are the most efficient and appropriate available. Be aware that it is very easy for technology wants to supplant technology needs. The following information is accurate at the time of writing. However, by the time you read this, the specifications and prices will probably have doubled and been cut in half respectively—further proof that if you blink, you're behind the times.

Computers

Basically, the computing power of the machines necessary to create TBT exceeds the technical specifications of the systems used to distribute it. The common platform for personal and professional computers, the IBM-compatible or personal computer, is supplemented in creative fields such as TBT production by the use of Apple's Macintosh. Graphic artists coming from Macintosh backgrounds are largely responsible for this dual-platform development, and the reason that so many Macs are still common in the industry. Figure 1.10 presents a ballpark *minimum* of the specifications of the computers used today to create TBT.

Figure 1.10
Minimum Requirements for a TBT Development Computer

Feature	PC	Macintosh
Processor	Pentium II; 200 MHZ	Mac G3; 200 MHz
RAM	64 MB	64 MB
Operating System	Windows 98 or NT	Mac OS 8
Media Cards	4 MB video; 16-bit sound	Built in
Drives	24-speed CD-ROM	24-speed CD-ROM
Monitor	17''; preferably high resolution	17''; preferably high resolution
Accessories	Speakers; pointing and input devices (mouse, keyboard, writing tablet, etc.)	Speakers; pointing and input devices (mouse, keyboard, writing tablet, etc.)
Price Range	$1,100–$2,200	$2,000–$3,000

In addition to these computers, peripherals not tied to one user are necessary. The two most notable are at least an eight-speed CD burner (the low end of which can now be purchased for $600) and a color scanner (from $200 to $400).

Audio-Video Equipment and Software

To produce audio and video for multimedia projects independently, here are some basic requirements. For audio, which in most cases will be voice-over, you will need a suitable environment in which to record sound. A soundproof studio is always best but an economical alternative is a small, one-person sound-deadening enclosure such as a Whisper Booth. You will additionally need a quality microphone (ranging from twenty to thousands of dollars but averaging $250), and a variety of supporting hardware. You will need to route your microphone signal through a separate preamplifier or a mixer with pre-amp capabilities, either of which can be obtained for $500. An investment in a compressor will help retain sound quality and avoiding synchronization error if you later have to decrease the sound's bit-depth, a measure of the complexity of the representation of a sound in computer code. The audio product can then be recorded straight to digital audiotape and digitized afterward, or recorded directly into a computer using applications such as ProTools, Sound Forge, SoundEdit, or a nonlinear video system such as Media 100 or Avid. These applications can also be used to edit the content, and most can add any specific effects that might be needed.

To record video for multimedia, you will first need to choose a format and purchase a camera. For optimized image quality, a digital format such as DVCPro is best. A DVCPro camcorder package can be purchased for about $6,000. The image is crisp and with the appropriate equipment you can transfer your footage to an editing suite without going to analog first. Even though the majority of video for multimedia today is compressed, the best thing you can do to achieve quality compressed video is begin with the best picture possible.

Depending on your budget and the quality of video you require, additional items ranging from production lights and backgrounds to a teleprompter may be required. All of these can be rented, or if more cost-effective, purchased.

After you have acquired your footage, you will need to transfer it to an editing station. You will need to purchase a video deck appropriate to your selected format. Recorder-player decks vary greatly in price depending on format and features, with a basic DVCPro deck running $7,000. Your decision about which editing system to purchase depends on the system's intended primary use as well as cost, speed, and platform. Some may find that a software application such as Adobe Premier suits their needs, while others will need a professional nonlinear system such as Media 100, AVID Media Composer, or Trinity.

Instructional Design and Writing

Not many equipment costs are associated with instructional design, because most personnel will use common word processors with specific script templates. Design products such as Designers Edge from Allen Communications, a step-by-step product for creating CBT scripts, do exist and are frequently used at a relatively low cost.

Graphic Art

The software needed by graphic artists ranges wildly based on productivity needs and designer preference. There is an overlap of products used to create multimedia and Web products, but specialized Web tools are required for optimal performance. See Figure 1.11 for a brief list of these tools.

Figure 1.11
Graphic Design Tools Used in Creating Art

Tool	Specialty	Price (at time of writing)
Adobe Photoshop	Pixel-based graphics; Photo manipulation	$500
Adobe Illustrator	Vector-based graphics	$400
Autodesk Studio 3D Max	3D models and animation	$2,500
Silicon Graphics Maya	3D models and animation	$7,000
Macromedia Flash	Animation	$300
Macromedia Fireworks	Optimize graphics	$200
Equilibrium Debabilizer	Optimize graphics	$150

Authoring

Authoring applications typically use a metaphor, such as an icon-based or slide-based interface, to make the structuring of content and the combining of media elements into a cohesive program accessible to the nonprogrammer. The term *authoring system* commonly refers to both multimedia production applications in general and those intended specifically for the creation of training materials. Deciding between the more than one hundred different authoring systems entails a serious undertaking, shaped by costs, needs, specialties, and preferences. The icons and flowline systems Authorware and IconAuthor and those that rely on scripted statements, Director and Toolbook, are the most commonly used systems for creating training applications.

WBT creation requires a different tool set, because the tools function as filters that create the languages HTML, DHTML, JavaScript, and Java, which make up Web environments. These tools include Microsoft's FrontPage and Visual Interdev, Macromedia's DreamWeaver, and Allaire's ColdFusion and Homesite, to name a few. The discussion of authoring systems contained in Chapter Eight of Brandon Hall's *Web-Based Training Cookbook* (1997) is a perfect resource with which to begin exploring development tools.

Figure 1.12
Costs to Equip a TBT Production Team

Tool	Price Range
Computer (PC or MAC)	$1,100–$3,000 per computer
Additional computer hardware (scanner, CD burner, etc.)	$1,000
Audio/video equipment and software	$25,000
Instructional design software	$500–$1,000
Graphic art software bundle	$3,000
Authoring software	$2,500
Total	$35,000–$41,500 (assuming three computers)

The Full TBT Production Suite

Figure 1.12 summarizes the hardware and software issues detailed in this chapter. The total cost represents a minimum for a small but well-equipped production team. It does not reflect any type of labor or training costs or overhead outside of those directly incurred by production.

CONCLUSION

In keeping with proper instructional design, you now have an opportunity to assess your own understanding of the content presented in this chapter by answering the following questions. The answers provided after the questions are only examples. In addition to using the self-test, examine how the test reflects the learning objectives presented at the beginning of the chapter.

Self-Check!

1. Give a brief definition of TBT.

2. List three synonyms for TBT.

3. Describe three modes of TBT.

4. Create an example of a good and a bad interactivity in TBT.

5. Recall one advantage to the trainer and one advantage to the learner of applying TBT.

6. List five members of the project team.

7. Detail five tools that are needed to create TBT.

8. Name three ways that this exercise could be different or more effective if presented within the realm of TBT.

Answers

1. Give a brief definition of TBT.

   Using technology to deliver training and educational materials; referred to by the acronym TBT.

2. List three synonyms for TBT.

   - CBT: computer-based training
   - CBL: computer-based learning
   - WBT: Web-based training

3. Describe three modes of TBT.

   - Tutorial: straightforward presentation of content based on principles of instructional systems design
   - Simulation: recreation of realistic scenarios that puts learner in control of variables
   - Performance support system: tool presented when needed to increase job effectiveness

- Instructional game: learning exercise with creative elements to increase learner interest

- Test, record-keeping mechanism, or prescription generator: automated tools for assessment, clerical duties, and course guidance.

4. Create an example of a good and a bad interactivity in TBT.

- Good interactivity: multiple-choice questions, the selection of answers for which determines the learner's path through a track of instruction

- Bad interactivity: trumpet sound presented at the start of every page of a tutorial

5. Recall one advantage to the trainer and one advantage to the learner of applying TBT.

- Advantages to the trainer: reduced cost, reduced learning time, increased retention, consistent delivery, expert knowledge captured, proof of completion

- Advantages to the learner: on-demand delivery, self-pacing, interactivity for increased engagement, increased confidence

6. List five members of the project team.

Client-sponsor, project manager, subject matter expert, instructional designer, writer, graphic artist, audio-video producer, programmer, quality reviewer, administrator

7. Detail five tools that are needed to create TBT.

- Multimedia computer with specifications outlined in Figure 1.10

- Audio equipment, including a soundproof studio, microphone, mixer or pre-amplifier, editing system, and software

- Video equipment, including a camera, grip equipment, editing deck and suite like those produced by Media 100 or Avid

- Instructional design software such as Designer's Edge and word processing software

- Graphic arts software such as Adobe Photoshop, Macromedia Flash, and Equilibrium Debabilizer

- An authoring system, possibly Macromedia Authorware or Aimtech IconAuthor

8. Name three ways that this exercise could be different or more effective if presented within the realm of TBT.

- Reveal answer immediately after each question is attempted.
- Give specific feedback to correct and incorrect responses.
- Provide links directly to content areas where incorrect responses occurred.
- Provide audio pronunciations of terms.
- Include animation and sound to increase engagement.

Choosing the Right Technology

In Chapter One we reviewed the many modes of technology-based training, and the terminology and jargon that exists in the field. In this chapter we'll focus on the technologies most commonly used for the actual delivery of training programs, with special emphasis on CD-ROM and the Web. The chapter is not meant to be a detailed or comprehensive look at all technology but rather an overview that will provide a useful framework for the average training professional.

What You Will Learn in This Chapter

- The technical fundamentals of CD-ROMs and the Web

- The advantages and limitations of CD-ROMs

- The advantages of Web-based training (WBT)

- The two limitations of Web delivery that will likely disappear within ten years

- How to select the most appropriate technology for each new training initiative

TECHNOLOGY USED IN TBT

TBT has been around for many decades. In its earliest form it was stored on huge mainframe computers attached to terminals that could display only green text. But beginning with the invention of the personal computer and continuing more recently with the advent of Web browsers, there have been great advances in the field of educational technology.

Some organizations and individuals are early adopters who immediately embrace the newest technology. But for most organizations it takes time to evaluate, purchase, and implement new hardware and software. This means that there will always be new, recent, and old technologies in use simultaneously. This chapter discusses the variety of data storage technologies—things that hold programs and data—that have defined the limits of multimedia, and introduces Web technologies that have drastically changed the face of TBT.

Floppy Disks

In the late 1980s and early 1990s, training programs were primarily delivered on floppy disks. Floppy disks hold 1.44 megabytes of information, which is the equivalent of about 1.5 million text characters or seven hundred pages of straight text. Compression software can increase the amount a floppy disk holds approximately fivefold, but the software must be installed on a computer's hard drive before the disk's data can be run. This storage amount is relatively small, given the large file size of audio and video files. Using uncompressed files, one floppy disk can hold only six seconds of low-quality video. Because of this, computer-based training delivered via floppy disk is usually text-based with limited graphics. It isn't that multimedia can't be delivered via floppies; the issue is that it takes an impracticably large number of floppy disks to hold even a relatively small multimedia program.

But it will not be much longer before floppies become completely obsolete. Newer portable storage devices exist that have much more capacity (for example, Zip disks). But the whole need for portable storage devices is disappearing with the emergence of high-speed network connections at the office and at home.

CD-I

CD-I, which stands for *compact disc interactive,* is a multimedia system developed in the late 1980s that was designed to be used at home, in schools, and in business. A CD-I player is a relatively inexpensive device that connects to any TV, much like a VCR. CD-I disks hold text, computer animation, and digital audio, along with video that can be displayed full-screen.

The CD-I format gained popularity initially because it was easier and cheaper to implement than a complete multimedia CD-ROM-equipped computer system, and the quality of the multimedia was much higher. However, a major limitation was that there was no hard drive or floppy disk system attached to CD-I, and data (such as student test scores and bookmarking features) could not be saved. As multimedia computers rapidly came down in price, the popularity of CD-I technology declined.

CD-ROM

CD-ROM, which stands for *compact disc–read only memory,* is a system for delivering multimedia to a personal computer. This five-inch disc looks identical to an audio CD that is played in a home or car stereo. It requires a CD-ROM drive, which has come as standard equipment with all new computers for several years.

Each CD-ROM has a storage capacity of 650 megabytes. In other words, one CD-ROM can hold as much as 450 floppy disks, or approximately one hour of low-quality video. Because of this vast storage capability, CD-ROMS are a relatively easy and inexpensive way to distribute large files and programs, including audio, video, and complex animations. Through the mid-1990s, TBT was primarily delivered using CD-ROMs.

DVD-ROM

DVD-ROM, which stands for *digital video disc–read only memory,* is essentially a bigger, faster CD-ROM. It is a new standard that is being embraced to provide training and business information as well as home entertainment. DVD-ROMs look identical to standard CD-ROMs but can hold 4.7 gigabytes of information, or two hours and thirteen minutes of full-screen digital video. Figures 2.1 and 2.2 illustrate the relative storage capacities of these different media.

DVD-ROMs are already quickly replacing CD-ROM technology. New computers are being equipped with DVD drives as standard equipment, and these drives are compatible with the older CD-ROM technology. In other words, consumers and employees can switch to the new DVD technology but still access all of their old CD-ROMs using the DVD drive.

Internet and Intranet

The Internet started in 1969 as a Department of Defense research project to create a secure means of communication in the event of war. Originally it was called ARPAnet and consisted of computers dispersed around the globe that would pass messages to each other using a technical standard called TCP/IP (transmission control protocol/Internet protocol). In the 1980s, funding for the network was

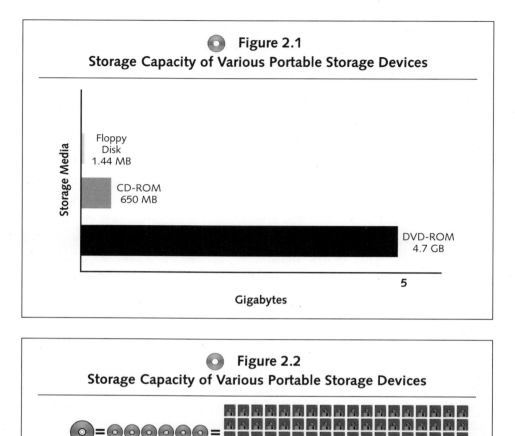

Figure 2.1
Storage Capacity of Various Portable Storage Devices

Floppy Disk 1.44 MB

CD-ROM 650 MB

DVD-ROM 4.7 GB

Storage Media

5

Gigabytes

Figure 2.2
Storage Capacity of Various Portable Storage Devices

1 DVD-ROM = 7 CD-ROMs = 3,157 Floppy Diskettes

taken over by the National Science Foundation and only a few hundred computers, mostly owned by government agencies and academic institutions, were attached to the Internet.

Initially, the Internet was difficult for nontechnical people to use, but the invention of Web-browser software changed all that. A Web browser is simply a piece of software that sits in the user's computer and provides a point-and-click graphical interface to the World Wide Web. The Web is a global network of millions of "pages" of information that contain text, graphics, and links to other pages or pieces of information. With advances in browser technology, Web pages now often contain multimedia elements, too. Browsers made it easy for everyone, regardless of their level of computer expertise, to "surf the 'net" and gain access to a vast, worldwide library of information (see Figure 2.3).

WBT didn't take off until 1996. Initially, the more common term was *Internet-based training* (IBT), but the reality was that most corporations never put their private training programs and internal information on the Internet, which is open to the public. Instead, Web pages were held on organizations' private internal networks, called Intranets. Intranets are smaller, private networks that work

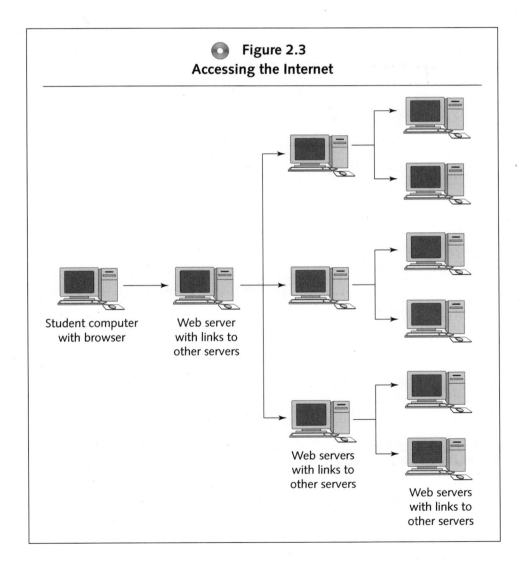

**Figure 2.3
Accessing the Internet**

Student computer
with browser

Web server
with links to
other servers

Web servers
with links to
other servers

Web servers
with links to
other servers

on the same TCP/IP technology as the Internet. Because a Web browser provides an interface to both Internet and Intranet education, the term WBT is more dominant today.

USING CD-ROMS TO DELIVER TRAINING

Although WBT is already the dominant delivery technology, the use of CD-ROMs and DVD-ROMs will continue for some time. Their vast storage capability still makes them a good choice for the delivery of video-intensive programs. Furthermore, programs developed for CD-ROM delivery tend to be much more stable and have better overall performance than those developed with the latest Web technologies.

Technical Requirements for Using CD-ROMs

To use a CD-ROM-based training program, students need the following:

- *Computer:* either a Windows-based personal computer (PC) or an Apple Macintosh. If using a PC, a Pentium processor with speeds of two hundred megahertz or better will get best results. If using a Macintosh, a PowerPC is recommended for multimedia.

- *Operating system:* Windows 95 or later if using a PC, or System 7 or later if using a Macintosh.

- *RAM (random-access memory):* any late-model computer is likely to have more than enough RAM (at least thirty-two megabytes) installed standard.

- *CD-ROM drive:* comes in various speeds (2x, 4x, 8x). Today's CD-ROM drives are very fast, and anything over 4x will perform fine.

- *Audio system:* consists of a soundboard inside the computer and a pair of speakers. These components come in eight–bit and sixteen–bit levels of quality, with sixteen–bit preferred.

- *Video:* Windows-based PCs come equipped with a video standard called AVI, and Macintosh computers use QuickTime. QuickTime is a higher-quality format and can be used on Windows-based PCs, too, but it will need to be installed manually. An even better video format is the MPEG system for Windows, which enables video to be played in a larger window and at more video frames per second (the frame rate). This video format requires either special hardware or software for playback.

Advantages of CD-ROM

When compared to instructor-led programs, the features and benefits of CD-ROM training include all those shared by other types of TBT: it is self-paced and highly interactive, and it fosters increased retention rates and reduced costs.

Compared to WBT, the benefits of CD-ROM come largely from the fact that CD-ROMs usually provide a more engaging learning experience, with text, audio, video, and animations all used to convey information. Typically, a graphic will be displayed along with bulleted text as an audio narration provides the primary content. Video clips can be used to show human behaviors or complex operations. This use of multiple media means that learning is optimized for all three learning styles: auditory, kinesthetic, and visual.

Student engagement is also increased with the use of creative themes or metaphors. Whether the topic is sales training or understanding a new computer system, today's programs are often wrapped in a classic Hollywood genre: science fiction, mystery, adventure, or even television talk shows and game shows. Students can play the role of starship captain, private eye, or swashbuckling archeologist as they explore their way through knowledge and conquer the learning objectives.

Finally, because people learn best from experience, the multimedia capability of CD-ROMs provides the power to create realistic job simulations. For example, a sales training program could put the student face-to-face with a tough prospect ("Your prices are 10 percent higher than what I'm paying now!"). Medical education programs put new doctors in front of simulated patients ("Would you choose chemotherapy or surgery?"). Soldiers choose tactics on a realistic battlefield ("Enemy tank is flanking five hundred yards to the right"). CEOs can hone their approach to crisis management ("Ms. Jones, the six o'clock news crew is in the lobby demanding a statement about our product recall. What should we do?"). In each case, a discovery-learning simulation can be developed using disk-based CBT or it can be delivered via the Web, but with bandwidth limitations the simulations would consist of only text and graphics. Learning is enhanced with multimedia CD-ROM because students are able to see the body language and hear the voices of on-screen video participants, and interact in real-time using more of their senses.

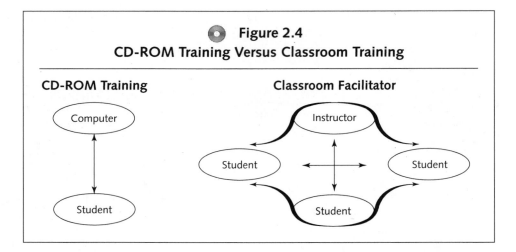

Figure 2.4
CD-ROM Training Versus Classroom Training

CD-ROM Training

Computer

Student

Classroom Facilitator

Instructor

Student

Student

Student

Limitations of CD-ROM

One of the disadvantages of CD-ROM based training, compared to instructor-led delivery, is the lack of peer-to-peer learning opportunities. After all, good instructors are really supposed to be *facilitators,* who bring out experience-based lessons and realizations from the students themselves. Figure 2.4 compares the different learning access points of CD-ROM training and live facilitation. There are also other benefits from the socialization that takes place in a physical classroom, including higher motivation, team building, and creation of relationships that can be supportive long after the training is over.

The biggest drawback of CD-ROM-based training relative to WBT is the difficulty of updating or changing the content. Once a CD-ROM is created, the information on it cannot be changed. For example, if a widget manufacturer uses CD-ROMs to train its sales force and they create a better widget, a new training CD-ROM will have to be created, duplicated, and distributed to the sales force. Depending on the size of the sales force, distributing new CD-ROMs could cost thousands of dollars. But more important than the higher cost is the additional time required. Figure 2.5 shows a typical production and distribution sequence.

Finally, CD-ROM programs present a challenge when it comes to student tracking. Because the CD is a distributed system without a direct link back to a training manager, other types of media must also be used for the reporting of student

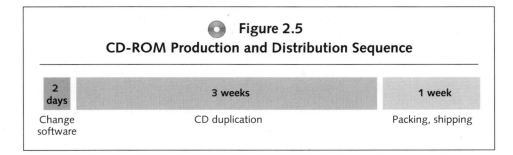

Figure 2.5
CD-ROM Production and Distribution Sequence

2 days	3 weeks	1 week
Change software	CD duplication	Packing, shipping

scores and completion certificates. Common methods include the following:

- Score report or certificate is printed out, then faxed or mailed to a manager or the corporate training department.
- Final score is saved as a small data file onto a floppy disk, which is then mailed back to the home office for processing.
- If students have e-mail access but no Intranet is available for automatic distribution, assessment score files can be attached to e-mail messages and sent to a training manager.

USING THE WEB TO DELIVER TRAINING

WBT, also known as *on-line learning,* began as a simple means of providing information to geographically dispersed students. But with advances in the technology, WBT has become more complex, with a variety of "flavors" that can be implemented. Here are some of the intricacies of this new medium.

Asynchronous Versus Synchronous Training

There are basically two types of WBT: synchronous training and asynchronous training (see Figure 2.6). *Synchronous* literally means "at the same time," and synchronous training involves interacting with an instructor via the Web in real time. *Asynchronous* means "not at the same time," and asynchronous training allows the student to complete the WBT on his own time and schedule, without live interaction with the instructor.

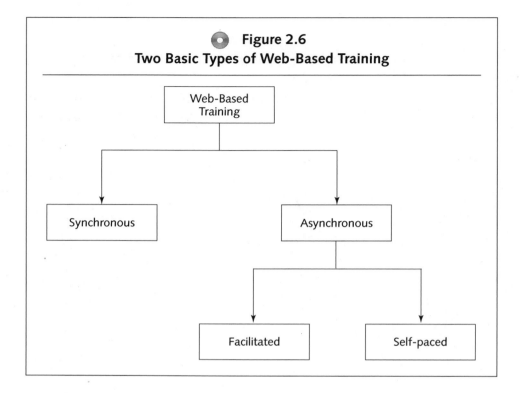

Figure 2.6
Two Basic Types of Web-Based Training

Synchronous education is a less common form of training. It involves geographically dispersed students accessing the same Web site at the same time as an instructor. The instructor and students can communicate with one another in a chat room in which they all type statements and questions that are viewed instantly by all participants. Another form of delivery involves the instructor "broadcasting" audio or video to the students, who are often linked to some type of visual slide show. Students can ask questions or provide comments through e-mail or the chat room. The instructor can use a more advanced technology, videoconferencing software, to link everyone in real time.

Asynchronous WBT is more common because it creates a just-in-time, on-demand student learning experience, and because low-speed network access is still the norm. Unlike synchronous training, students do not need to schedule their time around the predetermined plan of the instructor. There is complete flexibility with asynchronous training, which comes in two forms, facilitated and self-paced.

Facilitated asynchronous training involves an instructor and group of students, but the interaction is not in real time. The instructor posts assignments on a Web page, typically including on-line reading or research conducted on various Web sites. Students communicate with one another through threaded discussions (also known as *on-line bulletin boards*) and submit their homework to the instructor via e-mail. An advantage of this type of training is that students have a lot of peer interaction and can receive personalized attention and guidance from the human facilitator. The disadvantage of this form of WBT is that it tends to involve only one type of media—text. Additionally, even though the training isn't completed live, students still have scheduling concerns. Because a human instructor is posting assignments and grading homework, some kind of schedule needs to be kept, typically with each assignment lasting for one week.

Facilitated asynchronous training is common in the academic community, but the most common form of WBT used in corporations is *self-paced instruction*. This form of delivery consists of stand-alone instructional material that can be accessed and completed via the Web without additional interaction among students. Materials could include guided tutorials, discovery-learning simulations, and assessment exercises. Simple WBT programs are text-heavy and look like the original disk-based CBT. More technologically advanced WBT looks and feels as if the student were interacting with a multimedia CD-ROM.

Technical Requirements When Using WBT

To deliver WBT, a server-computer must be configured with Intranet server software. Student computers should be equipped with the following:

- *Computer:* either a Windows-based PC or an Apple Macintosh. WBT does not typically require as much processing power as CD-ROM training, but a Pentium-based PC or Macintosh PowerPC will deliver best results.

- *Operating system:* Windows 95 or later if using a PC, System 7 or later if using a Macintosh.

- *RAM:* any late-model computer is likely to have more than enough RAM (at least thirty-two megabytes).

- *Web browser:* intense competition in the browser market between Microsoft's Internet Explorer and Netscape's Navigator has led to rapid releases of new versions from each company. Therefore there is no browser that is commonly agreed upon as the standard. Version 3.0 of both browsers, which provides dependable performance for accessing text and graphics, is the minimum acceptable version for WBT. Versions 4.0 of both browsers support the language DHTML, which provides for more advanced on-screen animation, improved user interface control, and greater levels of interactivity, such as drag-and-drop questions and answers. At the time of this writing, version 5.0 browsers have just been released and include Shockwave and Flash technology for built-in support for multimedia. Figure 2.7 shows a standard browser interface.

• *Web connection:* students need some form of connection to the Intranet or Internet server. Remote users will typically need a modem and telephone line to gain access, though cable modems and DSL connections are increasingly common. Students who work in a more traditional office environment will need access to the Intranet through a standard Ethernet network connection.

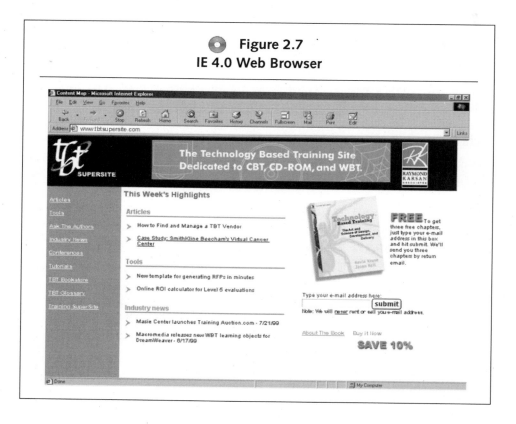

Figure 2.7
IE 4.0 Web Browser

Bandwidth

The primary factor that determines whether or not Web-based tutorials can incorporate audio, video, and animations is the amount of *bandwidth* that is available. Bandwidth, in simple terms, is the connection speed to the Internet or Intranet. The more bandwidth there is, the faster will be the connection, which is needed for downloading or "streaming" large media files such as audio and video. Often bandwidth is referred to simply as high bandwidth (or broadband), which means capable of delivering multimedia, or low bandwidth, which can handle text and graphics only.

Figure 2.8 shows several different types of network connections and the speed at which they operate. Bandwidth is measured in bits per second (bps), which is how many pieces of data can be transmitted every second during the connection. It is usually measured in increments of thousands (Kbps) or millions (Mbps).

As a rule of thumb, students who are dispersed geographically and accessing the Web using a dial-up modem are considered to have a low bandwidth connection. With current technologies, it is not practical to use audio or video extensively in training programs because of the long delays in downloading the files and the associated technical glitches. Even the latest video compression technologies display video only in postage-stamp-size screens using half the normal frame rate.

Figure 2.8
Bandwidths of Various Web Connections

Dial-up modems	14.4, 28.8, 33.6, or 56 Kbps
ISDN	56 Kbps or 128 Kbps
Ethernet (10baseT)	10 Mbps
T1	1.5 Mbps
T3	45 Mbps
Cable modems	Up to 10 Mbps
ADSL	From 1.5 to 9 Mbps
Satellite	From 400 Kbps to 4 Mbps

Students who work in a traditional office environment, in the same building or location as the Intranet server, are likely to have a high bandwidth connection. This is because employees are usually connected to the *local area network* (LAN) using a technology called Ethernet, or 10baseT. Figure 2.8 shows that this connection is almost one hundred times faster than traditional dial-up modems. This type of connectivity enables audio and video delivery with generally the same speed and quality as a CD-ROM.

Plug-Ins

The capability of the Web has been greatly enhanced with the addition of *plug-ins,* which are also often called *players.* Plug-ins are small pieces of software that integrate with Web browsers to greatly enhance their features. More than a thousand different plug-ins are available today. They are generally available free of charge and can be downloaded easily from the Internet. Many plug-ins facilitate the use of multimedia, others enable the viewing of special documents, and still others enable links to proprietary databases and graphing tools.

Because plug-ins are developed by many independent companies, a variety are available to choose from for each desired functionality. Among the common plug-ins used for WBT today are the following:

- *Shockwave,* from Macromedia, enables multimedia programs created in *Director* and *Authorware* to be played via an Intranet and the Internet. Shockwave is probably the most commonly used plug-in for the delivery of multimedia on the Web. It is now included in Microsoft's Internet Explorer 5.0 browser.

- *Flash,* also from Macromedia, greatly accelerates the display of most graphics and animations on the Web. Flash is commonly used for images within tutorials, as well as to add visual cues to user interfaces, such as highlighting buttons and other clickable areas. Flash is now included in Microsoft's Internet Explorer 5.0 browser.

- *Acrobat,* from Adobe, is a document-formatting standard. The Acrobat reader is a plug-in that enables you to download and view documents in a format that is true to their original hard-copy appearance.

- *RealPlayer,* from Real Systems, enables viewing of video and audio clips played directly from the server computer. This method, called *streaming,* results in much faster access than traditional methods that require the video or audio to be downloaded onto the user's hard drive first.

Audio and Video in WBT

The decision to use multimedia in WBT should be made after considering the dual factors of bandwidth and plug-ins. Figure 2.9 illustrates a decision tool that weighs the various factors. The lower left quadrant of the matrix indicates that with low bandwidth and no plug-ins, design is limited to text and small graphics. The upper left quadrant shows that with high bandwidth and no plug-ins, students can access text, large graphics, and animations very quickly. In the lower right quadrant, low bandwidth with plug-ins provides adequate performance for text, graphics, and animations, as well as limited streaming audio. In this case, even with streaming audio, after the user accesses the sound clip it is likely to take three to five seconds before it begins to play. This makes the use of audio as primary narration awkward but acceptable in unique cases, such as for simulations. Finally, the upper right quadrant is the high performance zone, with high bandwidth and plug-ins. With these capabilities, a Web-based program can perform the same as CD-ROM.

Advantages of WBT

Once again, the general benefits of WBT compared to traditional instructor-led training include all those shared by other types of TBT: the training usually is

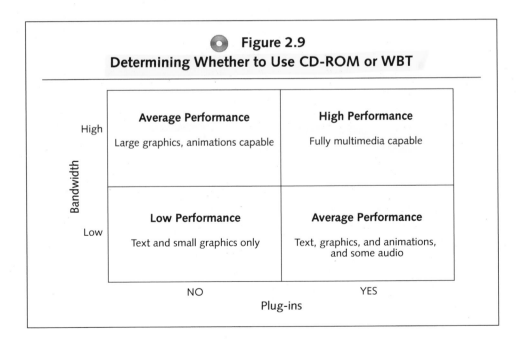

Figure 2.9
Determining Whether to Use CD-ROM or WBT

High	**Average Performance** Large graphics, animations capable	**High Performance** Fully multimedia capable
Low	**Low Performance** Text and small graphics only	**Average Performance** Text, graphics, and animations, and some audio
	NO	YES

Bandwidth

Plug-ins

self-paced and highly interactive, results in increased retention rates, and has reduced costs associated with student travel to an instructor-led workshop. When compared to CD-ROM training, the benefits of WBT stem from the fact that access to the content is easy and requires no distribution of physical materials. This means that WBT yields additional benefits, among them the following:

- *Access is available anytime, anywhere around the globe.* Students always have access to a potentially huge library of training and information whether they are working from home, in the office, or from a hotel room. As cellular modems become more popular, students will even be able to access training in a place that doesn't have a traditional phone line or network connection.

- *Per-student equipment costs are affordable.* Almost any computer today equipped with a modem and free browser software can access the Internet or a private Intranet. The cost of setup is relatively low.

- *Student tracking is made easy.* Because students complete their training while they are connected to the network, it is easy to implement powerful student-tracking systems. Unlike CD-ROMs that require students to print reports or save scores to disk, WBT enables the data to be automatically tracked on the server-computer. This information can range from who has accessed the courseware and what their assessment scores are to detailed information, including how they answered individual test questions and how much time they spent in each module.

- *Possible "learning object" architecture supports on-demand, personalized learning.* With CD-ROM training, students have access only to the information that can be held by one CD-ROM. The instructional design for this type of delivery, therefore, has included entire modules and distinct lessons. But with WBT there is virtually no storage limitation, and content can be held on one or more servers. The best WBT is designed so that content is "chunked" into discrete knowledge objects to provide greater flexibility. Students can access these objects through predefined learning paths, use skill assessments to generate personal study plans, or employ search engines to find exact topics.

- *Content is easily updated.* This is perhaps the single biggest benefit of WBT. In today's fast-paced business environment, training programs change frequently. With CD-ROM and other forms of training, the media must be reduplicated and redistributed to all the students. With WBT it is a simple matter of copying updated files from a local developer's computer onto the server-computer. The next time students connect to the Web page for training, they will automatically

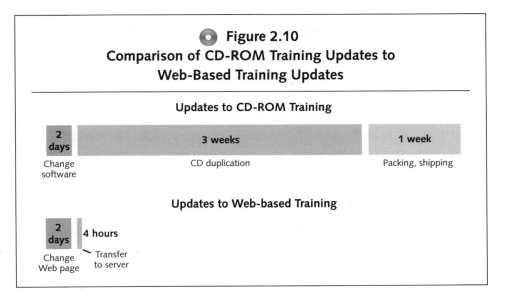

Figure 2.10
Comparison of CD-ROM Training Updates to
Web-Based Training Updates

Updates to CD-ROM Training

2 days	3 weeks	1 week
Change software	CD duplication	Packing, shipping

Updates to Web-based Training

2 days	4 hours
Change Web page	Transfer to server

have the latest version. Figure 2.10 compares the update time line for CD-ROMs and WBT.

Limitations of WBT

There are only two real disadvantages to WBT and both will be overcome in the next five to ten years as high bandwidth network connections become as common as telephones. The first drawback of WBT compared to live instruction is the lack of human contact, which greatly impacts learning. As reviewed earlier in this chapter, WBT is better than CD-ROM learning in this regard. Students can use their Web connection to e-mail other students, post comments on message boards, or use chat rooms and videoconference links to communicate live. Although this type of interaction is helpful and an improvement over CD-ROM learning, it still doesn't have the impact of a live workshop. With higher speed connections and improved conferencing software, one day students around the world will be able to communicate with each other in real time through full-screen video.

The second major drawback is the lack of multimedia in many WBT programs. The use of audio and video are critical to creating compelling metaphors and realistic job simulations, and to accommodating different learning styles.

Full multimedia delivered over corporate Intranets is possible, and many companies are doing it (see the case studies in Part Three of this book for examples). But in most cases, even if students have a high-bandwidth Intranet connection, corporate information technology departments don't want to use large media files because it slows down the entire network. The result is that most WBT programs are still composed of text and graphics alone. Once again, the bandwidth problem will be solved in the near future with advancements in network protocol standards and software compression.

WHEN TO USE WBT OR CD-ROM

A question often asked by training managers is, "I've got a new training program coming up; should I do it on CD-ROM or the Web?" Although we've seen the many pros and cons of each delivery method, the major advantage of CD-ROM delivery is its ability to delivery multimedia, and the major advantage of WBT is the ease of updating the content.

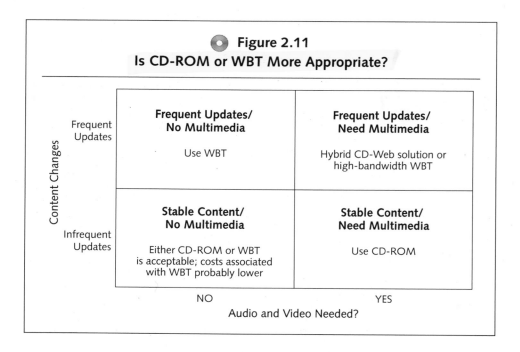

Figure 2.11
Is CD-ROM or WBT More Appropriate?

	NO	YES
Frequent Updates	**Frequent Updates/ No Multimedia** Use WBT	**Frequent Updates/ Need Multimedia** Hybrid CD-Web solution or high-bandwidth WBT
Infrequent Updates	**Stable Content/ No Multimedia** Either CD-ROM or WBT is acceptable; costs associated with WBT probably lower	**Stable Content/ Need Multimedia** Use CD-ROM

Content Changes

Audio and Video Needed?

Figure 2.11 shows a simple decision grid to help answer this question. It assumes that students have the technology to access both types of delivery. The horizontal access plots the need for video and audio while the vertical access plots the likelihood of changes to the content. If you think your content will change more than once a year, you should consider that change a frequent update. When determining the need for video and audio, think carefully about the true value it brings to your program. While talking-head narrators are nice to have, using text and graphics instead probably won't change the learning outcomes. However, if you are training certain behaviors (for example, selling skills, coaching, or interviewing) then the ability to view video clips of model behaviors in realistic scenarios is beneficial.

APPLYING IT ON THE JOB

Before starting any new TBT project, make sure to review all of the relevant technical details by considering the following questions.

General Questions

1. Will this be a CD-ROM or Web-based program?

2. Are we communicating and coordinating with our information technology department? What are their guidelines or standards?

3. Have all technical specifications been communicated to the vendors, consultants, and other team members?

4. Who will be responsible for testing the program?

5. Who is the single point of contact on our team to handle all technical questions?

6. Will this program place any files permanently on our students' hard drives? Will this have an impact on any other existing applications?

CD-ROM Questions

1. Are the audio and video formats used supported by student computers?

2. Is the installation procedure easy to understand?

3. Is there an uninstall procedure that is easy to follow?

4. Is student tracking required? How will students report their final test scores?

5. When will the program content need to be updated? Have the update, dupli-cation, and distribution costs been considered?

WBT Questions

1. Do the program's media files fit within our bandwidth constraints? What will be the longest time a student has to wait for a piece of content?

2. Do we have all the plug-ins required of the program?

3. Will the program integrate with our existing student-tracking system, or is it creating a new system?

Guaranteed Results with a Systematic Design Process

Before undertaking any journey it is a good idea to have a destination in mind. In training, the destination or end result might be to change a behavior, improve a skill, or impart knowledge that can then be applied in a specific work situation. This chapter describes classic instructional design processes modified to support technology-based training. Using a highly structured design process forces you to identify the destination desired—and in that way be more sure to reach it. Technology itself does not make the training but is simply a means to accomplishing an end. The proven design processes outlined here are the real secrets to developing effective TBT.

What You Will Learn in This Chapter

- The importance of a systems approach in the design of training programs
- The five major steps in the ADDIE model
- How analysis identifies needs and keeps training on target
- What rapid prototyping adds to the ADDIE model
- The eight major elements in every script or storyboard

- Important ways in which video for multimedia differs from traditional video
- What you can hope to accomplish with alpha and beta testing
- How to roll out Web-based training and CD-ROMs
- The four levels of the Kirkpatrick Model for Summative Evaluation

WHAT IS INSTRUCTIONAL SYSTEMS DESIGN?

The most widely used methodology for developing new training programs is called *instructional systems design* (ISD). It is also known as *instructional systems design and development* (ISDD), the *systems approach to training* (SAT), or just *instructional design* (ID). This approach provides a step-by-step system for the evaluation of students' needs, the design and development of training materials, and the evaluation of the effectiveness of the training intervention.

ISD evolved from post–World War II research in the United States military to find a more effective and manageable way to create training programs. These efforts led to early ISD models that were developed and taught in the late 1960s at Florida State University. Today, Walter Dick and Lou Carey are widely viewed as the torchbearers of the methodology, with their authoritative book, *The Systematic Design of Instruction* (Dick and Carey, 1996).

Why Use a Systems Approach?

A system is any set of components that work together to achieve a specified outcome or goal. Think of the cruise control system on your car. You set the desired speed (or goal) and the cruise control sets the gas injection to the proper level. An important aspect of any system is the feedback mechanisms that ensure the goal is achieved or maintained. Using the cruise control analogy, the car does not just lock the gas pedal in one position. If you begin to drive uphill, the car briefly slows down until the speedometer information is fed back to the cruise control system, which then increases the amount of gas and the desired speed is reached again.

Just as a systems approach with its requisite feedback makes cruise control a viable system for maintaining driving speed, so too does the systems approach provide the smoothest means for developing training programs.

The ADDIE Model

There are more than one hundred different ISD models, but almost all are based on the generic ADDIE model, which stands for analysis, design, development, implementation, and evaluation (see Figure 3.1). Each step in the model has an outcome that feeds the subsequent step. During *analysis,* the designer develops a clear understanding of the gaps between the desired outcomes or behaviors and the audience's existing knowledge and skills. In the *design* phase, the instructional designer then documents specific learning objectives, assessment instruments, exercises, and content. The actual creation of learning materials is completed in the *development* phase by programmers, artists, and audio and video producers. During *implementation* these materials are delivered or distributed to the student group. After delivery, the effectiveness of the training materials is *evaluated.*

Alternate Design Models

The ADDIE model has been criticized by some as being too systematic, that is, too linear, too inflexible, too constraining, and even too time-consuming to implement. As alternatives to the *systematic* approach, there are a variety of *systemic* design models that emphasize a more holistic, iterative approach to the development of training. Rather than developing the instruction in phases, the entire development team works together from the start to build lessons rapidly, to test them with the student audience, and then to revise them based on the students' feedback.

The systemic approach to development has many advantages when it comes to the creation of TBT. To create engaging metaphors or themes, artists and writers work together in a process that validates the creative treatment with students

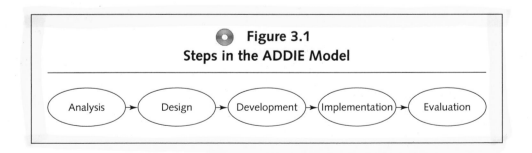

Figure 3.1
Steps in the ADDIE Model

Analysis → Design → Development → Implementation → Evaluation early in the development cycle. Programmers and designers garner agreement from the client as to which learning activities are both effective and possible given the constraints of the client's computers or network.

Despite these advantages, there are practical challenges with a purely systemic design approach—namely, in the management of resources. In most cases, training programs must be developed under a fixed—and often limited—budget and schedule. While it is very easy to allocate people and time to each step in the ISD model, it is harder to plan deliverables when there are no distinct steps in the process. The holistic approach begs the following questions: How many iterations and how much time will it take to finish the program? and Do the contributions made in the design phase by programmers and artists, who have no formal background in instruction, warrant the extra time required and additional compensation for this time?

Introducing a Rapid Prototyping Phase

For best results, the development process for CD-ROM or WBT programs should follow a modified ADDIE model, which borrows from the most valuable aspects of the systemic approach (see Figure 3.2). Specifically, a rapid prototype phase is inserted after or as an extension of the design phase. A rapid prototype is simply a quickly assembled module that can be tested with the student audience early in the ISD process. The evaluation of the prototype typically looks at such things as how well the learners responded to the creative metaphor, how effective the learning activities are, and how well the program performs on the chosen technology platform. Based on the feedback, the design can be revised and another prototype developed. This iterative process continues until there is agreement on and confidence in the prototype.

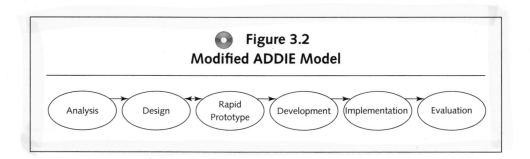

Figure 3.2
Modified ADDIE Model

Analysis → Design ↔ Rapid Prototype → Development → Implementation → Evaluation

In this process, only after the prototype is completed is additional development work done. This work often moves more quickly, however, than in the traditional ADDIE model. Instructional designers and writers are able to proceed more efficiently because they know exactly what the program will look like and what it will be capable of doing. Additionally, with all of the major technical issues resolved, final programming becomes a simple matter of assembling media components.

A more detailed look at each step in the ADDIE–rapid prototype model follows.

ANALYSIS

The analysis phase simply identifies the gap between actual behaviors and desired outcomes, and obtains information about the learner, environment, and technology that are relevant to closing the gap. This phase is the first and most crucial phase, and all subsequent work is based on the outcomes of the analysis. Despite this fact, the analysis phase is frequently omitted from the process because it is perceived as unnecessary or too time-consuming.

Many corporate training managers or executives believe they intuitively know what students need in a training program. Their preconceptions are expressed in statements such as "Our employees are conservative; don't use any games or themes" or "Our students really don't have any experience with this topic, so we'd better cover everything" or "We all love the Internet; let's put everything on-line." The danger with assumptions such as these is that programs will be rolled out that are boring, too long, or technically flawed. Even if time is limited, an expedited analysis phase will uncover and document key items about learners, content, and technology.

The tools that can be used to gather analysis information include the following:

- A *survey* or *questionnaire* is the most commonly used method of posing specific questions to a representative sample of the student population. Survey results are reviewed and summarized.

- In *direct observation,* the designer personally observes employee tasks being performed in the workplace.

- *Indirect observation* involves examining relevant performance data such as safety records, error rates, help-desk call reports, sales data, or customer satisfaction surveys.

- *Interviews* put the instructional designer in touch with experts, a random sample of students, or both through one-on-one interviews.
- *Focus groups* are similar to interviews except the designer poses questions to a group of experts or students. Data come from direct answers as well as from conversations among the focus group participants.

Evaluate Business and Instructional Goals

The first step in analysis is determining or clarifying the goals or desired outcomes. Entire systems have been developed just to handle goal analysis, but in simplified terms you need to answer the question, What are we really trying accomplish? The goal need not be stated in behavioral terms but rather in the context of big-picture impact. Examples of various goals include the following:

- Improve sales among new representatives by 30 percent.
- Reduce the defect rate of widgets by 10 percent.
- All administrative assistants should be at an intermediate competency level with their computer applications.
- Deli workers need to master the safe operation of the meat slicer.

Business goals often need to be further analyzed to select the proper intervention. In the first example of the preceding list, there may be nontraining solutions to the problem. Perhaps increasing the sales representatives' commissions or changing to a team selling system would have the desired impact on sales. If a training intervention is appropriate, the goal needs to be modified into an instructional outcome such as "New representatives must be able to demonstrate each product's features and benefits."

Analyze Required Tasks and Behaviors

After the business or instructional goal is understood, further analysis of all the subordinate skills necessary to achieve the goal is required. This is a critical step toward developing behavioral learning objectives and it becomes the foundation for all of the content.

For example, the goal to have all deli operators properly operate a meat slicer can be broken into more specific tasks such as the following:

- Set the blade to the desired thickness of cut.
- Turn the slicer on.
- Place the food on the slicer and lock the food in place.
- Safely cut the meat or cheese.
- Turn the slicer off.
- Clean the blade after each use.

Assess Learners

After the desired goals and subordinate tasks are understood, the target audience has to be analyzed. Information obtained from learners affects everything from appropriateness of metaphor to selection of content. Topics to be explored in assessing learners include the following:

- *Demographics:* What are the general characteristics of the audience? Is there uniformity of gender, age, or educational background?
- *Psychographics:* What is the psychological makeup of the target audience? Do they want the information provided in a very direct manner or do they prefer a more time-consuming but engaging game format?
- *Attitude:* What are the learners' attitudes about the content or about training itself? What are their attitudes about the use of TBT?
- *Experience with technology-based training:* Will this be employees' first experience using the corporate Intranet for learning or are they already accustomed to navigating on-line material?
- *Motivation:* What are the learners' work and career goals? How can the training program assist them with the realization of those goals?
- *Prior knowledge and experience:* What skills and knowledge will the learners bring to the training? To what extent are they currently working toward achieving the desired business goals?

The audience profile can be used to direct both the design of the interface and instructional design. For example, an older workforce might not respond well to a music video theme or review questions embedded within an arcade game. Students for whom English is not their first language typically prefer audio narration over on-screen text. A young student audience may not understand allusions to historical events that occurred before they were born.

Conduct a Technology Assessment

Finally, the technology available to the student audience must be investigated. What type of computers do they have? What kind of software is installed? What kind of network connection exists? What limitations will the information technology department put on the program? Specifications should include the following (examples in parentheses):

- Speed and processor type (200 megahertz Pentium)
- Amount of memory or RAM available (64 megabytes)
- Type of operating system (Windows 3.1, Windows 95)
- Whether or not CD-ROMs are available
- Whether or not there is audio capability
- Screen resolution available (800 x 600)
- Video standards available (Windows AVI, MPEG, QuickTime)
- Whether or not there is an Intranet or Internet connection
- Whether the connection is high bandwidth (Ethernet) or low bandwidth (dial-up modem)
- Browser and version available (MS Internet Explorer 4.0)
- Browser plug-ins available (Shockwave, Flash, RealVideo)

Instructional designers should consult with programmers or other technical supervisors to gain an understanding of the limitations of the technology. Some common limitations include the following:

- Without speakers or headphones, the training program will not be able to use audio narration as the primary teaching media.

- Without a fast-enough processor or enough RAM, complex animations may not run smoothly.

- With Windows' standard AVI video format, video windows will be small and the video itself may be choppy and grainy.

- Only if there is some type of connection to an Intranet or the Internet is WBT possible.

- If the connection is low bandwidth, the time it takes to download big files (large graphics, animations, audio, and video) will be prohibitively long; designers will have to stick to text and simple graphics.

- Web-based multimedia is possible only with the use of certain plug-ins.

- Complex activities, such as drag-and-drop exercises, can be implemented only using later versions of popular browsers, using advanced technologies such as DHTML, Java, and Javascript.

Analysis Data

After completing a thorough analysis, the instructional designer can use a series of worksheets, questionnaires, and other information to influence the outcomes of the design phase.

DESIGN

In the design phase, the outcomes from analysis are used to create a blueprint for the instruction. This blueprint, called a design document or design report, covers the training need, instructional strategies, content, and creative treatment. The document is used by the designer and project manager to communicate with all members of the development team and is invaluable for keeping the project on track and focused on the real training goals.

Determine Learning Objectives

The first step in the design phase is to examine the tasks or subordinate goals that were listed in analysis and from these create a set of behavioral learning objectives. Objectives should be short, specific, and testable.

For example, let's assume that a task analysis for a sales training program reveals that new representatives have three needs:

- To understand product features and benefits
- To know the competition
- To be able to handle customer objections

Corresponding learning objectives, which are specific and testable, might be written as finishing the following sentence: After completing this course students will be able to

- List five product features and identify an associated benefit for each feature.
- Identify five major competitors and list the name of each competitor's product.
- Classify an objection as either a misunderstanding, a smokescreen, or a valid objection.

Develop a Content Outline

Learning objectives determine the actual content of the program. After reviewing source materials, interviewing subject matter experts, or both, a content outline is developed by the instructional designer. The outline provides a lesson-by-lesson breakdown of topics, as well as a summary of any motivational strategies that will be employed.

The content outline lays out a plan for the sequence of instruction. The order of information depends on the subject matter at hand but typically goes in sequence from beginning to end when process is being taught and from easy to hard when concepts are being taught. A common exception is to begin with an overview lesson that presents the big picture before going into the details.

One of the strengths of the ISD process is that it excludes background information and tangential content, which might be interesting but are not related to the specific learning objectives at hand. By paring down content, development time and learning time are reduced and retention of relevant information is increased.

Indicate Practice Activities

In addition to presenting content, the design document specifies the strategies for practice. Practice and feedback are critical elements of effective instruction and should be planned carefully.

Although the specific activities themselves are not created until the development phase, a general description of practice should be given. The design document might include brief descriptions of simple questioning (multiple choice, true-false, or fill-in), simulations, instructional games, on-the-job application exercises, or situational analysis activities.

Specify Technology and Media

In TBT, the availability of CD-ROMs, audio speakers, bandwidth, and plug-ins always helps to determine the choice of media. The design document formally identifies the learners' available technology, which drives many of the implementation decisions later in the project. This specification should include not just what is available but what is allowed by an organization's information technology department. Sometimes technical specifications expand into the choice of development tools, including specific authoring systems, databases, or student-tracking systems.

The choice of media should also be justified from an instructional standpoint. Just because a computer can display video does not mean that video has to be used. In fact, many designers with a video or instructor-led background overuse video. Audio narration with appropriate graphics and interactivity will always be a better choice than "talking head" video clips that are passively viewed.

Determine User Interface and Creative Treatment

The graphical user interface is the critical link between the student and content. The design document spells out the buttons and navigational features that will be available, what their labels or names will be, and where on the screen they will be located. Ideally, an artist creates the actual screen designs and these images can be imbedded within the design document.

The following list indicates commonly prescribed interface items:

- *Next* button, which advances the user to the next screen
- *Back* button, which moves the user back to the previous screen
- *Screen counter* to indicate progress through a lesson
- *Menu* button to move user directly to the main menu
- *Exit* button to exit the program.

- *Glossary* button to access an on-line glossary
- *Help* to access context-sensitive information or navigational assistance
- *Notepad* for students to use to record notes
- *Bookmark* for tagging the existing screen for future quick access

The interface section of the design document should also describe or show the look and feel of the program. With consideration of the learners' profile and the client culture, the visual treatment can be a conservative, functional screen or something more creative. Training programs use a variety of metaphors or themes to increase student engagement. Among common examples are the science fiction adventure, James Bond espionage, film noir mystery, music video, TV game show, simulated work environment (virtual reality), and animated cartoon host or narrator.

Final Sign-Off

Once all revisions have been made, the "client" should officially approve the design document as the blueprint for the entire program. If you are managing a project inside an organization, the internal client, such as your boss or the project contact in the sponsoring department, should sign a release document (or at least acknowledge approval in an e-mail or memo) so that the other phases of the project can proceed based on the design document. If you are managing an outside vendor, you should provide written approval of the design. This final acknowledgment step helps to communicate the importance of the design, and the fact that changing the program at a later stage of development will be considered out of scope.

RAPID PROTOTYPE

In this phase, an instructional software module is created for quick testing with a sample of the student audience. The rapid prototype creates an early iteration loop that provides valuable feedback on technical issues, creative treatment, and effectiveness of instruction. The design document itself is then changed to reflect this feedback, and in some cases a new prototype module is developed for subsequent testing of the refinements.

Value of a Rapid Prototype

With the addition of the rapid prototype phase, the value of the ADDIE model for TBT is greatly enhanced. The prototype overcomes the limitations of the traditional ADDIE approach in that it involves all team members earlier in the project cycle and enables both the client and students to provide early feedback.

This early review process is critical to software development and can catch actual errors as well as identify client preferences. Many people without a programming background do not realize the complexity involved with multimedia programming. Sometimes seemingly simple changes, such as moving the location of navigation buttons, adding a new student-tracking feature, or increasing the size of the font, have a tremendous ripple effect throughout the program. Even when there is no apparent link between a requested change and another program feature, there often are connections within the software itself.

Changes to source code can potentially add dozens or hundreds of hours of programming time to a project. In fact, revisions are almost always the root cause of missed deadlines and exceeded budgets. Vendors even have a name for it—scope creep—which typically means that the client requested changes that exceed the original scope of the project. A detailed design document and prototype are the best insurance policies against last-minute alterations.

Create a Vertical Slice of the Program

Some developers consider a prototype to be nothing more than a couple of screen designs that show the look and feel of the program. For reviewers to provide truly valuable feedback, however, the prototype must include a cross section of the entire program. This cross section is sometimes called a *vertical slice,* which is depicted on the simple program flowchart in Figure 3.3.

A vertical slice of the program typically includes the title screen, the main menu, one complete lesson, and sometimes a portion of the post-test. All features that will be available from within a lesson should be tested in the prototype phase. These often include glossary, notepad, and bookmark. Make sure that all types of media, such as video and audio, are included to reveal any technical problems. Finally, creative themes or metaphors are the most subjective element of any program, and among the most time-consuming to change, so they should also be included in the prototype.

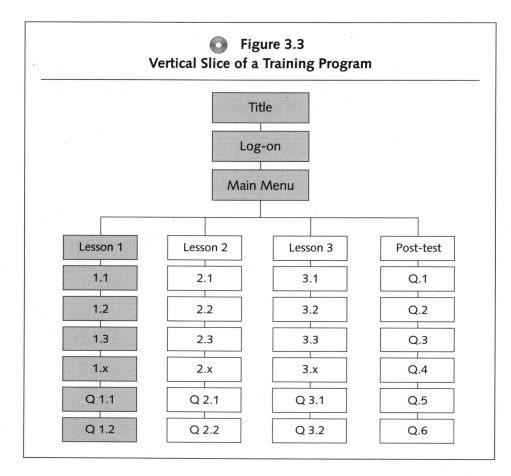

Figure 3.3
Vertical Slice of a Training Program

Evaluate the Rapid Prototype

Ideally, four to eight individuals selected from the student audience review the rapid prototype. What often occurs, however, is that three or four training managers or subject matter experts review the prototype. In the latter case, to provide an accurate and useful evaluation the reviewers must have a clear understanding of the learner population in terms of demographics, culture, and level of technical expertise.

The main purpose of the review is not to evaluate the content or instructional design but to evaluate the ease of navigation, the screen design and layout, the appropriateness of the metaphor, and the technical performance of the prototype.

Specific questions the designers should ask of the reviewers include the following:

- Did the program immediately capture your attention?
- Was the creative theme or metaphor engaging and appealing?
- Were the look and feel appealing? Was the program acceptable to corporate standards and culture?
- Was it easy to navigate the program? Did you ever feel lost or confused? Were the functions of the buttons easily identified?
- Was the quality of the audio acceptable?
- Was the quality of the video acceptable?
- Were waiting times acceptable during the loading and playback of graphics, animations, and video? (This is especially important for Web-based programs.)
- Was the tutorial lesson interactive and engaging?
- Did program features such as the glossary, notepad, and bookmark perform flawlessly?

DEVELOPMENT

After the design and prototype are finalized, the team is ready to begin actual development, which is often conducted in the following phases (see Figure 3.4).

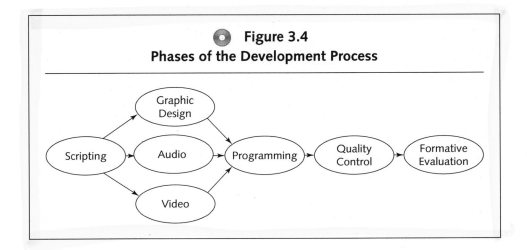

Figure 3.4
Phases of the Development Process

Develop Scripts or Storyboards

The development of scripts is the first step in the creation of programmer-ready materials, or PRMs. The script or storyboard is simply a screen-by-screen description of what students will see, hear, and do when running the program. Once the designer completes the script, it becomes the guidebook for all other team members: artists, audio-video producers, and programmers.

Depending on the project and the background of the development team, designers will create either scripts *or* storyboards. Both formats serve the same purpose and include the same descriptive elements, but they vary in their layout and their treatment of graphics. Scripts typically use verbal descriptions of on-screen graphical items (see Figure 3.5) while storyboards use sketches or clip art to depict required art elements visually (see Figure 3.6). Because of the time it takes to create even rough composite artwork, a scripting approach typically takes less time, but storyboards provide a more complete picture of what the final program will look like.

Regardless of the format chosen, every script or storyboard has the following eight major elements:

• *Project information* includes the name of the client, the curriculum title, the course title, the date, the draft or version number, and the script page number.

• The *screen label* indicates which screen of the program is being described. Sometimes screens are called frames or events. Screen labels are generally coded with both a lesson number and a screen number. For example, screen 03–0090 refers to lesson three, screen nine. The extra zero at the end of the screen counter leaves room to fit additional screens into the script in the future. If you wanted to add a new screen in lesson six, between the existing screens twelve and thirteen, the revised script would reference the new screen as 06–0125. Although this labeling system might seem arcane at first glance, it can save a lot of time and energy later. Because artists name graphical images using these numerical screen labels as file names, this system avoids the need to renumber all the screens in the script whenever a new page is added.

• *Audio-narration* is specified in the script if the technology used supports it. Typically an audio voice-over (sometimes labeled VO in the script) of the narrator is used. Sometimes the audio segment of a script specifies "Play dramatic music," "Buzzer sound on incorrect answer," or some other sound effect.

Figure 3.5
Sample Program Script

EVENT #00100
INTERVIEW RESULTS—MAIN MENU

[User selects Interview Results from the list of training topics on the Module Menu.]

GRAPHICS:
Graphic Interview Results icon from Module Menu is displayed in the top left corner of the screen.
RKA Management Results title is at the top of the screen. The main menu choices are prominently
displayed center screen; secondary menu choices are displayed vertically screen left; the program's
standard navigational tools are grouped together at the top of the screen.

PRIMARY MENU CHOICES:	SECONDARY MENU CHOICES:
• Planning the Interview	• Assessment
• Conducting the Interview	• Resources
• Finishing the Interview	• Site Map

ADD TEXT IN SYNC WITH NARRATION:	NARRATOR (VO):
• Human Resources drive organizational success and growth. • Finding, hiring, and retaining high-quality employees is crucial.	One of the most important driving forces behind the success and growth of an organization is its human resources. The process of finding, hiring, and retaining high-quality employees is crucial for a company in today's competitive marketplace.
• Interviewing is the most widespread selection method. • Well-planned and well-executed selection interviews help to place the right person in the right position.	There are many variables that managers must weigh in the employee-hiring equation, but interviewing is consistently the most widespread and relied-upon selection method. Well-planned and well-executed selection interviews provide valuable information about the applicants and help to place the right person in the right position.
• This training course provides essential knowledge and skills for interview success.	This training course provides you with the essential knowledge and skills to be a successful interviewer. By following the step-by-step process outlined in this course you will improve your understanding of the overall process and be able to plan and conduct more effective interviews.

NAVIGATION:
Planning the Interview = #20000
Conducting the Interview = #30000
Finishing the Interview = #40000
Assessment = #50000
Resources = #60000

Home = #00100
Index = #70000
Search = #80000
Help = #90000

HYPERTEXT:
Step-by-Step Process = #10020

RKA Management Results Interviewing Results   *March 4, 1999*   *Draft 1.0*   *Page 7*

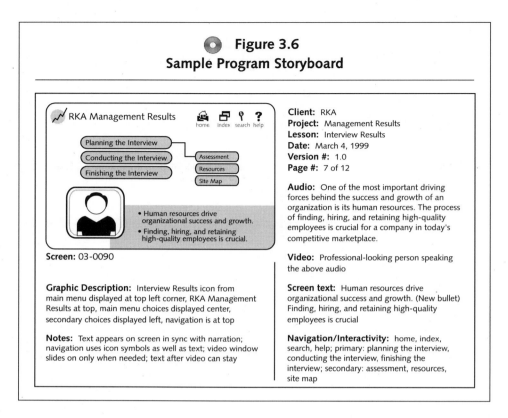

Figure 3.6
Sample Program Storyboard

RKA Management Results
home index search help

Planning the Interview
Conducting the Interview
Finishing the Interview

Assessment
Resources
Site Map

• Human resources drive organizational success and growth.
• Finding, hiring, and retaining high-quality employees is crucial.

Screen: 03-0090

Graphic Description: Interview Results icon from main menu displayed at top left corner, RKA Management Results at top, main menu choices displayed center, secondary choices displayed left, navigation is at top

Notes: Text appears on screen in sync with narration; navigation uses icon symbols as well as text; video window slides on only when needed; text after video can stay

Client: RKA
Project: Management Results
Lesson: Interview Results
Date: March 4, 1999
Version #: 1.0
Page #: 7 of 12

Audio: One of the most important driving forces behind the success and growth of an organization is its human resources. The process of finding, hiring, and retaining high-quality employees is crucial for a company in today's competitive marketplace.

Video: Professional-looking person speaking the above audio

Screen text: Human resources drive organizational success and growth. (New bullet) Finding, hiring, and retaining high-quality employees is crucial

Navigation/Interactivity: home, index, search, help; primary: planning the interview, conducting the interview, finishing the interview; secondary: assessment, resources, site map

• *Video clips,* if used, are described in the script, both giving camera direction and writing out the actual dialogue for on-screen actors. Descriptive notes to the director are included, such as "executive at her desk," "prestigious environment," or "slow zoom as she reaches her conclusion."

• *Graphics* are provided in the script as a verbal description of what should appear on screen or as a sketch. The purpose is to help both the reviewer (client or subject matter expert) and the artist who must create the final images to visualize what the designer has in mind. Descriptions might be "Show group of businesspeople around a conference table, gender balanced and multiculturally diverse," or more vague, such as "Computer on desk." General descriptions enable artists to apply their own creativity and resources. At the same time, given only a loose interpretation, the final graphic the artist creates may not match what the designer had in mind.

- The *on-screen text* section of the script describes the words that will appear on the screen. In many WBT programs that can not support audio, text is the primary learning media; thus this section of each script page may be quite long. In other programs where audio narration is the primary instructional media, the text is used to reinforce the audio. In these cases, the text is likely to appear as brief bullet points or short statements.

- *Navigation and interactivity* describe the action items of the program— What can the student do on this screen? and What will happen next? Standard navigation options include phrases such as "Next button moves to next screen in sequence" and "Menu button jumps back to main menu." These types of options, which are available from every single screen, are often excluded from the description. Once it is noted on the first script page, navigation is assumed to be constant. Other types of interactivity might be, "Answer A: Play buzzer sound and display in feedback window, 'That's incorrect. Try again,' " or even directions related to the theme or metaphor, "Clicking elevator doors causes doors to open, followed by interior elevator scene and movement to fifth floor (lesson five)."

- *Notes* is the final section of the script. It provides an area for recording any additional comments that do not fit easily into one of the preceding categories. This informal area allows the designer to communicate directly with an artist or programmer. Such comments might be, "The corporate culture is very Generation X. Let's make this opening screen colorful and extreme. Feel free to get creative!" or "This question segment needs to be tracked for final report purposes. We need to track specific answers in addition to correct or incorrect information."

Just as with the design document, once all revisions are made to the script, the client needs to approve it officially. This approval is critical because even small revisions to wording in audio narration or video segments will require the rehiring and scheduling of actors and voice talent, additional time in a studio or recording booth, and the digitizing and editing of sequences. Whoever has final approval rights of the scripts needs to know that they have to be perfect before production begins. An official sign-off memo makes this point explicit.

Create Graphic Art

Given direction, sketches, or both in the final script, graphic artists can begin to develop images that will be used in the actual program. Graphic art includes original illustrations and cartoons, manipulated stock images taken from a library, photographs scanned or taken with a digital camera, as well as animations. These images typically are saved with a filename that reflects the screen or frame on which they will appear. For example, if an image will be displayed on page five of lesson three, the graphic file might be named 3_005.bmp (where the bmp extension refers to the format of the graphic file, which is bitmap).

Produce Audio and Video

While the graphics are being developed, audio and video production can occur. For audio, professional voice actors are hired to record narration segments. This recording is done in a studio using soundproof booths and digital recording equipment. It is very important that the client or subject matter expert be on hand for this recording to ensure proper pronunciation of industry jargon and proper intonation. Developers can also purchase libraries of sound effects and music to include in their programs.

Video shoots can be done in a studio or on location and the client or subject matter expert should also be on hand to guarantee that the video will be created right the first time. Make sure that the team shooting the video is familiar with the peculiarities of multimedia production rather than just with traditional videotape. Playing video back from a CD-ROM or via the Web usually means that the video window will be small, the number of frames displayed per second will be much slower than in normal viewing, and the range of colors will be limited.

When shooting video for multimedia, follow these general guidelines:

- Actors and actresses should not wear white clothing that might "ghost" or glow on the screen.

- Wide-angle shots and panning should be avoided because they lose their effect when displayed in the small window.

- Try not to move the camera (tripods are a must); let the central objects on the screen do the moving.

- Even movement in the background requires a lot of data to be updated on the digital video stream, so avoid outdoor backdrops that might include trees blowing in the wind or cars or people passing by.

- Close-ups for talking-head shots should be tighter than normal, even to the point where the actor's head appears to be touching the top of the screen.

After audio and video have been created, the program is edited and cut into distinct segments. Each segment is saved with a file name that matches the script page to which it applies. All materials are now ready for the programmers.

Program the Instructional Software

Programmers, also known as multimedia authors or Web developers, take the media files and, using the script or storyboard as a guide, create the actual program. The time it takes to program training depends on the complexity of the course. Linear programs on CD-ROM or the Web are easier to create than nonlinear simulations, where the navigation and tracking is more complex. Programs that rely heavily on the presentation of information are easier to create than highly interactive programs.

Internal Quality Control (Alpha Test)

After the programmers are finished assembling the program, it undergoes an alpha test—several rounds of quality control testing—before the software is taken to the client or students. The term *alpha* (the first letter of the Greek alphabet) is a software-development term for the first version of software that is completed but that is not yet ready to be viewed by end users. The revised version of the program, which is ready for further testing by end users, is called the *beta* version.

Alpha tests consist of evaluations conducted by experienced multimedia developers as well as by "naive users" who have no direct role on the project. The developers look for problems in design and programming and know likely areas in which to find bugs. Naive users come at the program with a fresh perspective and are more likely to run through it in the same manner as actual students. In addition to finding bugs, these users may notice areas where additional user instructions are required, content is unclear, or graphics are confusing.

Quality reviewers should track their findings and observations on a simple log. Vague comments like "The program got stuck in lesson five" make the task of fixing the problem difficult. Programmers won't know where to look in lesson five, and they won't have any clues about how the program "got stuck." Efficient user comments should answer these questions:

- In which lesson and on which screen did the bug, typo, or error occur?
- What was the specific error? For example, if a typo, in which word? If a bug, what happened?

- What were the previous actions completed prior to the bug? For example, "I clicked 'True' to answer the question, feedback popped up, and then I clicked on the glossary button. The glossary did not display."

Conduct a Formative Evaluation (Pilot Test)

After internal quality control has been completed, training programs go through what is called a formative evaluation to "form" or revise the program. In this type of evaluation (also known as a pilot test, field test, or beta test), the program is rolled out to a small group of people, usually six to twenty, from the actual student target population. They complete the program in the same setting and with the same computers as the rest of the student audience will use.

This process serves as yet another check for technical bugs and glitches, but more importantly it checks the effectiveness of the instruction itself. Hard performance data are collected on whether or not the students achieved the learning objectives, based on the test results. Designers also gather attitudinal data through surveys (such as the one shown in Figure 3.7), observations of students' use of the program, one-to-one interviews, and focus group discussions.

The result of this step of the development process is a formative evaluation report summarizing students' test results and survey answers. The report also includes student comments and observer remarks, as well an outline of revisions necessary to improve the effectiveness of the program. Revisions could include changes to interface design, motivation and attention tactics, lesson structure, quantity or type of activities, features, and amount of practice and feedback; bug fixes; or even changes to the process for program completion.

Once revisions to the program are complete, the software undergoes another rigorous round of internal quality control. Even making small changes to text or graphics can have mystifying effects on other portions of the program. Although these types of edits should not create new bugs, you never know when a programmer might accidentally change or delete something that affects the logic and flow of the program. WBT is by its nature relatively easy to update. But the cost involved in reduplicating CD-ROMs to fix a bug can be quite high. These duplication costs typically include a fee, approximately $500, to create a glass master CD, followed by duplication at approximately $1 to $5 per unit.

Figure 3.7
User Evaluation Form

Pilot Test Evaluation Questionnaire

Student Information

Student Name:

Company:

Phone:

E-mail:

Learning Objectives

The objectives of the course were stated clearly.
(disagree) 1   2   3   4   5   (agree)

The objectives of the course are relevant to my job. (Y/N)
(disagree) 1   2   3   4   5   (agree)

Design

The course content and activities are engaging.
(disagree) 1   2   3   4   5   (agree)

The course is easy to move through.
(disagree) 1   2   3   4   5   (agree)

The design is flexible enough for me to move around at my own pace.
(disagree) 1   2   3   4   5   (agree)

Activities

There are an ample number of activities.
(disagree) 1   2   3   4   5   (agree)

The placement of activities makes sense.
(disagree) 1   2   3   4   5   (agree)

The activities helped to reinforce my understanding of the content.
(disagree) 1   2   3   4   5   (agree)

Content

The content is accurate.
(disagree) 1   2   3   4   5   (agree)

The course content is covered to an appropriate degree of breadth.
(disagree) 1   2   3   4   5   (agree)

The course content is covered to an appropriate degree of depth.
(disagree) 1   2   3   4   5   (agree)

The content is clearly explained.
(disagree) 1   2   3   4   5   (agree)

Navigation and Instructions

The navigation is intuitive.
(disagree) 1   2   3   4   5   (agree)

The program directions are clear.
(disagree) 1   2   3   4   5   (agree)

The exercise directions are clear.
(disagree) 1   2   3   4   5   (agree)

Logistics/Performance

How long did it take you to complete the course?

Did you complete it in one sitting? (Yes/No)

If not, were you able to pick up easily where you left off? (Yes/No)

There were no delays in accessing the content; performance was sufficient.
(disagree) 1   2   3   4   5   (agree)

Have you taken computer-based or Web-based training courses before? (Y/N)

If yes, how does this course compare?
(worst) 1   2   3   4   5   (best)

Global Transferability of Content

Is the content relevant to your geographical region and company?

If not, specifically what was included in the course that was not relevant to your geographical region and company?

What specific additions would make this material more relevant to your geographical region and company?

Miscellaneous

What would enhance this learning experience?

What additional content would you like to see developed in the future?

IMPLEMENTATION

The TBT program is finally ready to be released to the general student population. This step involves more logistical elements than instructional ones but is critical nonetheless. After all the hard work and effort exerted so far, you don't want your program to fail because of a delivery flaw.

Rollout of Web-Based Training

If the program is Web-based, it is likely that the software already exists on a private and secure server computer, either on the Internet or on a corporate Intranet. Changes are typically uploaded to the server and reviewers are provided with log-on passwords to gain access. Assuming that this is the case, releasing the Web-based training program is a simple matter of transferring it from the test server to the final location of the program. Often two copies of the program will be maintained. One copy is the live version accessible to the students, the other is the development site for new changes, which is kept on a mirrored or shadow server.

Rollout of Multimedia CD-ROM Training

Releasing a CD-ROM-based program is a bit more difficult than the rollout of a Web-based one in that it requires the duplication and distribution of CD-ROMs. The developer copies the final program to a master CD-ROM in a process known as "burning the gold master." The master CD is usually sent to an outside duplication company that is equipped to produce a large volume of CDs, along with their labels and jewel (plastic) cases.

Even though the training program is technology-based, it is a good idea to provide an accompanying quick reference card or printed set of instructions. Depending on the computer literacy of the audience, some students may have problems installing the software onto their computer or launching the program directly from the CD-ROM. It is a good idea to have the instructions on both a quick reference card or the case cover and on the CD label. Although the instructions on the CD label cannot be read once the CD is inserted into the computer, they will be there long after the printed instructions have been lost.

Internal Marketing

The internal marketing of your training program to the student audience is a step that is usually overlooked. In some cases, the training is mandatory and internal marketing is not an issue. In other cases, the training is optional support for those who need it. Don't assume that students will use a program just because you made it.

If CDs are shipped on an as-needed basis from the training department, or if Web-based tutorials are sitting on a training home page, students need to be notified and reminded that these resources exist. A communication plan announcing the release of a new title, curriculum, or virtual corporate university might include all of the following elements:

- Broadcast voice mail
- Broadcast e-mail
- Internal-mail announcement postcards
- Posters or banners displayed prominently in lobbies, cafeterias, and elevators
- Article in corporate newsletter
- Demonstrations and announcements at company meetings
- Prizes for first students to complete the course
- Prizes for high scores on self-assessment games

End-User Technical Support

As part of implementation, a plan needs to be made to support the end users, the students. This is not necessarily support for content questions but rather technical support to handle questions about installing or accessing the program, performance problems, or hardware issues. If the deployment of the software is small, a training manager or the vendor that created the program will often handle these types of calls directly. For larger audiences, the normal help desk or information technology department should handle technical support telephone calls.

EVALUATION

The final step in the revised ADDIE model is a summative evaluation in which you measure how effectively the training program accomplished its stated goals. This step in the training process is usually ignored because of the added time and cost required. Training departments with limited budgets often assume that new programs are effective and put dollars that should go into evaluation into the next program. However, as senior executives demand more accountability from training efforts, interest in measuring and reporting results is certain to increase.

The Kirkpatrick Model for Summative Evaluation

In 1975, Donald Kirkpatrick first presented a four-level model of evaluation that has become a classic in the industry:

- Level One: Reaction
- Level Two: Learning
- Level Three: Behavior
- Level Four: Results

These levels can be applied to technology-based training as well as to more traditional forms of delivery.

Level One: Students' Reaction In this first step, students are asked to evaluate the training after completing the program. The evaluation forms are sometimes called smile sheets or happy sheets because in their simplest form they measure how well students liked the training. However, this type of evaluation can reveal valuable data if the questions asked are more complex. For example, a survey similar to the one used in the formative evaluation (see Figure 3.7) could also be used with the full student population. This questionnaire moves beyond how well the students liked the training to questions about the following:

- The relevance of the objectives
- The ability of the course to maintain interest
- The amount and appropriateness of interactive exercises
- The ease of navigation
- The *perceived* value and transferability of the training to the workplace

With TBT, the survey can be delivered and completed on-line and then printed or e-mailed to a training manager. Because this type of evaluation is so easy and cheap to administer, it is conducted in most organizations.

Level Two: Learning Results In this second step, learning results are measured. Did the students actually learn the knowledge, skills, and attitudes the program was supposed to teach? To show achievement, have students complete a pretest and post-test, making sure that test items or questions are truly written to the learning objectives. By summarizing the scores of all students, trainers can accurately see the impact the training intervention had. This type of evaluation is not as widely conducted as Level One but it is still very common.

Level Three: Behavior in the Workplace Students typically score well on post-tests, but the real question is whether or not any of the new knowledge and skills are retained and transferred to the job. Level Three evaluations attempt to answer whether or not students' behaviors actually change as a result of new learning.

Ideally this measurement is conducted three to six months after the training program. By allowing some time to pass, students have the opportunity to implement new skills and retention rates can be checked. Observation surveys, sometimes called behavioral scorecards, are used. Surveys can be completed by the student, the student's supervisor, individuals who report directly to the student, and even the student's customers. For example, a survey to evaluate a sales training program might include the following questions:

- Did the representative open each customer dialogue with a product benefit statement followed by a request to proceed?

- Was the representative able to analyze and describe customers' objections as either valid, misinformation, or a smokescreen?

- Did the representative use the appropriate model answer in response to each objection?

- Did the representative close each sales call with a request for purchase?

- If the prospect did not buy anything, did the representative end the call with specific future action steps?

- Did the representative complete call-history records that include summaries of who, what, where, when, and why?

Level Four: Business Results The fourth step in this model is to evaluate the business impact of the training program. The only scientific way to isolate training as a variable would be to isolate a representative control group within the larger student population and then rollout the training program, complete the evaluation, and compare the results against a business evaluation of the nontrained group. Unfortunately, this is rarely done, because of the difficulty of gathering the business data and the complexity of isolating the training intervention as a unique variable. Even anecdotal data is worth capturing, however. Following are sample training programs and the type of business impact data that can be measured.

- *Sales training:* Measure change in sales volume, customer retention, length of sales cycle, and profitability on each sale after the training program has been implemented.
- *Technical training:* Measure reduction in calls to the help desk; reduced time to complete reports, forms, or tasks; or improved use of software or systems.
- *Quality training:* Measure a reduction in number of defects.
- *Safety training:* Measure reduction in number or severity of accidents.
- *Management training:* Measure increase in engagement levels of direct reports.

APPLYING IT ON THE JOB

Whether you evaluate your own project plan or the development plan obtained from your training vendor, you should be able to answer yes to the following questions:

- Is there a suitable analysis of business goal, audience, technology, and content?
- Will there be a detailed design document that serves as a blueprint for the whole program?
- Will a rapid prototype be built for evaluation early in the project lifecycle?
- Is the script or storyboard format clear and easy to understand?
- Will subject matter experts be included in audio and video recording sessions?
- Are adequate resources and time allocated for a formative evaluation (pilot test) to be conducted?
- Is there a clear plan for implementation and technical support?
- Is a plan in place and are resources allocated to conduct a program evaluation?

Designing Lessons
for Adult Learners

No matter what kind of training you are developing, all adult learning programs need to be based on proven principles of instruction. Although the training should look appealing and engaging, above all it must be designed to teach. Adults bring different attitudes, expectations, life experiences, and goals to the training experience than children or even teens do. By applying what is known about adult learners to your training program, you can make it more effective, no matter what technology you choose to employ. Instruction, not technology, should always be the most important design consideration of any TBT program.

What You Will Learn in This Chapter
- The four main points of Knowles's theory of andragogy
- How Gagné's nine instructional events help learners retain information
- How instructional events can be applied to a training program
- How behavioral objectives help to evaluate the effectiveness of a training program
- How to maximize learning by understanding what motivates learners
- How constructivism differs from other theories of adult learning

THE VALUE OF PROVEN INSTRUCTIONAL DESIGN STRATEGIES

The most profound statement uttered in the training community over the last ten years was the simple declaration in 1998 by M. David Merrill that "information is not instruction" (Zemke, 1998). Although Merrill, professor of instructional technology at Utah State University, was reacting to the inadequacies of many Web-based training programs, his statement reflects that it has always been too easy to become enamored with the technology portion of TBT—at the expense of proper design and learning outcomes.

In the early days of disk-based computer-based training, there was a rush to pour content into electronic tutorials. At the time, computers could display only black and white text. Audio, video, and graphics were years away. A few innovative designers made the most of the limited media and created engaging simulations, quizzes, and even games. But this was the exception to the rule, and most early programs were nothing more than books on a computer. Learners were forced to read the text passively on the screen, often clicking the enter button or space bar to move on. Eyestrain and boredom, rather than improved learning and performance, were often the end results. These types of programs, derisively known as *page-turners,* tainted the image of CBT for many years.

With the advent of interactive videodisks and multimedia CD-ROMs, designers gained the ability to add graphics, animation, audio, and video to their CBT. Today's CD-ROM training programs often use creative themes and production elements that make them look more like the latest blockbuster movie or Nintendo video game. These bells and whistles can keep students engaged, but many of these programs still lack implementation of sound principles of instructional design. Frequently, development budgets are consumed by dramatic themes and Hollywood production values, leaving few resources to spend on instructional activities. The result is an audience that has been entertained but has not acquired new skills or knowledge.

More recently, there has been an unprecedented move toward Web technology as a training and education medium. Consider recent changes: at the 1996 annual conference of the American Society for Training and Development there was only one seminar devoted to the topic of WBT. Two years later more than a dozen *conferences* were held on the topic. In 1997, total expenditures on WBT were estimated at $197 million, with spending in the year 2002 projected to be $6 billion, representing a 95 percent annual growth rate (International Data Corporation, 1998).

Most early WBT programs were nothing more than on-line documents. Trainers created electronic versions of traditional printed student manuals, articles, tip sheets, and reference guides. Although these are valuable and accessible resources, their conversions on the Web cannot be considered true training programs. The rush to the Web without giving consideration to instructional design led to Merrill's passionate defense of a scientific approach to learning. In a June 1998 interview in *Training* magazine, Merrill put it simply, "If you don't provide adequate practice, if you don't have an adequate knowledge structure, if you don't provide adequate guidance, people don't learn" (Zemke, 1998, p. 37). To guarantee the effectiveness of any training program, remember that although technology will always change, the way adults learn will not.

HOW ADULTS LEARN

The birth of the modern theory of adult learning, known as *andragogy,* occurred in 1946 at a Boston YMCA. A young director of adult education organized a course on astronomy and arranged for a local university professor to teach the class. Although the students were initially enthusiastic, they quickly became bored with the passive lecture experience, and attendance dwindled until the course was finally canceled.

Trying again, the YMCA director rescheduled the course and this time invited a member of the amateur astronomers club to lead the group of students. As soon as the students arrived for their first class, the new teacher escorted them to the roof of the YMCA and asked them to gaze into the night sky. While they looked up, the teacher asked them what they noticed most and what they wanted to learn. Their questions formed the basis for the rest of the course, and the teacher led discussions with a telescope on hand for ready use. This experiential method of teaching was popular with the students and the class enrollment swelled.

The young YMCA director, Malcolm Knowles, took note of different teaching styles and their dramatically different outcomes. The method of teaching to adult learners' interests and actively engaging the students in their own discovery became the structure Knowles would use for all of the YMCA courses. The astronomy class also marked the beginning of Knowles's lifelong exploration of adult learning.

Knowles did not adopt the term *andragogy* until 1970 with the release of his book *The Modern Practice of Adult Education: Andragogy Versus Pedagogy.* The word *pedagogy,* defined as the art and science of teaching, has its origin in Greek and traditionally has applied to the teaching of children. Knowles's seminal work clearly drew a new distinction between classic methods of pedagogical instruction and adult learning principles.

Knowles's theories of adult learning are complex but his conclusions can be summarized in four main points:

- Adults need to know why they are learning something; they should be told how it effects them directly.

- Adults have a repository of lifetime experiences that should be tapped as a resource for ongoing learning; similarly, adult learners bring various levels of prior exposure to any topic and that fact should be acknowledged.

- Adults use a hands-on problem-solving approach to learning; rote memorization of facts and figures should be avoided.

- Adults want to apply new knowledge and skills immediately; retention decreases if the learning is applied only at some future point in time.

Andragogy and TBT

Regardless of whether a training program is delivered via CD-ROM or the Web, Knowles's assumptions about adult learners can be used for designing effective instruction.

For example, assume that you are creating a self-paced course on team building. Because adult students need to know why they are learning about a topic, the course should begin with an emphasis on the specific benefits of teamwork that the learner can apply directly to his or her work, as shown in Figure 4.1.

Knowles's theory acknowledges that adult students come to the course with previous work experiences and expect to participate in the learning process. Figure 4.2 illustrates how students can be engaged by the content. They have been asked to recall how they've solved problems in the past and how teamwork could be beneficial in the future.

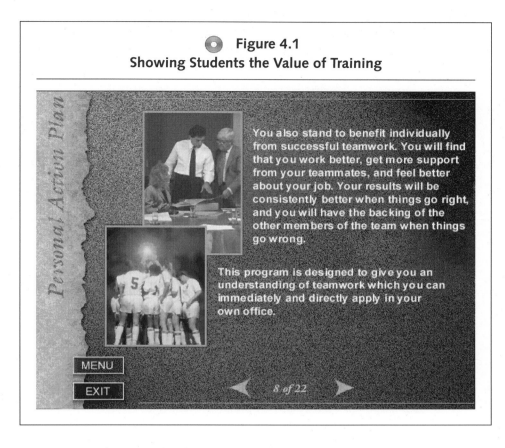

Figure 4.1
Showing Students the Value of Training

Personal Action Plan

You also stand to benefit individually from successful teamwork. You will find that you work better, get more support from your teammates, and feel better about your job. Your results will be consistently better when things go right, and you will have the backing of the other members of the team when things go wrong.

This program is designed to give you an understanding of teamwork which you can immediately and directly apply in your own office.

MENU

EXIT

8 of 22

As an example of Knowles's hands-on approach to adult learning, Figure 4.3 shows a game in which the student interacts with computer-controlled survivors on a raft at sea. The purpose of the exercise is to teach students about the concept of *synergy,* in which a team's group decision is better than that of any one individual.

According to Knowles, knowledge should be applied immediately to increase retention. Figure 4.4 shows an example of a personal action plan that can be completed on-line and accessed on a daily basis.

(Gahnyā)

GAGNÉ'S SYSTEMATIC APPROACH TO TRAINING

Just as Malcolm Knowles is widely regarded as the father of adult learning theory, Robert M. Gagné is considered to be the foremost researcher and contributor to

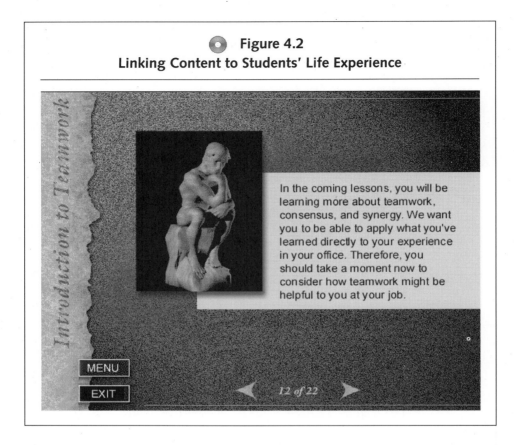

Figure 4.2
Linking Content to Students' Life Experience

Introduction to Teamwork

In the coming lessons, you will be learning more about teamwork, consensus, and synergy. We want you to be able to apply what you've learned directly to your experience in your office. Therefore, you should take a moment now to consider how teamwork might be helpful to you at your job.

MENU

EXIT

12 of 22

the systematic approach to instructional design and training. Gagné and his followers are known as behaviorists, and their focus is on the outcomes, or behaviors, that result from training.

Gagné's Nine Events of Instruction

Gagné's book *The Conditions of Learning and Theory of Instruction,* first published in 1965, identified the mental conditions for learning. These conditions were based on the information processing model of the mental events that occur when adults are presented with various stimuli. (Chapter Five covers the details of the information processing model.) Gagné created a nine-step process called the *events of instruction,* which correlate to and address the conditions of learning

Figure 4.3
Game for Teaching Concept of Synergy

Synergy Simulation

Now you will have 4 minutes to ask each of the other six survivors their opinions about which items are important. They will share with you their ideas when you click on their faces.

I think I read someplace that most people are rescued within the first 48 hours.

First Mate

MENU

EXIT

(Hint: Each survivor has a lot to say. Click on them more than once.)

12 of 21

(Gagné & Medsker, 1996). Figure 4.5 lists these instructional events and their associated mental processes.

1. *Gain attention.* For learning to take place, you must first capture the attention of the student. A multimedia program that begins with an animated title-screen sequence accompanied by sound effects or music startles the senses with auditory and visual stimuli. An even better way to capture students' attention is to start each lesson with a thought-provoking question or interesting fact. Curiosity motivates students to learn.

2. *Inform learners of objectives.* Early in each lesson, students should encounter a list of learning objectives. This list initiates the internal process of expectancy and helps motivate the learner to complete the lesson. These objectives

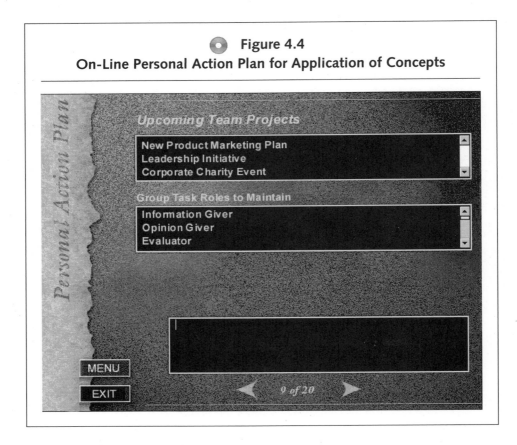

Figure 4.4
On-Line Personal Action Plan for Application of Concepts

Personal Action Plan

Upcoming Team Projects

New Product Marketing Plan
Leadership Initiative
Corporate Charity Event

Group Task Roles to Maintain

Information Giver
Opinion Giver
Evaluator

MENU

EXIT

◄ *9 of 20* ►

should form the basis for assessment and for possible certification as well. Typically, learning objectives are presented in the form of "Upon completing this lesson you will be able to. . . ." (The phrasing of the objectives themselves are covered under Robert Mager's contributions later in this chapter.)

3. *Stimulate recall of prior learning.* Associating new information with prior knowledge can facilitate the learning process. It is easier for learners to encode and store information in long-term memory when there are links to personal experience and knowledge. A simple way to stimulate recall is to ask questions about previous experiences, about understanding of previous concepts, or about a body of content.

Figure 4.5
Events of Instruction and Associated Mental Processes

Instructional Event	Internal Process
1. Gain attention	Stimuli activates receptors
2. Inform learners of objectives	Creates level of expectation for learning
3. Stimulate recall of prior learning	Retrieval and activation of short-term memory
4. Present the content	Selective perception of content
5. Provide learning guide	Semantic encoding for storage in long-term memory
6. Elicit performance (practice)	Responds to questions to enhance encoding and verification
7. Provide feedback	Reinforcement and assessment of correct performance
8. Assess performance	Retrieval and reinforcement of content as final evaluation
9. Enhance retention and transfer to the job	Retrieval and generalization of learned skill to new situation

4. *Present the content.* This event is when the new content is actually presented to the learner. Content should be chunked and organized meaningfully, and it is typically explained and then demonstrated. To appeal to different learning modalities, a variety of media should be used if possible, including text, graphics, audio narration, and video.

5. *Provide learning guidance.* To help learners encode information for long-term storage, additional guidance should be provided along with the presentation of new content. Guidance strategies include the use of examples, nonexamples, case studies, graphical representations, mnemonics, and analogies.

6. *Elicit performance (practice).* In this event, the learner is required to practice the new skill or behavior. Eliciting performance provides an opportunity for learners to confirm their correct understanding, and the repetition further increases the likelihood of retention.

7. *Provide feedback.* As learners practice new behavior, it is important to provide specific and immediate feedback on their performance. Unlike questions in a post-test, exercises within tutorials should be used for comprehension and encoding purposes, not for formal scoring. Additional guidance and answers provided at this stage are called *formative feedback.*

8. *Assess performance.* Upon completing instructional modules, students should be given the opportunity (or be required) to take a post-test or do a final assessment. This assessment should be completed without the ability to receive additional coaching, feedback, or hints. Mastery of material, or certification, is typically granted after achieving a certain score or a percentage of correct answers. A commonly accepted level of mastery is 80 to 90 percent correct.

9. *Enhance retention and transfer to the job.* Whether the skills learned from a training program are ever applied back on the job often remains a mystery to training managers—and a source of consternation for senior executives. Effective training programs have a performance focus, incorporating design and media that facilitate retention and transfer to the job. The repetition of learned concepts is a tried-and-true means of aiding retention, although it is often disliked by students. (There was a reason for writing spelling words ten times as grade school students.) Creating electronic or on-line job aids, references, templates, and wizards (step-by-step instructions on completing complex tasks) are other ways of aiding performance.

Applying Gagné's nine-step model to any training program is the single best way to ensure an effective learning program. A multimedia program that is filled with glitz or that provides unlimited access to Web-based documents is no substitute for sound instructional design. Although those types of programs might entertain or be valuable as references, they will not maximize the effectiveness of information processing, and learning will not occur.

Applying Gagné's Events of Instruction

For an example of how to apply Gagné's events of instruction to an actual training program, let's look at a high-level treatment for a fictitious software training program. We'll assume that we need to develop a CD-ROM tutorial to teach sales representatives how to use a new lead-tracking system called STAR, which runs on their laptop computers.

1. *Gain attention.* The program starts with an engaging opening sequence. A space theme is used to play off the new software product's name, STAR. Inspirational music accompanies the opening sequence, which might consist of a shooting star or an animated logo. When students access the first lesson, the vice president of sales appears on the screen in a video clip and introduces the course. She explains how important it is to stay on the cutting edge of technology and how the training program will teach them to use the new STAR system. She also emphasizes the benefits of the STAR system, which include reducing the amount of time representatives need to spend on paperwork.

2. *Inform learners of objectives.* The vice president of sales presents students with the following learning objectives immediately after the introduction:

Upon completing this lesson you will be able to

- List the benefits of the new STAR system.
- Start and exit the program.
- Generate lead-tracking reports by date, geography, and source.
- Print paper copies of all reports.

3. *Stimulate recall of prior learning.* Students are called on to use their prior knowledge of other software applications to understand the basic functionality of the STAR system. They are asked to think about how they start, close, and print from other programs, such as their word processor, and it is explained that the STAR system works similarly. Representatives are asked to reflect on the process of the old lead-tracking system and compare it to the process of the new electronic one.

4. *Present the content.* Using screen images captured from the live application software and audio narration, the training program describes the basic features of the STAR system. After the description, a simple demonstration is performed.

5. *Provide learning guidance.* With each STAR feature, students are shown a variety of ways to access it—using shortcut keys on the keyboard, drop-down menus, and button bars. Complex sequences are chunked into short, step-by-step lists for easier storage in long-term memory.

6. *Elicit performance (practice).* After each function is demonstrated, students are asked to practice with realistic, controlled simulations. For example,

students might be asked to generate a report that shows all active leads in the state of New Jersey. They will be required to use the mouse to click on the correct on-screen buttons and options to generate the report.

7. *Provide feedback.* During the simulations, students are given guidance as needed. If they are performing operations correctly, the simulated STAR system behaves just as the live application would. If the student makes a mistake, the tutorial immediately responds with an audible cue, and a pop-up window explains and reinforces the correct operation.

8. *Assess performance.* After all lessons are completed, students are required to take a post-test. Mastery is achieved with an 80 percent or better score, and once it is obtained, the training program displays a completion certificate, which can be printed. The assessment questions are directly tied to the learning objectives displayed in the lessons.

9. *Enhance retention and transfer to the job.* Although the STAR system is relatively easy to use, additional steps are taken to ensure successful implementation and widespread use among the sales force. These features include on-line help and wizards. Additionally, the training program is equipped with a content map, an index of topics, and a search function. These enable students to use the training as a just-in-time support tool in the future. Finally, a one-page laminated quick-reference card is packaged with the training CD-ROM for further reinforcement of the learning session.

MAGER'S BEHAVIORAL LEARNING OBJECTIVES

Robert Mager is the third titan of instructional design. His 1962 book, *Preparing Instructional Objectives,* influenced school systems for decades and continues to shape the vast majority of corporate training programs developed today. Mager argued for the use of specific, measurable objectives that both guide designers during courseware development and aid students in the learning process. These instructional objectives, also known as *behavioral* and *performance* objectives, can be applied directly in Gagné's second event of instruction (to inform learners of objectives).

In the design of instructional materials, first training needs are analyzed and then the learning goals of the program are determined. Mager's central concept is that a learning goal should be broken into a subset of smaller tasks or learning objectives. According to his definition, a behavioral objective should have three components:

- *Behavior:* The behavior should be specific and observable.
- *Condition:* The conditions under which the behavior is to be completed should be stated, including what tools or assistance are to be provided.
- *Standard:* The level of performance that is desirable should be stated, including an acceptable range of answers that are allowable as correct.

Consider the following behavioral objective: *Given a stethoscope and normal clinical environment, the medical student will be able to diagnose a heart arrhythmia in 90 percent of effected patients.* This example describes the observable behavior (identifying the arrhythmia), the conditions (given a stethoscope and a normal clinical environment), and the standard (90 percent accuracy).

Today, the performance objectives in most training programs ignore an indication of the conditions and standards. When these are omitted, it is assumed that the conditions involve normal workplace conditions and that standards are set at perfection. What is always included, however, is the most important criteria for a valuable objective: a written indication of the behavior using measurable or observable verbs. According to Mager, vague verbs such as *understand, know,* or *learn about* should be replaced with more specific verbs. The list that follows provides some of the verbs appropriate for use with the statement, "At the conclusion of this lesson you will be able to"

- List
- Identify
- State
- Describe
- Define
- Solve
- Compare and contrast
- Operate

For an example of how behavioral objectives can be developed, let's assume that we are creating a training program for receptionists. The goal of the program is simply to train people in proper phone use. What specific tasks and associated learning objectives might be included?

An example of a poorly defined objective is, *In this course you will learn how to operate the phone and properly talk to callers.* This statement is not an objective but a description of the course contents.

Another example of poorly written objectives is the following: After completing this course you will be able to

- Operate your phone
- Know how to greet callers
- Understand the procedure for transferring a call

These objectives do not indicate observable behaviors, making assessment of their mastery impossible. How does one know if a person knows or understands something? What does it really mean to operate the phone?

The following performance objectives are good examples of the use of observable behaviors: After completing this course you will be able to

- Place a caller on hold
- Activate the speaker phone
- Play new messages on the voice mail system
- List the three elements of a proper phone greeting
- Transfer a call to a requested extension

These objectives are built around very discrete tasks. Instead of the vague objective to "operate the phone," the learner knows exactly what is expected for successful operation—namely, using the hold feature, speaker phone, and voice mail system. More importantly, these behaviors are observable. A student can be watched as she activates the speaker phone or listened to as she describes the elements of a good phone greeting. Because there is no ambiguity, learner expectancy is achieved and a proper evaluation can be made.

MOTIVATING LEARNERS

Motivation is the most overlooked aspect of instructional strategy, and perhaps the most critical element needed for employee-learners. Even the most elegantly designed training program will fail if the students are not motivated to learn. Without a desire to learn on the part of the student, retention is unlikely. Many students in a corporate setting who are forced to complete training programs are motivated only to "pass the test." Designers must strive to create a deeper motivation in learners so they will learn new skills and transfer them back into the work environment.

As a first step, instructional designers should not assume that they understand the target audience's motivation. To analyze needs, the designer should ask prospective learners questions such as the following:

- What would the value of this type of program be to you?
- What do you hope to get out of this program?
- What are your interests in this topic?
- What are your most pressing problems?

The answers to these types of questions are likely to provide insight into learner motivation, as well as desirable behavioral outcomes.

Keller's ARCS Model for Motivation

John Keller and T. W. Kopp (1987) synthesized existing research on psychological motivation and created the ARCS model. ARCS stands for attention, relevance, confidence, and satisfaction. This model is not intended to stand apart as a separate system for instructional design; rather, it can be incorporated within Gagné's events of instruction.

Attention. The first and single most important aspect of the ARCS model is gaining and keeping the learner's attention, which coincides with the first step in Gagné's model. Keller's strategies for attention include sensory stimuli, inquiry arousal (thought-provoking questions), and variability (variations in exercises and use of media).

Relevance. Attention and motivation will not be maintained, however, unless the learner believes that the training is relevant. Put simply, the training program should answer the critical question, What's in it for me? Benefits should be clearly stated. For a sales training program, the benefit might be to help representatives increase their sales and personal commissions. For a safety training program, the benefit might be to reduce the number of workers getting hurt. For a software training program, the benefit to users could be to make them more productive or reduce their frustration with an application. A health care program might have the benefit that it can teach doctors how to treat certain patients.

Confidence. The confidence aspect of the ARCS model is required so that students will feel they should put a good-faith effort into the program. If they think they are incapable of achieving the objectives or that it will take too much time or effort, their motivation will decrease. In TBT programs, students should be given estimates of the time required to complete lessons, or a measure of their progress through the program.

Satisfaction. Finally, learners must obtain some type of satisfaction or reward from the learning experience. This can be in the form of entertainment or a sense of achievement. A self-assessment game, for example, might end with an animation sequence acknowledging the player's high score. A passing grade on a posttest might be rewarded with a completion certificate. Other forms of external rewards would include praise from a supervisor, a raise, or a promotion. Ultimately, though, the best way for learners to achieve satisfaction is for them to find their new skills immediately useful and beneficial on their job.

CONSTRUCTIVISM

Practitioners of instructional systems design are called *objectivists.* In Gagné's own words, "Objectivism is the view that knowledge exists in the external world, and learning is the learner's attempt to represent that external reality internally" (Gagné & Medsker, 1996). More recently, new theories of learning have emerged that are collectively known as *constructivism* (Duffy & Jonassen, 1992).

Constructivism has its roots in ideas of discovery-learning (Bruner, 1961). It asserts that learners must "construct" their own knowledge and behaviors through undirected experiences. Constructivism is more a philosophical or theoretical approach to learning than a specific model for the development of training programs.

The Theory of Constructivism

The basic tenets of constructivism are that

- Knowledge is constructed from and shaped by experience.
- Students must take an active role and assume responsibility for their learning.

- Learning is a collaborative process and students create their own meaning from obtaining multiple perspectives.
- Learning should occur in a realistic setting.
- Learners should choose their own path through content and activities.
- Content should be presented holistically, not broken into separate, smaller tasks.

Applying Constructivism to TBT

With computer technology, a constructivist approach to training is easier than ever before. The calculation capabilities of computers enable complex quantitative simulations, which can be applied to simulated chemistry experiments or

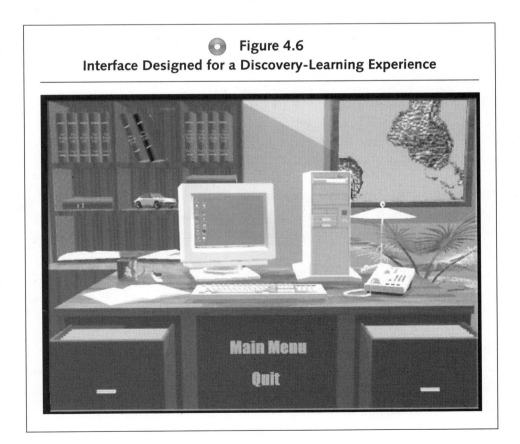

Figure 4.6
Interface Designed for a Discovery-Learning Experience

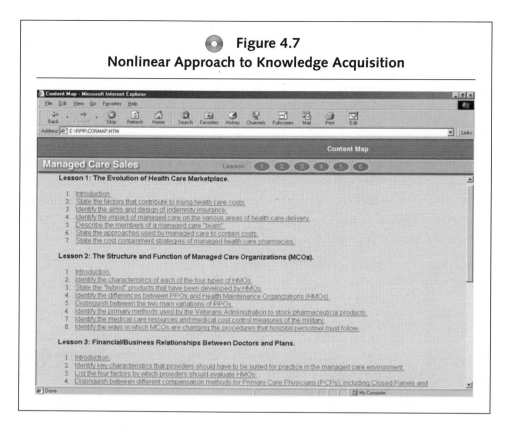

Figure 4.7
Nonlinear Approach to Knowledge Acquisition

business finances. CD-ROMs provide a rich media context for simulations. Realism is obtained with the use of audio, video, and possibly even virtual workspaces. The very nature of Web sites facilitates learner-controlled navigation of content with hyperlinks.

The case study presented in Chapter Nine of this book provides a good example of how a constructivist approach was used to teach pharmaceutical representatives about cancer. The design included the creation of complex simulations of the diagnosing, staging, and treatment of patients with cancer.

Figure 4.6 shows a screen from another program in which international sales managers learn how to manage the launch of a new product. Learners use the mouse to click on various objects in their office to learn how to obtain relevant marketing and planning information.

A Web-based instructional program that provides an interface to a knowledge database is depicted in Figure 4.7. In a constructivist fashion, learners are required to select content, thus creating their own sequence of instruction.

SUMMARY

Until recently, many theorists considered instructional systems design and constructivism to be diametrically opposed. But now some similarities between second generation instructional design and the approach of constructivists are becoming apparent (Duffy & Jonassen, 1992). If the two theories are not converging, they are at least viewed as compatible. Within the context of Gagné's events of instruction, there is certainly room for applying constructivist-inspired simulations and other experiential exercises, collaboration with peers in threaded discussions and chat rooms, and multiple paths to content and learning activities.

APPLYING IT ON THE JOB

Whether you are evaluating your own instructional design efforts or those of your training vendor, a yes answer to all of the following questions is evidence of a high-quality instructional design program:

- Does the program immediately capture attention when it is run?
- Does the training program explain its relevance to learners? Does it answer the student's question, "What's in it for me?"
- Are learning objectives presented near the beginning of each lesson?
- Are learning objectives specific and observable?
- Is the presentation of content made interesting with a variety of media or through an engaging treatment?
- Does the program provide a variety of interactive exercises beyond simple multiple-choice questions?
- Are learners given the opportunity for frequent practice?
- Is feedback on practice immediate and specific?
- Does the program include a post-test for final certification?

Secrets of User Interface Design

For many people, the user interface *is* the training program. Much in the same way that an attractively designed book jacket becomes a reader's visual image of a novel, the interface creates the graphical association of the training program in the mind of the user. Because the interface plays such an important role in a training program, considerable thought and planning must be devoted to its creation. By following proven design principles, the user interface facilitates rather than impedes the learning process.

What You Will Learn in This Chapter

- The importance of a well-designed user interface
- Common design flaws that create user frustration
- The proper order of menu items for maximum ease of use
- How mental models help people understand complex information
- How to put the user in control and improve learning
- The many ways in which consistent design elements contribute to an effective training program

USE VISUALS TO MAKE COMPUTERS EASIER TO USE

The single most neglected topic in the field of TBT is the *interaction* between students and computers. Typically, instructional design and the creation of media assets receive the sole emphasis, while crafting an effective interface between the student and the content is left to chance. Often when students complain about computer-based training or express a preference for classroom-based instruction, it's not the training they object to but rather it's confusing menus, unclear buttons, or illogical links. The success of any training program is largely dependent on the student's own motivation and attitude. If a poorly designed interface has them feeling lost, confused, or frustrated, it will become a barrier to effective learning and information retention.

The culprits behind bad interfaces are the designers themselves. Just as it is difficult to proofread your own written work, many designers, artists, and programmers are just too close to the program to have a "beginner's mind" when they try to create easily used training programs. When building the program from the ground up, they sometimes assume that it is clear what each on-screen button does and how the content is organized. The good news is that the most common errors are easily observed and remedied—if you know what you're looking for.

What Is the User Interface?

Generally you can think of an interface as anything that enables a person to interact with or use something. A soda machine has a simple interface: a series of buttons, large or small, lighted or not, that allow you to purchase a beverage. A car has a more complex interface, including a gas pedal, brake, and steering wheel, that enables the driver to control the vehicle. A computer's interface is the keyboard, the mouse, and the software that appears on the monitor and enables you to use the computer to perform a wide array of tasks.

Since the initial release of the Macintosh computer and the subsequent development of Microsoft's Windows software, most people automatically think of a graphical user interface (GUI, pronounced gooey) when they think of an interface. Although on-screen visual objects go a long way toward making computers easier to use, they are only part of a menu of items that dictate user-computer interactions: menus, language, options, screen layout, commands, and even the relationships between visual objects.

Common User Frustrations

Interface design flaws can be found in all kinds of software. These flaws, while not necessarily consciously noticed, make the software more difficult to use. What are some of the specific complaints that students express when working with courseware that has a poorly designed interface?

- "What am I supposed to do now?" This frustration is often the result of poor instructions or lack of visual cues. Sometimes the title screen is programmed to remain on-screen until the student presses a key to continue; but without a prompt, the student waits and waits. Some linear tutorials that use audio narration don't provide guidance as to when to move forward in the program. Students will click forward prematurely during a long verbal pause, or will linger too long, waiting for more audio to begin.

- "Did I finish everything?" Students are feeling this anxiety more than ever before with the move to Web-based training. Unskilled developers sometimes provide too many hyperlinks to various locations in the program and offer too many layers of content. Without a recommended path of navigation or an excellent tracking system, students find themselves "lost in hyperspace."

- "How do I get out of this thing?" Students have the flexibility of accessing TBT wherever and whenever they want. This means they might need to exit the program quickly—to respond to an urgent task at work or perhaps to attend to a crying baby at home. Without a clear and easy exit path, students can feel stuck inside the program and might be reluctant to use it as a just-in-time resource in the future.

- "What's it doing? Is it hung up?" Computers can be slow to process large programs; they can "crash" or simply "freeze." Computer slowdowns typically occur during software installation, when accessing student records in a database, or when performing some kind of calculation. Crashes and freeze-ups occur when the computer gets conflicting messages that it can't process. Some of these technical glitches are unpredictable. But some student anxiety can be anticipated and eliminated by simple messages that inform the student what the computer is busy doing—for example, "Loading program, please wait." Without adequate information, students are likely to assume the worst and may shut off the computer thinking that it isn't working properly.

HELP THE USER REMEMBER

Although human brains are still vastly more powerful and intelligent than computers, computers are much better than people when it comes to remembering things. Much of the work done in human-computer interaction is focused purely on ways to reduce the load on the human user's memory. By understanding how humans remember things, we can develop effective strategies for aiding memory—and improve training programs.

How Human Memory Works

Educational psychologists still do not know for certain how people process and remember things. The information processing model is the best explanation to date. It is the model for both instructional systems theory and user interface design. Figure 5.1 shows step by step how humans process information obtained from a computer. First, the computer provides external stimuli in the form of text, pictures, and audio that gain the attention of the receptors in the eyes and ears. The receptors pass this information into sensory storage for automatic processing. Sensory storage processes all stimuli in real time, so as new information comes in, it replaces the previous information.

Stimuli, or information, that has any value to the perceiver will be passed along into short-term memory, also known as working memory. Scientists have shown that short-term memory can hold only about seven to nine items at a time, and these items will be held for only about thirty seconds, unless a memory aid such as repetition or chunking is used.

For an everyday example of the use of a short-term memory aid, consider how you try to remember a phone number given to you when you don't have pen and paper handy. You might repeat the number several times to keep it present in your short-term memory ("908-555-1212, 908-555-1212, 908-555-1212"). Of course, rather than memorizing one long string (9085551212), you "chunk" the numbers into three smaller pieces (908-555-1212) to aid your memory.

The ultimate goal of training and education is to get relevant information through short-term memory and into long-term memory, where it can be

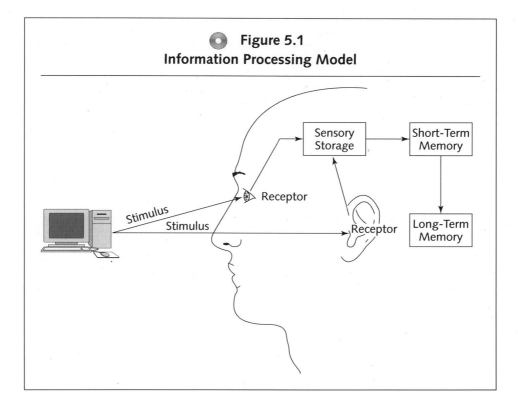

Figure 5.1
Information Processing Model

accessed at a later time. Long-term memory is like a giant warehouse where you keep many of your previous experiences and knowledge, such as memories of your high school prom, details of a play you saw, or important information about business competitors.

The real challenge when working with long-term memory is not just how to store information in that memory area but rather how to get it back out again when needed. Research indicates that there are many tactics that will improve a person's ability to find and access information locked up in long-term memory. Among devices used to aid in future recall are mental pictures, emotional intensity, word associations, and use of multiple senses.

These techniques are often put to practical use in our everyday surroundings. Anybody who has ever been in the vast O'Hare Airport parking garage in Chicago has probably chuckled at how they remember where their car is parked.

Instead of using alphanumeric location indicators—such as parking deck C, level 2, section 11—O'Hare uses such designations as Chicago Bulls, Michael Jordan, and Red Section. A traveler returning from a trip several days later would be less likely to remember something like C–2–11 and more likely to think, "Oh yeah, I was in the Chicago Bulls Section, with Michael Jordan, and Red."

Chunking Information and Organizing Menu Structure

Using what we know about short-term and long-term memory, we can apply the following strategies to maximize the effectiveness of a program's menu system.

• *A menu should ideally contain no more than seven items.* If a menu has more than seven items, see if it can be split logically into a higher-level menu and a submenu. This helps students remember which menus contain certain items.

• *The order or placement of menu items should match the structure of the tasks.* For example, Figure 5.2 depicts the main menu from a sales training program

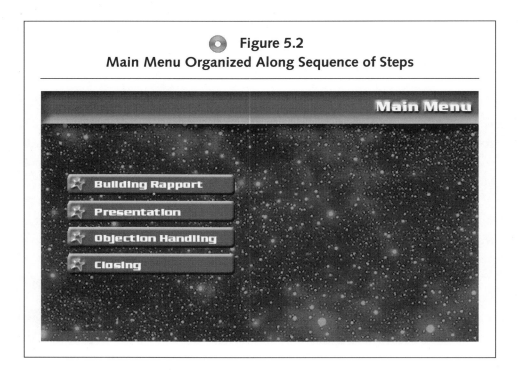

Figure 5.2
Main Menu Organized Along Sequence of Steps

Main Menu

Building Rapport

Presentation

Objection Handling

Closing

with lessons on building rapport, presentation, objection handling, and closing, which are the classic steps in a sales call. In turn, the objection-handling submenu shown in Figure 5.3 is sequenced along the consecutive steps of classifying objections, responding to objections, and confirming satisfaction.

- *If there is no sequence associated with menu items, place the most commonly used options at the top of the menu and the least-used items on the bottom.*
- *Submenus should have titles that reflect the selected option from the previous menu.* The submenu in Figure 5.3 enables students to see clearly that they are now choosing options from the objection-handling menu. It serves as a simple reminder of where they've been and how to get to this menu again in the future, without taxing their memory.

Using Mental Models or Visual Metaphors

A mental model or visual metaphor is the internal picture we create to help us understand how things work. Even though we are not conscious of our mental

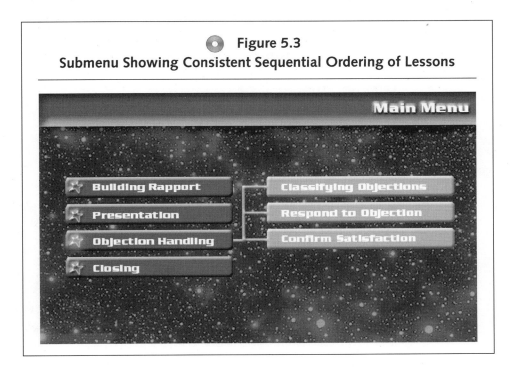

Figure 5.3
Submenu Showing Consistent Sequential Ordering of Lessons

models, they help us to use computers effectively. Similar to models, visual metaphors are used by designers to take advantage of what we already knew when helping us to understand something new.

A good example of a visual metaphor is a computer's directory structure presented by the Microsoft Windows Explorer program, shown in Figure 5.4. While the computer actually stores files and data haphazardly on its hard drive, the visual metaphor presented to the user is that of file folders and a vertical ordering system.

This metaphor gives an artificial but clear sense of order to the system. As users we imagine that our documents are being held in these little folders and that there is some kind of depth to these folders. We even use this model in our everyday language when we say things such as "It's not in that folder; move up

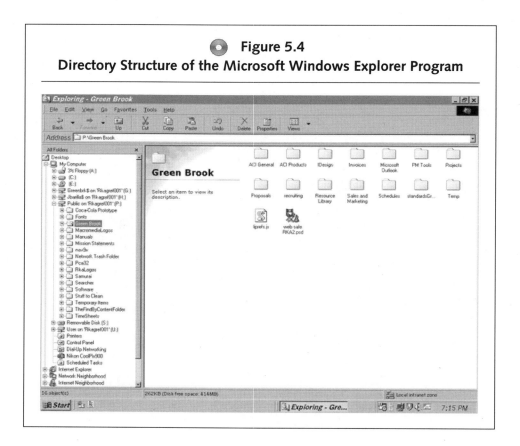

Figure 5.4
Directory Structure of the Microsoft Windows Explorer Program

one level" or "I can't remember where I put that file; I must have buried it somewhere" when speaking of our computer files.

Mental models and metaphors are still subject to short-term memory restrictions, however. Most users begin to get lost when their model contains more than three layers or paths. Imagine a training program that has a main menu (the first level) from which students gain access to a specific lesson (the second level) and eventually click on a hyperlink called More Information, which displays some additional text (the third level). At this point, most students will still have a clear understanding of where they are in the program and how to retrace their steps if necessary. But if students are once again presented with a link for more information, such as to a case study within the More Information section, they will begin to lose track of their location or the relationship of the on-screen content to the overall lesson.

Visual metaphors can include simple items like on-screen folders, tabs, or buttons. They can also consist of more elaborate, simulated environments. Figure 5.5, which was also shown in Chapter Four (Figure 4.6), illustrates an office metaphor used in a strategic selling simulation. In this program, student managers use the mouse to click on the image of the computer to gather relevant information from a database, they click on the phone to speak to industry experts, or they click on the bookshelf to study journal articles.

Don't Overload the Sensory System

The human sensory system processes all external stimuli and can be easily overloaded by too much stimulation. Information overload can occur even from background noise or peripheral images and animation. A multimedia program that plays continuous background music or repeats a complex animation on a screen to engage the user is just as likely to distract him or her. In reality, this type of overuse of visuals, or "eye candy," can conflict with the processing of more relevant content.

Using Multiple Access Points

A simple way to relieve the burden on users' memories is to provide multiple ways in which they can locate and access the content. Following are descriptions of some common methods.

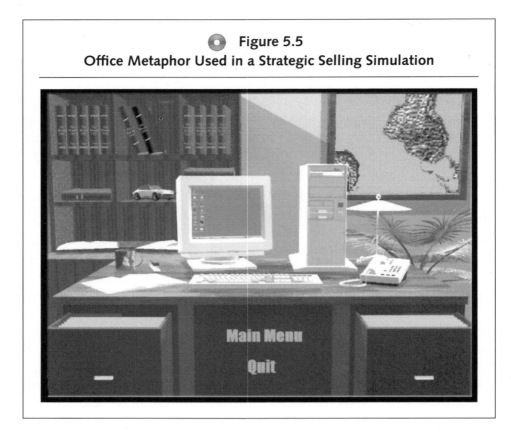

Figure 5.5
Office Metaphor Used in a Strategic Selling Simulation

- *Main menu.* The primary access point is always the program's main menu, which should be well organized and descriptive. Rather than using generic names, such as Lesson 1 or Lesson 2, use descriptive headings such as "1: Overview to Customer Service" and "2: Dealing with Difficult Customers."

- *Bookmark and student history.* A bookmarking system enables students to exit from any screen in the program and, upon reentering at a later date, resume exactly where they left off. This tracking information is often stored in a student history file.

- *Index.* An index of key topics or of all learning objectives helps users find specific information. A well-indexed system will enhance any training program's subsequent use as a just-in-time support tool.

- *Keyword search.* The keyword search enables students to type in a word and have the program scan the entire textual contents for all occurrences. Although this is a very powerful feature, a keyword search looks only at on-screen text and cannot identify information presented as audio narration.
- *Site map or content map.* A visual representation of the order of the topics in the entire program, or content outline, is called a site map. Typically it displays the entire menu system graphically, extending down to individual learning objectives.

PUT THE USER IN CONTROL

An effective interface puts the user in control of the program, or at the very least lets them *feel* like they are in control. By giving users control, you ease their anxieties, minimize confusion, and create an environment conducive to learning. Descriptions of a number of time-tested ways of putting the user in the driver's seat follow.

Status Messages

If the computer is busy for longer than four seconds, the program should display what is called a *status message.* This message alleviates the user's concerns that the software may have frozen or hung up. Though the message in itself doesn't provide control to the user, the communication to the students helps them to feel that they are still in control. The initial software installation almost always requires a status message. Typically a meter is used to show the installation progress from 0 to 100 percent. Other operations that might occupy the computer and require a status message include accessing student records, calculating test scores, and printing completion certificates or other documents.

Reversible Actions (Undo)

Well-designed software protects users from making incorrect choices or errors. Knowing that the software is "forgiving" also increases a student's confidence and reduces their anxiety. Following are several of the most important checkpoints where actions should be reversible.

- *Log-in screens.* Most programs require students to log-in with their name, an identification number, or both at the beginning of the program. This information is used for bookmarking purposes, test reporting, and other administrative activities. Because of the critical importance of this information, students should have the opportunity to review their log-in data for accuracy. Figure 5.6 provides an example of a log-in screen.

- *Exiting the program.* Users may mistakenly click the exit button when they want to access the main menu or leave an exam. Rather than closing the program and returning them directly to the operating system, clicking the exit button should make a window pop up with a confirmation message such as, "Do you want to exit this program and return to Windows?" The option buttons available should be labeled *exit software* and *return to program.*

Figure 5.6
Log-In Screen for On-Line Training Program

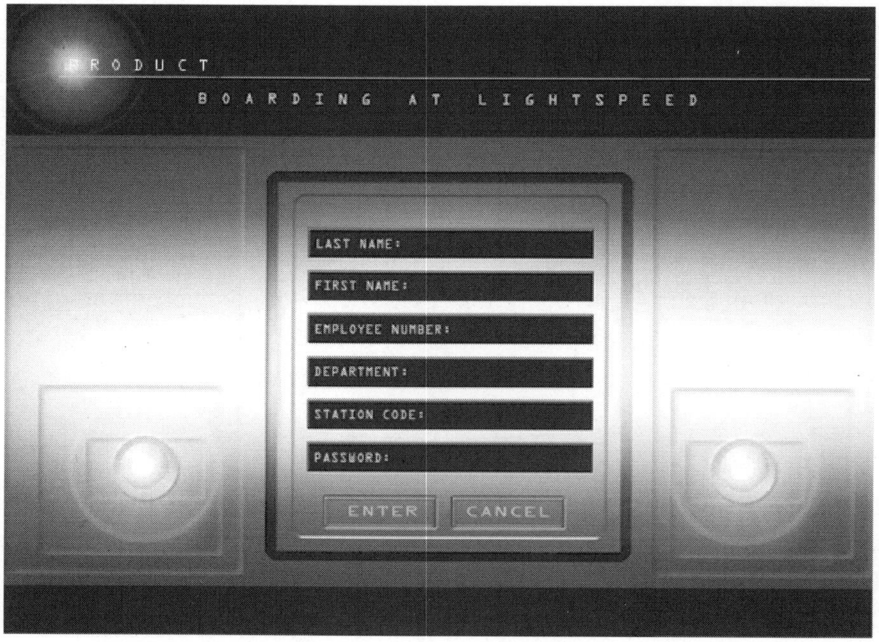

- *Taking a test.* Final exams are often timed and intentionally prevent the student from leaving the test module until they are finished with the test. This kind of program control is designed to keep students from looking for correct answers in the lessons. Before the test is started, a confirmation message should appear that advises the student, "You are about to begin the test. Once you start this test you will have to finish it in one sitting. You will not be able to take the test again. Are you sure you are ready to take this test now?" Action buttons should be clearly labeled *take test* or *return to main menu*.

- *Previous page.* Perhaps the most obvious undo feature is the *previous page* button or *back* button in a linear tutorial. In addition to giving students the control to move forward in a program, an effective interface also enables them to move back to a previous page.

- *Replay audio.* Related to undoing a function is *redoing* a function, the most common being an on-screen button that replays the audio narration.

Mouse and Keyboard

The mouse and keyboard are two common hardware components of the user interface and the most commonly used controls. Less common hardware interfaces include touch screens and voice-recognition systems. Although most computer users today prefer to use the mouse, many experienced users gain greater productivity using the keyboard. A good interface supports both options.

An example of where keyboard and mouse should both be supported is on question screens. When presenting a multiple-choice question, students should be able to use the mouse to click on answer A, B, C, or D *or* press the desired letter on the keyboard. Similarly, confirmation message windows that require the user to click on a yes or a no button should also allow the keyboard letters Y and N to indicate the same action. Finally, the most common use of dual support is accepting the keyboard right- and left-arrow keys as equivalents to the *next* and *back* buttons.

One-Click Access to Help, Menus, and Exit

Users need instant access to the functions they use most frequently and especially to those features that help them to escape or end their current session. Buttons or links that jump directly to help, the main menu, or the exit procedure should appear on every screen.

CREATE CONSISTENT AND LOGICAL DESIGNS

Users can quickly learn a new visual metaphor or a new mental model, but they can also quickly create expectations that the interface they see will be consistent.

Everyday we create expectations in our physical environment. Imagine, for example, that you are walking down a long hallway in a building and you must pass through several doors. When you get to the first door, you won't know whether to pull it or push it open, unless it is clearly marked. You grab the handle and pull but the door doesn't budge, so you push and it opens. When you get to the second door, you notice that it seems identical to the door through which you just passed. Perhaps unconsciously you push the door first this time, and it opens.

As you approach door after door, your mind creates a model and expectation of how the doors will behave: "This door has the same shape, size, color, position, and handle as previous doors. I need to *push* this door open." A problem occurs, however, if the interface is inconsistent and conflicts with your expectations. If the tenth consecutive identical door is a *pull* door and you push it but it doesn't open, you will probably feel frustrated and a bit confused. You may wonder, "What's going on? Is this door locked or stuck?"

A program's interface is the door between the student and the instruction. To facilitate access and reduce confusion, consistency in interface appearance and behavior are paramount.

Use Clear and Logical Screen Layouts

An intuitive interface begins with the overall layout and design of the screen. Following are four principles of screen layout:

- Place screen objects together in a logical order.
- Place buttons where the user's eye can easily find them.
- Give buttons clear symbols or labels.
- Group buttons together based on their function and frequency of use.

It is usually assumed that users in western countries read the screen in a "Z" pattern from left to right and from top to bottom. Figure 5.7 shows how a user's

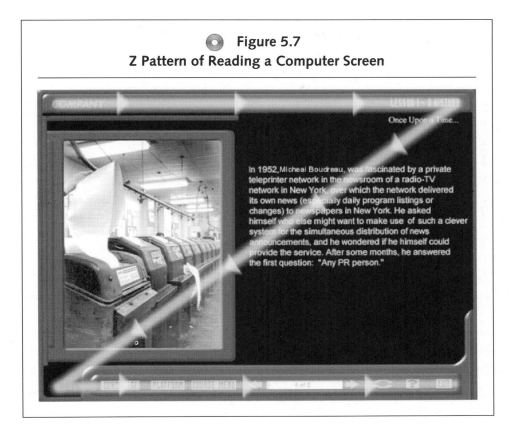

eyes track an entire screen and then read the text on the screen. Note where the eyes remain focused after processing the information.

Given the Z pattern of reading, the proper layout of information becomes obvious. The top of the screen should include location information and any critical instructions that can't be missed. This information will immediately fulfill users' need to know where they are and what the screen is about. Instructional material should dominate the middle portion of the screen. A navigation bar should appear on the bottom of the screen.

Web-based training programs often have navigation bars running vertically down the left side of the screen. This is because scrolling text windows are a consistent user interface element on the Internet, making horizontal buttons on the bottom of the screen impractical. In some cases, technical limitations hinder ideal button placement.

Buttons should always be given clear labels, with both text and graphical indicators, if at all possible. Common button-naming rules include the following:

- Use *menu* to label the button that accesses the main menu. Don't use the ambiguous word *main*.

- Use *help* to access navigational guidance. Don't use *hint* or *panic*.

- Use *exit* to end the program. Don't use *quit, end,* or *stop,* which might refer to "quitting" the immediate exercise or lesson at hand.

- Use *forward* and *back* to designate page turning, as in a book. Don't use *up* or *down*.

- Use complete screen counters like "1 of 30," not partial counters like "page 5."

- If your program runs on Windows computers, refer to the keyboard enter key as *enter,* not *return*.

Be Consistent in Visual Cues

Early seafaring explorers used celestial navigation to make their way across the high seas. Like the North Star, the appearance or location of the buttons your students navigate with should never change. Button identification is a fundamental part of a mental model. Changing a button's location or appearance will cause users to think that they are seeing a *new* button with *new* functions.

As an extension of this design principle, on-screen graphics that are not intended to be buttons should not have any of the same design characteristics as buttons. The screen in Figure 5.8 illustrates this problem. The giant question mark is intended to be just a visual design to engage the learner. But because it is the same shape and color as the actual buttons, many users will be confused, believing that it is a hint button or the way to display the answer.

The most obvious way to indicate to a user that an action can be taken is to use a three-dimensional button. But other cues also indicate that an object is clickable—most notably, a change in the mouse cursor or a rollover effect. That is, by default the mouse cursor appears as an arrow, but a program can change the arrow into a hand when the mouse is rolled over a clickable object. If this extra guidance is provided, however, it must be done consistently for every click-

Figure 5.8
Example of a Poorly Designed Graphic

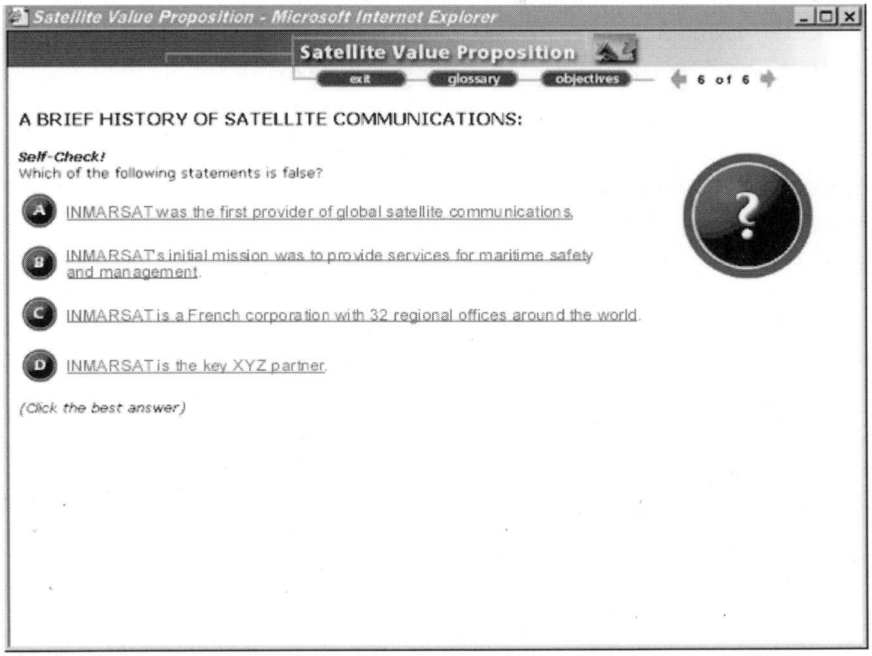

able object. If the user sees what appears to be a button but a hand doesn't appear when they roll the mouse cursor over it, they will be confused.

Similarly, buttons and icons sometimes have a rollover effect in which they glow or brighten as the mouse cursor rolls over them. Again, this is an excellent cue to students that they have located a clickable item. But regardless of what effect is used, it should be identical for all clickable objects.

Use Clear Messages and Be Consistent in Media Choices

Consistency and clarity are important for all information presented, whether text, audio, graphics, or video, and whether for new information or feedback. Indirect, confusing, or pedantic messages are misleading and should be avoided.

Consider the vague feedback for the question shown in Figure 5.9 and how it is improved in Figure 5.10. In addition to using vague language, the feedback in Figure 5.9 covers up the student's answer. This type of window placement error is known as *destructive messaging* and must be avoided.

Although some designers claim that adult learners should never be told they are wrong because they may become discouraged or feel challenged, in our experience adult learners do appreciate honest and direct feedback.

Consistency in use of media is important as well. If audio narration is the primary learning media in a linear tutorial, it should be used on every screen. If students encounter a text-only screen, they wait for the audio to begin. When they hear nothing, they may assume that there is a glitch in the software or that they have done something wrong. Similarly, if a video-based coach provides

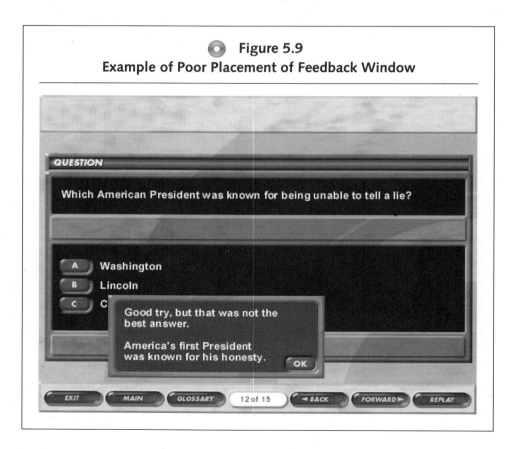

Figure 5.9
Example of Poor Placement of Feedback Window

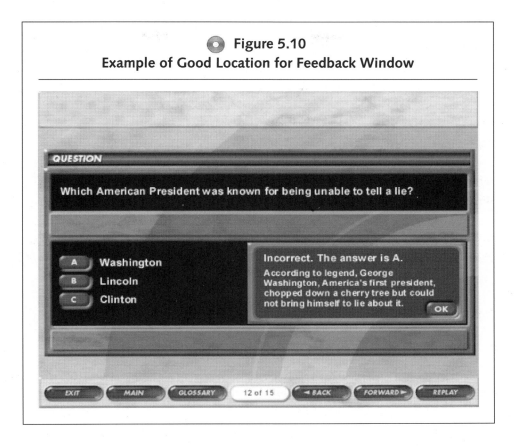

● Figure 5.10
Example of Good Location for Feedback Window

QUESTION

Which American President was known for being unable to tell a lie?

A Washington
B Lincoln
C Clinton

Incorrect. The answer is A.
According to legend, George Washington, America's first president, chopped down a cherry tree but could not bring himself to lie about it. OK

EXIT   MAIN   GLOSSARY   12 of 15   ◄ BACK   FORWARD ►   REPLAY

feedback to questions, the feedback should be used consistently or students may wonder why their coach suddenly left them stranded.

Have Menus Behave Predictably

Menus are the key structures for organizing and accessing information and must be planned with great care. In addition to being logically sequenced and having no more than three layers of menus (see the earlier discussion of organizing menu structure), the menu action must be consistent throughout the program. Similar actions must occur for each menu item on which the student clicks.

Main menu items that are clicked can lead to submenus, or the buttons can directly launch a lesson or simulation. But don't mix the two actions on the same menu. For example, if clicking on "Module 1: The Cardiovascular System" launches a submenu but clicking on "Module 2: The Nervous System" directly launches a thirty–screen linear tutorial, students can get confused. They may think, "Oops, where is that submenu? Did I accidentally click something to launch this tutorial?" or "What's going on? Will I get to the submenu after this tutorial?"

PROVIDE INFORMATIVE GUIDANCE AND FEEDBACK

TBT has significantly transformed training, replacing many traditional classroom sessions. But students of all ages are still students, and they perform best when given guidance and feedback. Just as in personal relations, in all TBT situations politeness and courtesy should be extended.

Include Page Counters

Every linear tutorial should have an on-screen page counter that tells users which screen or page they are on and how many more exist in the lesson. The simple message "Screen 5 of 25" clearly describes what is required to finish the lesson in the program and engenders student confidence. With self-paced programs that can be taken at any time, this type of progress marker helps users answer questions like "I have a meeting in fifteen minutes. Can I finish this lesson or should I quit now?"

Some designers recommend the use of time estimates rather than page counters. For example, "Lesson 1: Overview (10–15 minutes)." However, estimating the time needed for self-paced training is difficult. Be aware that even though a range is given, some students may feel anxiety from the implied time limitation. For example, some students may self-impose pressure to finish the lesson in fifteen minutes or less, while others may feel inadequate if they take much longer than the time estimate. Because a major benefit of TBT is that it is *self*-paced, measuring time rather than screens artificially imposes time expectations and can be counterproductive to the learning process.

Make Help and Instructions Easily Accessible

Even if a program's interface is simple and intuitive, it won't appear to be that to 100 percent of its audience. Always include a "How to Use This Program" section on the main menu for new users who may need specific directions on how to use menus, buttons, and other features.

These navigational instructions should also be accessible as help from any screen in the program. Make sure that when users exit the help screens they return to their last location within the tutorial.

Write Clear Error Messages

Most error messages are written at the last minute by programmers. Make sure they don't sound like "techie" messages. Figure 5.11 shows a student log-in error message that uses database terminology and causes undue concern. Figure 5.12 shows the same information conveyed in a friendlier message using common language.

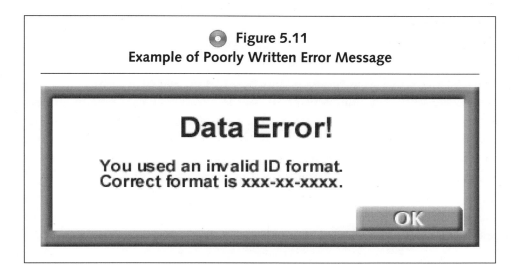

Figure 5.11
Example of Poorly Written Error Message

Data Error!

You used an invalid ID format.
Correct format is xxx-xx-xxxx.

OK

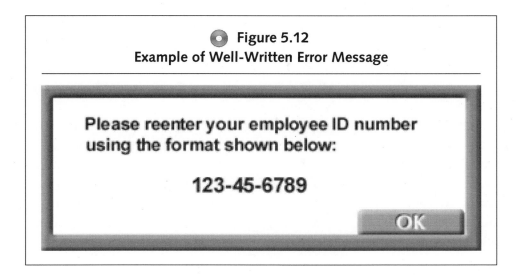

Figure 5.12
Example of Well-Written Error Message

Please reenter your employee ID number using the format shown below:

123-45-6789

OK

Give Appropriate Warnings

Providing information and feedback includes a responsibility to warn the user of the consequences of their actions. As previously described in the discussion of reversible actions earlier in this chapter, users should be stopped and presented with a confirmation request before accepting log-in data, taking a test, or exiting the program.

Make Messages Polite

In *The Media Equation,* Byron Reeves and Clifford Nass (1996) present conclusive research that people treat computers like real human beings. Even when great care is used to create androgynous on-screen narrators (such as a talking, animated floppy disk) or sterile messages within plain display windows, users will project both gender and personality onto (or into) the computer.

As Reeves and Nass explain, "This is pivotal for the design of interactive media, because the biggest reason for making machines that are polite to people is that people are polite to machines. Everyone expects reciprocity . . . when a technology (or a person) violates a politeness rule, the violation is viewed as social incompetence and it is offensive" (pp. 28–29).

Simple TBT politeness rules include the following:

• *Say hello and goodbye.* After the log-in procedure, greet students warmly with a message like, "Welcome back, <Name>. Would you like to resume where you left off, or go to the main menu?" Upon exiting, a simple "Goodbye" message provides easy closure.

• *Don't use exclamation points.* In error messages or feedback to wrong answers, exclamation points are unduly severe. Even for positive reinforcement, such as "That's correct!" exclamation marks become pedantic with overuse.

• *Blame the computer, not the user.* When displaying error messages or providing feedback, construct text so that the user is not accused of the mistake.

• *Use audio effects sparingly.* Playing audience cheering noises for correctly answered questions or buzzing sounds for incorrectly answered ones is suitable in self-assessment games. But these types of audio effects can be annoying to students and distracting to those around them and should be used infrequently within tutorials.

APPLYING IT ON THE JOB

When reviewing and evaluating the computer interface of your TBT program, you should be able to answer yes to the following questions:

- Do all buttons and icons have a consistent and unique appearance?
- Are visual cues like mouse cursor changes and rollover highlights used consistently on all buttons?
- Are buttons labeled with text descriptions (or with rollover text)?
- Do buttons "gray out" or disappear when they are inactive?
- Do nonbutton graphics have their own design properties distinct from those of buttons?
- Are navigation buttons displayed in exactly the same screen position every time they appear?
- Are buttons grouped logically and located where the user is likely to be looking?
- Do users have one-click access to help, exit, and the main menu?
- Are users returned to where they left off after closing the help window and canceling out of the exit screen?
- Does every menu have a title?
- Does every menu screen include an option to return to the previous or main menu?
- Are there fewer than three levels of menus?
- Do menus have nine or fewer items on them?
- Are menu items descriptive rather than general?
- Are menu items listed in a sequential or logical order?
- Do menus indicate which items the student has completed?
- Are confirmation messages used in areas such as student registration, exit, and final exams?
- Are clear instructions associated with menus, questions, and other tasks?
- Are error messages written in plain language?
- Are status messages displayed during delays greater than four seconds?

- Are exclamation points and sound effects used sparingly?
- Is there a bookmarking feature that enables students to exit and resume later where they left off?
- Can students move backward as well as forward in linear tutorials?
- Are page or screen counters used to show progress within linear lessons?
- Is the visual metaphor consistent and intuitive in nonlinear simulations?
- Are all pop-up windows positioned on the screen so they do not cover up relevant information?
- Does text appear clearly and with normal margins and spacing?
- Do information input screens force all capital letters and is the evaluation of inputs case-insensitive?
- Can users interact with the program from either the keyboard or the mouse?
- Are text fonts used consistently?
- Are audio volume levels consistent?
- Do users have the option to replay video or audio narration?

part two

Managing Technology-Based Training

Measuring Costs and Benefits

Chapter Three noted that the final step in the ADDIE development model is evaluation. The classic evaluation model developed by Kirkpatrick (1975) looks at four levels: student reaction, learning, behavior, and business results. Critics of Kirkpatrick's model say that it doesn't take the business impact far enough and that the final step in any training program should be a fifth, ultimate level of evaluation: financial return on investment (ROI). This chapter discusses issues involved in cost-benefit and ROI analysis, and presents a step-by-step worksheet for you to use to measure your training programs.

What You Will Learn in This Chapter

- Seven key concepts that factor into a cost-benefit analysis
- Why TBT doesn't have a favorable ROI for small audiences
- What the hidden costs are that drive up the true costs of traditional instructor-led training (ILT)
- How much burdened costs typically add to classroom instruction
- The steps to use to complete a worksheet to calculate total cost savings of TBT

OVERVIEW OF COST-BENEFIT ANALYSIS

For a long time, organizations paid lip service to the human resource motto that people are an organization's most important asset. Now senior executives have come to believe that employees and the intellectual capital they create can uniquely differentiate their company in the marketplace. Training expenditures are now viewed as critical investments in human capital and as an effective method of increasing employee retention.

Because of these factors, the investment in corporate training programs is large, and growing rapidly. Total corporate spending on training in the United States was approximately $60 billion in 1998 (Lakewood Publications, 1998). The fastest-growing segment of the training budget is expenditures on TBT. By the year 2000, it is estimated that 50 percent of all training interventions will be delivered via CD-ROM or corporate Intranets (Lakewood Publications, 1998). Specifically, within the Web-based training marketplace, expenditures are expected to go from a mere $197 million in 1997 to more than *$6 billion* in 2002 (International Data Corporation, 1998). This projected 100 percent annual growth rate in TBT is being driven by increases in the availability of network bandwidth, the decreasing price of multimedia computers, and the development of more services and products from vendors.

Commensurate with this increase in training expenditures, senior executives are demanding more accountability from their training departments. In fact, 93 percent of training professionals surveyed at a 1996 conference said they are increasingly being asked to show the ROI of their programs (National HRD Executive Survey, 1997). Training managers need to be able to answer direct questions about total costs, benefits, and bottom-line impact. Visionary training managers embrace cost-benefit analysis as a way to justify bigger budgets for technology and new training programs.

The Value of Cost-Benefit Analysis

Proponents of TBT have long touted its many benefits, such as reduction in learning time, increase in knowledge retention rates, and cost savings. Brandon Hall, editor of *Multimedia & Internet-Based Training Newsletter,* was quoted in the August 1998 issue of *HR Magazine:* "There's about a 50-percent reduction in time and cost over classroom training" (Roberts, 1998, p. 99). The power of the cost-benefit analysis process is that it enables you to move from generalizations and assumptions to proof of the value of each and every program you develop.

This type of quantifiable measurement of value is critical in the overall management of a training function. It is also a powerful tool that can be used to keep or expand available training resources. Hall (1997) has conducted exhaustive research on ROI. His research, and that of others, has uncovered some compelling cases:

• *A computer storage media company* converted a four-day instructor-led course for 1,500 technicians into a multimedia CD-ROM format. Due to a reduction in learning time and elimination of travel expenses, the company reduced costs over three years by 47 percent and saved $1.5 million (Hall, 1997).

• *A major consulting firm* developed and delivered computer-based training for seven thousand consultants in fifty countries. The cost of the training was $106 per student, versus an estimated $760 per student for instructor-led delivery. Over the five-year life span of the program, TBT saved the firm more than $4.5 million (Hall, 1997).

• *A computer reseller* developed a Web-based training solution for its internal sales force and value-added resellers. Some forty on-line courses were developed, complete with self-assessment quizzes. According to the company's director of strategies technologies, "We saw a 50 percent increase in sales across distribution and integration resellers" (Fickel, 1998).

• *A branch of the U.S. military* estimated that their technicians' ability to troubleshoot problems increased by 90 percent after the adoption of multimedia training. Over a period of five years, they expect at least a twentyfold return on their investment (Jerram, 1994).

Key Concepts of Cost-Benefit Analysis

At the simplest level, cost-benefit analysis answers the question, Was it worth the money? In other words, what were the total costs to develop the program and what were the total benefits realized? Costs include direct costs, such as payments to vendors, as well as indirect costs, such as the value of time. Financial benefits can be in the form of cost savings or increases in productivity or revenue. The following key concepts are factors in a cost-benefit analysis.

• *Life of training.* Every project needs to be measured over time. TBT programs don't last forever. Their shelf life is determined by such things as changes to content, changes in technology, and changes in business need. According to Hall's (1997) research conducted over ten years, most ROI studies show that TBT is more expensive to develop and deliver over the short term than instructor-led training, but it pays off over time. Typically, three to five years of use is an accepted period for evaluating a training program.

- *Alternate delivery options.* Perhaps the most common method of showing the financial impact of TBT is to compare it with the costs of other forms of delivery. To come up with a comparison means asking the question, If we don't deliver the training via the Web, what would it cost for us to deliver it in a classroom setting?

- *Size of audience.* With TBT, the cost of development is not dramatically affected by the number of students using the program. The cost is basically the same to develop a two-hour CD-ROM or Web-based training program for ten people as it is for a thousand people. The only additional costs may be for CD-ROM duplication, student tracking, and end-user support. However, the size of the target audience is extremely relevant when comparing the costs against instructor-led delivery. With live workshops, the number of students has a direct impact on expenses due to instructors, locations, and travel.

- *Seat time.* The total amount of time that students spend with the course is called *seat time* (how long they will be in their seats). Seat time is always specified for ILT, but estimated for self-paced TBT. After all, a course that takes one student two hours to complete might take another only ninety minutes. Increasingly, effective Web-based training is blurring the lines between instruction and just-in-time performance support. This factor makes estimates of seat time additionally tenuous.

- *Burdened costs.* This accounting term refers to the total cost of an item, which may include some hidden costs. For example, you might quickly estimate that a classroom facilitator who earns a $60,000 salary costs $230 per day, simply by dividing the salary by the total number of weekdays ($60,000 ÷ 52 weeks ÷ 5 days). But the burdened cost for the instructor will be higher once you take into account payroll taxes, insurance, and other benefits. Additionally, when calculating day rates, make sure to subtract company holidays, vacation time, and sick days to get an accurate estimate of the burdened cost for each productive workday.

- *Estimated revenue impact.* Often the impact that a training program has on sales and expenses is indirect or difficult to measure. In these cases, the impact on revenue is projected or extrapolated from known data. For example, assume that a quality control training program in a factory was shown to reduce the number of defective cell phones produced each year from five thousand to three thousand (a net reduction of two thousand defective phones per year). Although the training program directly reduced errors, which led to a drop in the number of defective phones, you would have to estimate the revenue impact. To do this, you would need to research costs associated with wasted materials in each defective phone and with labor time for the manufacturing, identification, and disposal of each defective phone. With this methodology, a defect-reduction number can be translated into a revenue-savings number.

   • *Opportunity costs.* These costs are the lost revenues or increased costs associated with opportunities that will be missed because of the time students spend in training. This measure is increasingly being used in the competitive world of sales. Traditionally, for a sales representative spending time in training, a main measure of cost is the rep's salary while in the training program. However, a more advanced analysis measures the opportunity cost of the rep not being out in the field. According to Jim DeMaioribus, director of sales training at Ortho-McNeil, every day a rep spends in the field is worth approximately $1,000 in revenue (Booker, 1997). Therefore a major advantage of technology-based sales training is its ability to maximize time in the field and minimize the opportunity costs of sales training.

MEASURING COSTS

The first step in cost-benefit analysis is simply to measure all of the direct and indirect costs involved in the design, development, delivery, and maintenance of the program. Because different industries have different ways of doing business, this process calls for some careful examination of how your organization goes about its daily work activities. So often, time is money. If you can more efficiently train employees, then the time saved can be used for productive work. More work time is then translated into a financial benefit.

   To generate an accurate and valuable cost analysis, you must consider all of the direct costs of program development as well as the indirect costs associated with delivery and maintenance.

   For example, the hidden costs of ILT include the costs of student transportation, meals, and room rental. Indirect costs associated with CD-ROM training include the duplication and distribution of CDs to students. Costs associated with Web-based training include the purchase or maintenance of the server-computer that hosts the program.

The following example illustrates most of the direct and indirect costs that make up the true cost associated with training programs. Keep in mind that every organization and project is unique and other costs may apply in any particular instance.

The example shows a direct cost comparison between ILT and TBT. Such a comparison is ideally carried out during the planning stages of a project to determine the most appropriate form of delivery. However, even if you have already chosen CD-ROM or Web-based technology for reasons other than cost (such as learning effectiveness or an organizational requirement), such a comparison can help you analyze the potential savings of TBT over live workshops. Blank worksheets that you can use to evaluate your own projects can be found in Appendix D.

Acme Incorporated, a maker of widgets, has identified a need to train its field service engineers (FSEs) in the basics of customer service. The FSEs are located throughout the country. They install and repair widgets at customer locations. With the additional training, Acme hopes both to increase customer satisfaction ratings as well as to increase the amount of follow-on sales. Each FSE has a multimedia-ready laptop computer, so Acme wants to determine the potential cost savings of using CD-ROM technology rather than their traditional instructor-led methods.

Phase One: Assumptions

In the first phase, certain assumptions about the project should be clarified or certain data should be gathered that will be required for the analysis. Figure 6.1 shows the results of this phase for Acme.

- *Step 1.1: Life span of course.* A training course on customer service could in theory be used for many years. The principles and skills involved are not likely to change. However, examples and case studies within the course might be directly linked to specific products or services, so it can be assumed that the course will have a useful life of only three years.

- *Step 1.2: Total number of students.* Acme currently has four hundred FSEs, all of whom will be required to take the course during its first year. Additionally, the FSE is an entry-level position that attracts young recruits. Turnover has been

Figure 6.1
Acme Assumptions About TBT

Item	Assumptions
1.1 Life span of course	3 years
1.2 Total # of students over life of course	800
1.3 Total hours of training, measured in ILT	14 hours (2 days)
1.4 Estimated reduction in seat time for TBT	50%
1.5 Burdened compensation for one instructor	$304 per day
1.6 Burdened compensation for one student	$164 per day

approximately 50 percent per year; thus an additional two hundred FSEs will need to be trained in year two, and another two hundred in year three. That brings the total number of students completing the course to eight hundred.

• *Step 1.3: Student learning time.* After examining required learning outcomes and associated behavioral objectives, it was determined that this course could be delivered as a two-day instructor-led workshop. Assuming that actual classroom time is only seven hours each day, the total learning time for the course would be fourteen hours.

• *Step 1.4: Reduction in seat time.* Because the course does not yet exist, the true reduction in learning time when using TBT can only be guessed. For this analysis, Acme is simply using the rule of thumb offered earlier in this chapter by Hall, that TBT typically results in a 50 percent reduction in seat time.

• *Step 1.5: Burdened compensation for instructor.* Acme's instructors are paid an average of $65,000 per year. Using another rule of thumb, it is assumed that payroll tax, insurance, and other benefits will equal 20 percent of an employee's salary. This brings the one-year cost for an instructor to $78,000. This annual cost is then divided by the total number of productive workdays, 257, to get the cost per instructor day. In other words, $78,000 compensation ÷ 257 workdays = $304 per day.

- *Step 1.6: Burdened compensation for student.* Acme's FSEs are paid an average of $35,000 per year. Using the same rule of thumb, it is assumed that payroll tax, insurance, and other benefits will equal 20 percent of the FSE's salary. This brings the one-year cost for an FSE to $42,000. This annual cost is then divided by the total number of productive workdays, 257, to get the cost per student day. In other words, $42,000 compensation ÷ 257 workdays = $164 per day.

Phase Two: Design and Development

After documenting assumptions, the second phase is to estimate the costs for courseware development. Figure 6.2 shows the budgets required for Acme to create both a workshop and a self-paced delivery version of a customer service program.

- *Step 2.1: Create courseware.* To determine the cost of developing ILT on customer service, Acme could obtain bids from various vendors, total the time and expense of using in-house developers (assuming that staff are available), or use some kind of benchmark from their previous experience. In this case, Acme is using past experience and another training rule of thumb to estimate that it would cost about $3,500 per finished hour to have an outside vendor develop this type of instructor-led courseware. Using the number of hours of training estimated in step 1.3, Acme calculated that fourteen hours of training × $3,500 per hour = $49,000.

Similarly, to determine the cost of developing TBT on customer service, Acme could obtain bids from various vendors, estimate the costs of in-house

Figure 6.2
Design and Development Costs for Acme's
Customer Service Program

Item	Instructor-Led Training (ILT)	Technology-Based Training (TBT)
2.1 Create courseware	$49,000	$350,000
2.2 Train the Trainer	$10,560	—
Phase 2 Total	$59,560	$350,000

development (if possible), or use an assumption from the company's previous experience. Acme's previous multimedia training projects cost around $50,000 per finished hour. Using the 50 percent time-reduction estimate determined in step 1.4, it is assumed that the CD-ROM training would require only seven student hours. Therefore, the estimated cost of development is 7 hours × $50,000 per hour = $350,000.

• *Step 2.2: Train the trainer.* Acme plans to use its own training managers to deliver the course in a workshop format. However, the training vendor will need to conduct a train-the-trainer session in which Acme's managers are themselves taught the content and given a chance to practice facilitation techniques and review the daily course schedule. Acme will only need five managers certified in the delivery of the customer service program, so it is budgeting for a single three-day train-the-trainer session. Prior experience indicates that the course and materials will cost $6,000. Another cost to Acme will be the compensation of the training managers while they are in the three-day program, or 3 days × 5 trainers × $304 per day = $4,560. Thus the total cost for training Acme trainers will be $6,000 (vendor fees) + $4,560 (salaries) = $10,560.

Phase Three: Delivery

After the second phase of the cost comparison, TBT appears to be almost six times more expensive than ILT. In fact, the up-front cost to develop TBT is typically much higher than the development cost for ILT. However, Figure 6.3 shows how the delivery of training to a large audience over time is where the tables are turned and the hidden expenses of classroom-based training are revealed.

• *Step 3.1: Number of ILT sessions.* The first step in determining delivery costs is to ascertain the total number of workshop sessions that would be required. To get this number, Acme divides the total number of students (800) by their ideal student-to-instructor ratio (12 to 1). So 800 students ÷ 12 students per class = 67 required sessions over the three-year life of the course.

• *Step 3.2: Instructor costs.* This number is calculated by multiplying the number of hours required to deliver each workshop by the compensation rate of the instructor. At Acme, the students would be required to travel to the home office for training rather than the instructors flying to various meeting locations throughout the country. So Acme estimates that, in addition to the two days of actual training time, each instructor would need to spend a half-day

Figure 6.3
Costs of Delivering Training Program at Acme

Item	Instructor-Led Training (ILT)	Technology-Based Training (TBT)
3.1 # of ILT Sessions	67	0
3.2 Instructor costs • Prep and travel time • Time delivering training • Travel costs	$50,920	0
3.3 Student costs • Time in training • Opportunity cost • Travel costs	$969,600	$131,200
3.4 Location fees • Room rentals • Shipping • Storage	0	0
3.5 Equipment fees • Projectors • Shipping • Storage	0	0
3.6 Student materials • Workshop handouts • CDs • Miscellaneous	$6,400	$3,200
Delivery Total	$1,026,920	$134,400

preparing for the session. Therefore, total instructor costs are 67 sessions × 2.5 instructor days for each session × $304 instructor cost per day = $50,920. Because no instructors are necessary for Acme's CD-ROM based program, this cost is zero.

• *Step 3.3: Student costs.* In the case of ILT, the FSEs will be required to travel to the home office for training. Acme is assuming that in addition to the two days of training time, each student will spend an additional day traveling to and from the training, for a total of three days. The costs of student salaries will therefore be 800 students × 3 days × $164 = $393,600.

Additionally, the students will incur travel-related costs for airfare, transportation, lodging, and meals. Acme estimates that for each student these expenses will be $400 for airfare + $160 for two nights in a hotel + $60 for transportation + $100 for meals = $720 per student. Total travel-related costs will be $720 × 800 students = $576,000.

Total student costs for ILT will be $393,600 in salaries + $576,000 in travel = $969,600.

TBT is taken to the students (in the form of CD-ROMs) rather than the students going to the training. Thus, travel costs are eliminated. Additionally, instead of three days of total student time, each FSE will be required to spend only seven hours with the CD-ROM program, or approximately one day. Thus, 800 students × 1 training day × $164 compensation per day = $131,200.

• *Step 3.4: Location fees.* Many ILT programs are delivered in rented hotel conference rooms or resort centers. Fees to rent small meeting rooms can range from $200 to $500 per day. Organizations often have internal charge-backs to departments that use internal training facilities. Acme is planning to use its internal training rooms, but there are no associated fees. The cost, then, is zero.

• *Step 3.5: Equipment fees.* Because Acme is using in-house facilities, they will not have any additional equipment costs related to the delivery of ILT. If external locations are used for training, the cost of renting overhead projectors, flip charts, LCD projection panels, TVs and VCRs, and slide projectors can add many hundreds of dollars to each day of the workshop.

In TBT there can be costs associated with the purchase of computers and software. This is especially true if a special multimedia learning center is being built to support a particular training initiative or if a new server-computer will need to be installed to support Intranet-based training. In Acme's case, the training would be delivered via CD-ROM using the FSEs' existing laptop computers, so the cost of equipment would be zero.

• *Step 3.6: Student materials.* Acme is planning to provide each workshop participant with a detailed student manual. After consulting with a local print shop, it is determined that each manual will cost $8 to produce. Total costs for workshop materials will be $8 × 800 students = $6,400.

If Acme delivers the customer service training on CD-ROM, it will cost $4 per CD. This includes the CD duplication, the label, the jewel case, an insert that provides an overview of the program and loading instructions, and the postage required to mail the CDs to the students. Total material costs for technology-based delivery would be $4 per CD × 800 students = $3,200.

Phase Four: Administration and Maintenance

The final details to include when totaling the direct and indirect costs are those related to administering the training program and keeping it current and valuable. Figure 6.4 shows Acme's costs for these items.

• *Step 4.1: Tracking.* Organizations track registration or scheduling for ILT workshops in a variety of ways, from very simple index-card systems to complex computer databases. Similarly, some companies lean toward using tests for self-assessment purposes, while others maintain detailed records of student performance. It is assumed that all students involved in Acme's customer service training will be scheduled by a training manager, and managers will be responsible for grading students' final tests. Total time per workshop for these activities will be two hours. Therefore total time for administration would be 67 total sessions × 2 hours = 134 hours, or approximately 17 days. The cost of this time is 17 days × $304 per instructor day = $5,168.

The tracking cost for a CD-ROM-based solution is almost zero. All students take the courses concurrently, so no scheduling or preregistration is required. A built-in student log-in screen will be linked to a final assessment that is automatically

Figure 6.4
Training Program Administration and Maintenance Cost at Acme

Item	Instructor-Led Training (ILT)	Technology-Based Training (TBT)
4.1 Tracking • Student registration • Testing • Certificates	$5,168	0
4.2 Technical support	0	$8,000
4.3 Updates to content	0	0
4.4 Updates to technology	0	$8,200
Final Administration Total	$5,168	$16,200

scored by the computer. A simple printout of the score report or completion certificate will be submitted to the training department.

- *Step 4.2: Technical support.* For workshop delivery, no technical support is required. For CD-ROM delivery, some form of technical support is a must. Acme will use its in-house help desk to answer basic questions and fix simple problems. The help desk is managed by the information technology department, which has an internal charge-back of $50 for each call handled. A technical support rule of thumb is that 10 to 20 percent of a target audience will encounter some kind of problem and call for help. Acme conservatively estimates its technical support costs at 160 help-desk calls (20 percent of total audience size) × $50 per call = $8,000.

- *Step 4.3: Updates to content.* Acme is assuming that no change in content will be required during the three-year life of the training. For subject matter that changes frequently, such as product training or new-hire orientation training, updates can be quite expensive. In addition to new design and development costs, there are repeated distribution costs, too. This is where Web-based training has a major benefit. Because the content sits on a central server-computer, it is easily and affordably updated. There is no need for new CDs or workbooks to be distributed again to the target audience.

- *Step 4.4: Updates to technology.* ILT by its nature does not require an investment to update technology. However, the speed of technical innovation often requires rapid revisions to TBT programs. Typical scenarios include upgrades to student computers that involve a new operating system, new screen resolution, improved capability for multimedia, or a new Web browser. Acme is assuming that there will be one major upgrade to student computers, which will require a revision to the CD-ROM. Costs are estimated to be $5,000 to a vendor for revisions + $3,200 for reduplication (same cost as initial duplication and delivery of CDs) = $8,200.

Phase Five: Total Cost Comparison

The final step in the cost comparison is simply to transfer all of the subtotals onto one worksheet to obtain a total cost comparison. Figure 6.5 shows that the cost to Acme of creating and delivering instructor-led customer service training workshops would be approximately $1.1 million. The cost for equivalent training delivered via self-paced CD-ROMs would be just over $500,000. It is now a simple and defensible decision to invest in CD-ROM-based training, because it will save approximately $600,000 over three years.

Figure 6.5
Comparison of Costs of ILT and TBT at Acme

Item	Instructor-Led Training (ILT)	Technology-Based Training (TBT)
Design and Development	$59,560	$350,000
Delivery	$1,026,920	$134,400
Administration and Maintenance	$5,168	$16,200
Final Total	$1,091,648	$500,600

Although the Acme case is fictitious, it accurately portrays the drivers behind the costs of TBT. The largest cost is for initial development. This cost is the same regardless of whether there will be ten students or a thousand. The cost for delivery is negligible. Thus it is easy to see that for small audiences, TBT might be prohibitively expensive. For large audiences, however, the potential cost savings of CD-ROM and Web-based training is incredible. In Acme's case, if they had only four hundred students instead of eight hundred, the decision to use technology just to save money would have been harder to make.

MEASURING BENEFITS

The second half of cost-benefit analysis is identifying and measuring the beneficial results from a training program. Benefits come in two types. *Tangible benefits* are those that can be measured and assigned some kind of number or dollar value. *Intangible benefits* are those that cannot be measured or even quantified.

Tangible Benefits

Tangible benefits can be measured and ideally quantified in dollars. For example:

- A sales training program increased sales by $24 million.

- A customer service program increased customer satisfaction survey results by 10 percent.

- A safety training program reduced the number of accidents over one year by 30 percent.

- A quality-control program reduced defects from 832 to 654.

- A software training program reduced calls to the help desk by 30 percent.

- A communication training program increased the ratings of managers by their direct reports by .43.

These examples all show very real, measurable, tangible results. To get valuable ROI information, however, these results must be turned into dollar values.

Before translating results into dollars, though, make sure that you are studying an isolated control group. Similar to how scientists conduct experiments, the goal is to minimize the number of other variables that might be contributing to the results. Without an isolated control group, your peers will challenge your findings. Consider the following retorts to various training claims:

- "How do you know the sales training caused sales to go up in the third quarter? Maybe it was the new incentive plan we rolled out in September."

- "Maybe it wasn't the safety training that reduced accidents at that plant location. Perhaps the layoffs resulted in fewer total workers to have accidents."

- "I understand that you think the software training reduced calls to the help desk. But maybe the new operating system is simply easier to use."

- "You said that direct reports scored their managers higher because of the management training. I think everyone is just happier because of the profit-sharing results."

The easiest way to isolate a control group is to roll out new training programs in phases. Although this is not always practical, it will enable you to measure results obtained with the newly trained group and compare them to those obtained with the untrained group. Some examples of how this could be done follow.

- To create a control group for sales training, identify two regions that have historically produced consistent and similar revenue results. Distribute the new sales training program to one region and then measure growth in sales over the following three-month period. If the trained region has a significantly higher sales growth rate than the untrained group, it is likely that the training can be credited with the increase. Make sure, however, that there were no other significant differences between the regions, such as the rollout of new technology to one group, a change in senior management, or other factors explainable by geographic differences.

• When conducting quality control training, first analyze error rates over the previous year at different factories, or if there is only one factory, look at error rates among different shifts. Then, to create a control group, pick one factory or one shift of workers to complete the training. Measure the increase or decrease in product defects over the next three or four months. If there is a decrease in the trained group and no change in the control group, the training likely had an impact. Follow-up investigation should ensure that no other factors in the period could have caused the difference.

Once you have isolated and validated the measurable results of your training program, it is time to quantify it in dollar terms. Sometimes this is straightforward, other times it requires some additional industry benchmarking. Following are some examples of quantifying training results:

• *Sales training.* If a sales training program increased revenue generated in the control group by 2 percent, this increase can be applied to the entire sales force's revenues. For example, if in the previous period sales totaled $500 million, a 2 percent increase would be worth $10 million.

• *Interviewing skills.* A training program on recruiting is shown in the control group to reduce turnover from 20 to 15 percent due to interviewers' ability to find a better match between company and contact—a 25 percent improvement. This reduction can be applied to the total anticipated turnover rate. If in the previous year 1,000 people left the company, after training that number should drop to 750, a net savings of 250 employees retained. Additional research into human resource issues might uncover that it costs on average $18,000 to hire and train each new employee. Total cost savings can then be projected to be 250 employees × $18,000 = $450,000.

Intangible Benefits

These types of benefits are usually assumed to result from a training program, but they are difficult or impossible to measure. Although specific dollar values cannot be attached to intangible benefits, they are still important to discuss and document. Examples of intangible benefits from specific training programs might include the following:

- An increase in morale and employee engagement resulting from new-hire orientation training
- Improvements in teamwork resulting from diversity training.
- Additional sensitivity and a more professional workplace resulting from sexual harassment training
- Less stress among students who complete conflict management training
- Less anxiety after completing a change-management program.

EVALUATING RESULTS

After you've come up with the specific costs to develop your training program and estimated or measured its financial benefit, several simple calculations can be used to express the overall return you are achieving from your training investment.

Calculating Cost Savings over Traditional Delivery

The most basic and frequently used analysis is a simple comparison of how much money TBT will save over more traditional instructor-led workshops. Figure 6.6 shows the formula and presentation method for this data using the Acme example.

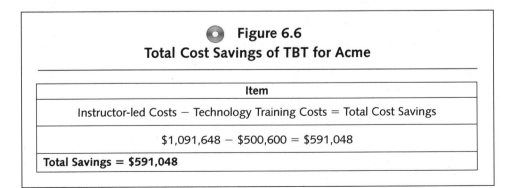

Figure 6.6
Total Cost Savings of TBT for Acme

Item
Instructor-led Costs − Technology Training Costs = Total Cost Savings
$1,091,648 − $500,600 = $591,048
Total Savings = $591,048

Conducting a Break-Even Analysis

The total savings in the Acme analysis does not, however, tell the whole story. Because TBT is initially more expensive to create than ILT, the payback often doesn't begin until year two or three. Using a break-even analysis will identify exactly when the program begins to "save" money. The value of this measurement is usually in terms of the number of students it will take to train in order to reach break-even. To put break-even analysis simply, it answers the question, How many students will we have to train for our up-front investment in TBT to begin to pay-off?

Figure 6.7 uses Acme's date to show the three-step formula for calculating the break-even point. Note that in this analysis the calculated cost to deliver the training to each student factors in both standard delivery costs as well as administrative and maintenance costs. The final result of 263 students as the break-even point is another indicator that the investment in TBT is a wise one because there are 800 students to be trained. If fewer than 263 students were to be trained

Figure 6.7
Break-Even Analysis for TBT at Acme

Step 1. Per-student delivery cost of technology-based training (TBT) = total TBT delivery costs ÷ total number of students

Step 2. Per-student delivery cost of instructor-led training (ILT) = total ILT delivery costs ÷ total number of students

Step 3. Break-even point =

$$\frac{\text{Total TBT development costs} - \text{total ILT development costs}}{\text{Per-student ILT costs} - \text{per-student TBT costs}}$$

Step 1. ($134,400 + $16,200) ÷ 800 students = $188.25 per student

Step 2. ($1,026,920 + $5,168) ÷ 800 students = $1,290.11 per student

Step 3. $\dfrac{\$350,000 - \$60,000}{\$\ 1,290 - \$\ \ \ 188} = \dfrac{\$290,000}{\$ - 1,102} = 263$ students during the three-year period, ILT would make more sense from a financial perspective.

Cost-Benefit Ratio

The cost-benefit ratio is a simple calculation that depicts the total financial return for each dollar invested in the training program. The example that follows is based on a fictitious case of a Web-based quality training program that cost $54,000 to develop and deliver and saved $430,000 in the first year due to a reduction in defective widgets. Figure 6.8 details the calculations.

Return on Investment

The ROI analysis is one of the more popular financial measures. It simply states the return on the training investment in percentage terms. Figure 6.9 details these

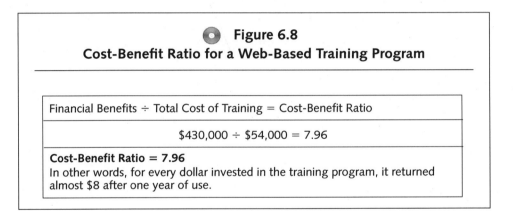

● Figure 6.8
Cost-Benefit Ratio for a Web-Based Training Program

Financial Benefits ÷ Total Cost of Training = Cost-Benefit Ratio

$430,000 ÷ $54,000 = 7.96

Cost-Benefit Ratio = 7.96
In other words, for every dollar invested in the training program, it returned almost $8 after one year of use.

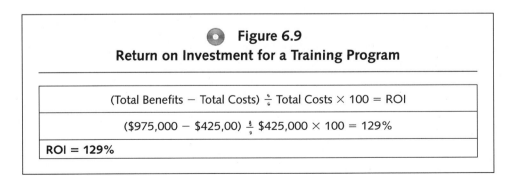

● Figure 6.9
Return on Investment for a Training Program

(Total Benefits − Total Costs) ÷ Total Costs × 100 = ROI

($975,000 − $425,00) ÷ $425,000 × 100 = 129%

ROI = 129%

calculations for a fictitious Web-based sales training program that cost $425,000 to develop and deliver and increased sales by $975,000 in the first year.

APPLYING IT ON THE JOB

Training programs should be implemented only if the benefits will outweigh the costs. Make sure that you or your vendor can defend any investment in training. Remember to measure indirect costs as well as direct costs. Wherever possible, turn measurable data on benefits into dollar estimates. Use the following measures when reporting program results:

- *Cost savings over ILT:* total cost savings = instructor-led costs − technology training costs
- *Break-even analysis:* break-even point = TBT development costs − ILT development costs/per-student ILT costs − per-student TBT costs
- *Cost-benefit ratio:* cost-benefit ratio = financial benefits ÷ total cost of training
- *Return on investment:* ROI = (total benefits − total costs) ÷ total costs × 100

Working with a Vendor

Once you have decided to use TBT and understand the basics of this form of delivery, the most challenging part of realizing your goals will be selecting a vendor and determining the necessary time and budget. By choosing the right vendor to partner with and properly managing the process, however, you will make your training project a great success.

What You Will Learn in This Chapter

- How to estimate the time and expense of completing a project
- How to create a request for proposals
- How to select a TBT vendor
- How to manage the development process

HOW TO DETERMINE THE PROJECT BUDGET

There is one question that training managers ask consultants and vendors more than any other. Consultants hear it in phone calls, at the end of their capability demonstrations, and at industry conventions. It causes vendors to cringe every time it is uttered. The seemingly simple question is, "What does it cost?" Variations include, "I need a sales training CD-ROM; what will it cost?" or "I want Web-based training to teach people how to use their word processor. What's a ballpark budget?"

Consultants squirm when asked how much a training project will cost. It is a lot like calling up a construction company and saying, "I want to build a house. What's it going to cost me?" The obvious answer is always, "It depends"—on many factors, including site preparation; total square footage; number of rooms; style and quality of construction; finishing details such as flooring, counters, and cabinets; landscaping; and even the construction schedule. (Is it a rush job that will require overtime labor?) So, too, does the cost of a training project depend on many factors.

Factors That Influence Price

When estimating the budget for a TBT program, you need to be able to answer at least these questions:

- How will the training be delivered—by CD-ROM or on the Web?
- If it will be Web-based, is it high bandwidth or low bandwidth?
- What is the content or subject matter?
- How long will it take the average student to complete the course or how many screens will it contain? (Though these are not exact measurements, they get at the basic issues of size and scope.)
- Will the program use audio, video, animations, or complicated illustrations?
- Where will the content come from? Are there existing training modules? Is a subject matter expert readily available?
- Will the program have student-tracking capabilities? Will it be complex?
- When will the project begin? When does it need to be delivered?
- What specific services will your organization provide—for example, script development, audio-video clips, quality control, or packaging and duplication?

With this information, an experienced vendor should be able to give you a rough estimate of the cost of program development. With some more details you can expect a firm price.

Pricing Rules of Thumb

Although the answer to "how much will it cost" is not simple, there are rules of thumb that are commonly used. These rules are often upheld wrongly as hard and fast and cast in concrete rather than as the general guidelines they are intended to be.

The most common price reference is that it takes approximately six hundred person-hours to complete one hour of high-quality multimedia training, which is usually delivered on CD-ROM. This includes all services—instructional design, audio and video, programming, quality control, and project management. For simpler Web-based or computer-based training without audio or video, the rule of thumb is that it takes three hundred person-hours, or half as much work, to complete one student-hour of training.

Most training vendors charge $100 to $125 per hour for their services, which puts the cost for multimedia CD-ROM training at $60,000 to $75,000 per finished hour. An hour of Web-based or computer-based training without audio or video might cost $30,000 to $40,000 to develop.

Problems with Pricing by the Hour

Although pricing by the hour is a very common practice, it is deeply flawed. The fundamental problem is the notion of the mythic student-hour. What is it really? Because the student controls the program's pace, it might take a slow learner two hours to complete a one-hour program of computer-based training. A fast learner might get through the same material in only thirty minutes. In fact, a well-designed program will purposely vary in length based on the experience of the student. Pretests enable some students to "test out of" certain lesson segments, thus reducing the total amount of learning time.

The complexities of the material to be taught and the instructional strategies deployed are other important factors in estimating the time it takes to create a training program. A one-hour simulation of open-heart surgery will certainly require more time and money to develop than a one-hour linear tutorial on how to use Microsoft Windows.

Significant programming tasks are required for the first hour of training that do not need to be replicated for subsequent hours of instruction. These programming tasks include developing the title screen, student log-in screens, student tracking, book marking, and the basic design of the graphical interface the user sees. It is inaccurate, therefore, to extrapolate that if a one-hour program costs $60,000, then a four-hour program would cost four times as much, or $240,000. Initial production requirements are involved in the project setup. Just as in producing a book, magazine, or newspaper, the first copy of the program off the press may cost thousands of dollars for the writing, art, typesetting, and design. Each additional copy costs less and less.

An alternative approach to per-hour pricing is pricing by the number of screens. Many multimedia training suppliers will quote $60,000 for 60 to 120 screens, or frames, of instruction. But problems arise that are similar to those in the learning-time approach. What really constitutes a screen? If one screen plays a thirty-second audio clip and another plays a five-minute video clip, shouldn't these costs vary? Are menus, glossaries, student tracking, and help screens included in the screen count? What about interactive questions that present a question, accept student input, and provide feedback? Is this interactivity counted as one, two, or three screens?

Simplistic per-hour or per-screen rates mask many factors that accurately describe and define the task at hand. Such flat-rate estimates do not adequately describe the quality of instruction, the number of features, or the amount of media in the program. Frequently, TBT projects that are initiated after the acceptance of a sparse three-page proposal conclude with the client being disappointed with the final program and the vendor disconcerted over the profit margin. The client may have imagined a program with much more interactivity. The vendor, who was continually asked to add complexity, may feel that the project was not fairly represented and should have been priced differently.

How Should a Project be Priced?

Developing TBT programs requires the time of many specialists, including programmers, writers, artists, audio and video specialists, and project managers. The most accurate way to price a project is to specify all of its design details and estimate the total amount of time each team member will contribute. Applying the respective hourly rates to each of these services will yield an accurate total project price.

Vendors typically make assumptions about the project that may or may not be expressed to you, the client. For example, an animated three-dimensional title-screen sequence with dramatic music can cost ten times more than a simple text screen, but you are not likely to be asked about this level of detail. If the production house typically creates Hollywood-style effects, and if they think your organization has a substantial budget for the project, they will likely assume that you want the deluxe opening, and they will price it accordingly.

These vendor assumptions should be presented to you as line items upon request. If you are surprised by how high or low a project estimate is, you should ask your vendors questions. Among the questions to ask to bring out assumptions are the following:

- How many interactive exercises are planned? What type of exercises are they?
- What are the plans for the post-test? Will it print a diploma upon reaching a mastery level?
- How many graphics and animations will be included? Are they all original or will some be clip art?
- How much total video and audio are to be used?

These questions will force vendors to show their cards and to examine their own plans if they are merely providing a generic per-hour price.

HOW TO FIND POTENTIAL VENDORS

Finding a qualified TBT partner does not have to be a difficult chore. Many training companies say they do multimedia, and many new media companies say they do training. But the field narrows considerably when you look at companies that truly place an equal emphasis on both instructional design and technology.

Using Associations

The single best way to find multimedia training companies is to search the ASTD *Buyer's Guide*. To purchase this guide, call ASTD (see Appendix E) or search the electronic version of the *Buyer's Guide* on the World Wide Web at <www.astd.org>. The guide provides an automatic first round of screening, because anybody who is anybody in the training industry will know of ASTD and will be listed in the guide. In other words, you are increasing your risk if you select a vendor who is not a member of ASTD.

Another good association to contact is the International Society for Performance Improvement (ISPI). The ISPI's annual directory of performance improvement resources lists dozens of vendors in the "Buyer's Guide" section. To purchase this directory call the ISPI (see Appendix E) or access it on the World Wide Web at <www.ispi.org>.

Do not limit yourself by considering the geographical location of a vendor. The best multimedia and Web-based training firms might not be in your own backyard. With modern communication tools such as e-mail, fax, express delivery, and secure, private Web sites, you can work with a firm across the country just as easily as with a local one. The quality of the work, the expertise, and the personal fit of vendor and client are much more important than location.

Using Trade Shows

One tried and true way to identify qualified multimedia training companies and to stay abreast of current industry trends is through trade shows and conferences. These multiday events typically include a full schedule of speeches by various practitioners, workshops by industry experts, and an exposition of hundreds of companies demonstrating their latest products and service offerings. The trade shows you should consider attending fall into three categories.

• *Trade shows dedicated to trainers and training in general.* These shows are offered by ASTD (see Appendix E) and ISPI (see Appendix E). The topics covered encompass the many aspects of training and typically include a technology and training track. Among the hundreds of exhibitors are many technology-focused companies.

• *Trade shows dedicated specifically to multimedia and Web-based training.* These shows include the On-line Learning convention sponsored by Lakewood Publishing, and the Society for Applied Learning Technologies conference sponsored by ASTD (see Appendix E).

• *Industry-specific training conferences.* Depending on the industry in which you work, there is a good chance that a training association exists that is dedicated to your industry's particular training needs. Examples of these types of organizations and trade shows include the National Society for Pharmaceutical Sales Trainers annual convention and the Society for Insurance Trainers and Educators conference.

When attending a trade show or convention, allocate a good amount of time to walking the exposition floor and visiting the booths of TBT vendors. Because they are all located under one roof, it is easy to meet representatives of many companies, look at samples of their work, gather marketing literature, and ask about their relevant experience.

Another excellent way to find qualified companies at trade shows is to attend the speeches or various sessions offered throughout the day. These talks are usually delivered by "experts" who present their latest work in the form of case studies. If you are impressed by a speaker's work, you can contact the presenter after the session (or after the conference) and request more information about his or her company. A sampling of topics from recent conferences includes the following:

- Building an on-line curriculum for sales training
- Multimedia new-hire orientation programs
- Selecting an on-line training management system
- Computer-based testing
- The power of games in multimedia
- Building virtual corporate universities

Narrowing the Field

Once you have found several TBT vendors that interest you, gather as much basic information about them as you can. Visit their Web sites, call and speak to an account executive, and review their marketing materials.

Your goal is to narrow down the field to perhaps three to five companies that will receive your official request for proposals, or RFP. If you ask more than five technology companies to submit proposals, the amount of time you spend evaluating them will be considerable.

What are important qualities to look for in a TBT vendor? Following are some key considerations:

- *Experience:* How many projects have they completed that are similar in size, scope, or content to yours?
- *Strength of company:* Do they have the financial resources and staff size to complete your project and maintain it in the future?
- *Understanding of instructional design:* Can they show evidence of understanding instructional systems design, constructivism, and performance-based learning objectives?
- *Quality of work:* Have they received professional awards, published articles in trade magazines, or otherwise been recognized for their work?

CREATING AN RFP

Training managers are often surprised when they receive vendors' proposals and see the wide disparity in prices and proposed solutions. One training manager at a pharmaceutical company received five proposals for the development of a CD-ROM to teach sales representatives about a new drug. The low bidder quoted $28,000 while the high bidder came in at $380,000. (The winning proposal was for $78,000.) What explains this huge disparity? Quite simply, the training manager was not specific enough in his request to receive comparable and valid responses from the vendors.

The Components of an RFP

An RFP is a document that explains the training need and provides details about the size and scope of the project. A complete RFP should include the following elements:

- Background on the student population
- Outline of the content or learning objectives to be covered
- Estimate of the total amount of learning time the finished program should include
- Samples of any existing subject matter or description of available subject matter expertise
- Description of the delivery technology, whether CD-ROM or Web-based
- Description of the types of media to be used, such as whether audio or video will be included
- Clear requests for vendor background information

  See Appendix A for a model RFP.

Key Points in a Model RFP

A fair amount of analysis and planning needs to be done by the client in order to provide an appropriately specific request to a TBT vendor. Ideally, a needs analysis and high-level design document should be created prior to sending out RFPs to vendors.

Sometimes one vendor is hired to conduct the needs analysis, outline the learning objectives, and produce a high-level design document. Then the same vendor or others are asked to propose how to create the actual solution. Such detailed front-end work helps ensure that the end product will be an effective training tool delivered on time and on budget.

Vendors should be given at least two to three weeks to complete their proposals. Some managers believe that mandating quick turnarounds of a proposal—three days, for example—tests how professional and committed the vendors are. The theory is that only the best companies will be able to respond on time. In reality, the best companies are very thorough with their proposed solutions and very busy with existing clients. The companies more likely to respond to quick turnaround RFPs are those that are desperate for new business or overstaffed for their current workload. A quality company might submit a proposal that is twenty to forty pages long, with detailed design strategies, sample screen images, and perhaps even an ROI analysis. The extra information you receive from such a company will be worth the wait.

SELECTING A VENDOR

The big day is at hand and the proposals are flowing into your office—some via overnight delivery, others by fax or e-mail. This is the first step to bringing your project to life as the vendors submit their most creative ideas, effective learning strategies, and step-by-step project plans.

Much preparation has gone into these proposals, but if you are like most managers, you will skip the first forty pages of each proposal and turn immediately to the price.

If your RFP was specific, the range in budget numbers should not be too great, perhaps plus or minus 30 percent. Now is your first chance to use the rule-of-thumb numbers given earlier in this chapter. If you were requesting two hours of high-end multimedia CD-ROM training on a topic of average complexity, you would expect to be looking at a price quote around $120,000. If you have a vendor who comes in significantly lower than this ballpark number—say $50,000—you would want to look into why the number is number so low. Did they not understand the specifications? Do they have some unique cost advantage? Are they a garage shop with no overhead, and no infrastructure?

If another proposal is significantly higher—say $220,000—you should similarly ask yourself why they are so high. Is the vendor recommending a more complex or lengthy solution? Have they uncovered some unique problems of which the other vendors are not aware? Are they really so good that they deserve a price premium?

After satisfying your initial price curiosity, you need to read the proposals carefully to understand fully what you will be getting from each vendor. Pay attention to specific elements that can greatly influence price, such as the following:

- Design strategies: linear versus simulations
- Features such as bookmarking and score reporting
- Amount of media to be used: audio, video, and artwork
- Number of animations and whether or not they are simple two-dimensional or more complex three-dimensional
- Unique offerings such as instructional games

Comparing Apples to Apples

You cannot evaluate the prices you have received until you understand exactly what you would be getting from each vendor and how much it would cost. A list of questions follows that you can ask vendors—in writing or on the phone—if their proposals do not give you the level of specificity you need to compare theirs with other proposals. Answers to these questions will help you make true comparisons of RFPs.

- How much learning time or how many screens will be provided?
- How much audio and video time will be incorporated?
- Will professional or amateur actors and narrators be used?
- How many graphics and animations will be used?
- What percentage of artwork will be original illustrations? What percentage will be stock photography or scanned photos?
- How many interactive exercises will be used throughout the training?
- What percentage of exercises will be simple multiple-choice questions? What percentage will be complex open-ended questions or simulations?
- How many questions will there be in the pretests and post-tests?

- What type of questions will be used in the tests (for example, multiple choice, true or false, matching, drag and drop)?

- What type of score reporting, tracking, or diploma printing will be provided?

Another price-analysis strategy is to ask vendors to break out their pricing according to different project tasks and provide their hourly rates for each task. Following are the most common tasks:

- Instructional design and writing
- Graphic art and illustration
- Audio and video production (shooting and editing)
- Programming
- Quality control
- Project management
- Out-of-pocket expenses

This price breakdown will enable you to see if one vendor is planning on spending much more time on instructional design than another might be planning.

How to Evaluate Previous Work

After reviewing all of the proposals, you should be able to weed out some of the responses based on obviously inappropriate solutions or pricing. If you have not already met face-to-face with the vendors or seen their work firsthand, it is time to do so. Make sure that the samples of work that are demonstrated are technically similar to the project at hand. If you want a low-bandwidth Web-based training program, you will have little to learn from a vendor who is demonstrating the latest whizbang effects on a multimedia CD-ROM. If you have a large project, you might want to ask the vendors that make your first cut to actually create a prototype or demo using your own materials. This is probably the best way to see the vendors' level of creativity and technical capability.

How to Check References

Checking references is a crucial step in the vendor selection process. Similar to a reference check for job candidates, this procedure requires that you talk directly to independent parties who have previous experience with the company. Any vendor that overstates his accomplishments or makes exaggerated claims will quickly be revealed through a few short calls to previous clients.

The key to effective reference checks is to request *many* references. Most RFPs ask a company for only three references, but every company has at least a few satisfied clients (or a brother-in-law who will claim to be a raving fan). You increase the odds of getting valuable client information if you ask for a minimum of five or six references.

When you call to check a reference, explain that you are considering working with Company X and would like to ask a few questions. You should start with general questions first, then probe for more detailed information. Questions can include the following:

- *Can you tell me about the project they completed for you?* After listening to the reference's answer you should examine how similar this previous project is to the one you will be doing. Consider whether the client's response is genuinely enthusiastic or cautiously subdued. Some references are reluctant to say anything specifically bad about another company, but the tone of their reply will be a clue to their sincerity.

- *Was the project delivered on CD-ROM or the Web?* Some TBT companies focus on only one type of delivery mechanism. Make sure that the vendor has experience with the specific technology you plan to use.

- *In what time frame was the project completed?* If the vendor has completed a similarly sized project in an equivalent time frame, they can probably handle your project's deadline, too.

- *Was the project completed on time?* If the vendor is not large enough, it may not be able to complete your project in the given period.

- *How responsive was the company to making changes and revisions?* How the reference answers this question will help you determine whether the vendor is customer-service driven. You can also ask whether the vendor tries to charge for every small change or only for changes to the size and scope of the project.

- *Was the project completed within the original budget or did the vendor ask for more money?* Frequently vendors will quote a low price to win a project but then repeatedly return for more money throughout the project to cover "unanticipated" costs.

- *What could the vendor have done better?* No company is perfect, but understanding a weakness in a previous project will help you avert potential problems should you choose that otherwise strong company as your vendor.

- *Who was the project manager on the project?* If you are dealing with a large vendor, you want to make sure you are getting references on the people who will actually be working on your project. The project manager, sometimes called the producer, is the key individual responsible for quality, budget, and schedule. Try to get personal references on the project manager for your project.

- *Would you work with the company again in the future?* This question gives the reference you are calling the opportunity to offer the ultimate testimonial and will reveal just how satisfied their company was with the project overall.

How to Negotiate Price

You should always pick the most qualified company to work for you, regardless of price, and then evaluate the costs associated with the proposed solution. As in all other areas of life, you can expect to get what you pay for. Vendors that have a proven track record of creating innovative and effective solutions while providing great customer service are likely to command a higher price than vendors with lesser qualifications.

However, if the price on the proposal is higher than the budget you are working with, do not despair. Although it is unlikely that a reputable vendor will arbitrarily drop its price, it may be willing to reshape the solution to fit your budget.

As described earlier in this chapter, you should work with the vendor to get a better understanding of where the costs are being incurred. You can often achieve your price target by reducing the total amount of video, animations, or three-dimensional effects without compromising learning outcomes. Be careful, however, about reducing the investment in instructional design and writing, as these are the areas that have the greatest impact on the quality of the instruction itself.

How to Use a Vendor Scorecard

If you have narrowed down the possible vendors to one that is the most qualified and customer service oriented, you need only confirm standard contract details and your search is complete. However, you may find that a few vendors all seem capable. In this case, a simple scorecard can be used to award each vendor points in various categories that you deem important. Figure 7.1 provides a sample scorecard with a scale of thirty-five total possible points.

Figure 7.1
Vendor Selection Scorecard

Item Description	Vendor #1 Points	Vendor #2 Points	Vendor #3 Points
Quality of Work **(10 possible points)** • Company has received awards and honors, published articles • Samples, demos, and prototypes show high quality • Has worked on similar projects			
Customer Service **(10 possible points)** • Positive feedback was provided by five references • Exhibited friendly, prompt service through proposal process • Showed flexibility of project manager			
Company Stability **(5 possible points)** • Firm has been in business several years • Is financially strong and growing • Has depth of talent and experience in staff			
Price (5 possible points) • Competitive and reasonable fixed budget • Estimate for expenses • Good track record of completing project on time, on budget			
Quality Proposal/Presentation **(5 possible points)** • Reflected research into client company and detailed solution; not a canned proposal • Attractive layout and presentation • Submitted on time • Followed all RFP directions and answered all questions			
Total			

TIPS FOR REDUCING PROJECT COSTS

After receiving all the proposals, you may discover that even the lowest-priced proposal costs more than you have budgeted for the project. There are some judicious ways to reduce costs and not necessarily jeopardize the ability of the program to teach.

• *Tip 1: Use repetitive screen layouts.* Most multimedia and Web-based training programs use a variety of screen designs to keep the program's appearance creative and engaging. Laying out each individual screen, however, can be very time-consuming, and costly. To reduce costs, use one or two screen layouts for the whole program. For example, one layout might have the text on the left side of the screen with a picture on the right, and a second style might reverse the positioning. Long text blocks can be placed in scrollable windows so they do not have to be broken up into a different layout.

• *Tip 2: Use only simple interactive exercises.* The best TBT will use a variety of simple and complex interactive exercises. Complex interactivities might include drag-and-drop questions, open-ended short-answer questions, or brief simulations. The easiest types of interactivity to program, however, are closed-ended questions (multiple choice, true or false, and fill-in). Choose these simple types of exercises as an easy way to reduce the budget. Be aware, however, that you will not be testing the capabilities of your students to recall information.

• *Tip 3: Use amateur actors and narrators.* If your program requires a substantial amount of video and audio narration, your vendor probably has budgeted for card-carrying union professionals to do the work—at a very high hourly rate. Many organizations choose to use their own employees for these parts and save thousands of dollars on the project. Depending on the role, using a real employee might add to the impact of the training program. For example, using your salesperson of the year to host a sales training program would provide credibility to the message. Having workers from an assembly line talk about quality control procedures would provide real-world relevance. However, if your employee-actors seem stiff or overly dramatic, students will focus on their poor performances more than on their messages. Choose your actors carefully and provide careful direction.

• *Tip 4: Use stock art images.* Creating original artwork is one of the most expensive production areas for TBT. Meticulously hand-drawn images, such as a cartoon character, a heart, or a computer, or the increasingly popular three-dimensional images of buildings or rooms, involve artistic talent and time to render digitally. Almost all programs use some stock images, also known as clip art. Today you can affordably access thousands of photographs, cartoons, and three-dimensional models that provide a high-quality alternative to original art. The proper mix of original and clip art will be kind to your budget and keep the visual quality of your program high.

TRICKS, TRAPS, AND OTHER VENDOR SHENANIGANS

Many vendors use certain practices that give them short-term advantages or lower prices, but with long-term negative consequences to you, the client. Make sure you investigate your vendor's approach to these topics and avoid falling into these common traps.

- *Who owns the source code?* The source code is the actual program, or lines of instruction, in an unencrypted format. Many vendors keep the source files and hold the copyright to them, which prevents you, the client, from making changes to the program on your own. Retaining the source code gives the vendor tremendous power over the client. If you are dissatisfied in the middle of the project, you cannot fire the vendor without being willing to start the project all over from scratch. More commonly, when you return to the vendor in the future for minor updates to the program, you may discover that exorbitant rates will be charged for the updates. Without ownership of source code, you have no choice but to pay the high fees; it is still cheaper than creating the program again from the beginning.

Make it clear in your RFP or contract that all unencrypted source files and programmer notes will be turned over to you and that you have the right to maintain the program yourself in the future. Many vendors intentionally encrypt their work to prevent others from accessing it.

- *Who owns the content?* Ownership of the content itself is as important as ownership of the source code. If the vendor holds exclusive copyright to the words, images, and videos that appear in your program, then only that vendor has the legal authority to change the content or to reuse it in a modified program.

Most vendors have a legitimate need to protect their "intellectual property" and need to be able to reuse part of the content on other projects. As the client, however, you need to make sure that you have the right to use, modify, and reuse the content for your internal purposes.

- *Are project expenses extra?* Some vendors bundle all expenses into the project fee while others bill for individual items. Just be sure you know in advance how your vendor operates. Vendors can charge for photocopies, phone calls, postage, faxes, office supplies, administrative assistance, and travel. These fees add an additional 5 to 15 percent to a project total. If your vendor charges for expenses, make sure to get a detailed list of which items will be charged, find out the exact cost per item, and insist on receiving all receipts or detailed records of materials used.

- *What will program updates cost in the future?* If you own the copyright to the source code and content, you are likely to get competitive rates for time and materials because you can always turn to another vendor. Never accept flat fees or percentage fees for changes. For example, some vendors will charge $2,500 plus $1,000 per day for changes. If you sign such an agreement, you could pay $3,500 for the vendor to make a simple text change that might require only an hour of time. The best deal is for the vendor to charge normal hourly rates ($100 to $150) and expenses for any future updates.

- *Is the vendor using a software engine or proprietary tools?* A software engine, sometimes called a black box, is a program that automatically processes content such as data stored in a separate database. For example, an engine might specify where to place text on a screen and where to place a photograph. Because an engine is built once and the content is easily added or changed, a large amount of multimedia training can be developed for a relatively low cost. Typically, however, engines result in linear page turners, where each page looks the same and there is little interactivity or room for creativity. Many vendors consider their engine to be proprietary technology and refuse to turn it over to their clients.

Similarly, many vendors have created proprietary development languages or models that enable them to reduce the time and cost of program development. While this may cut development time for the vendor, it also means that you, the client, will have to always return to the same company for future updates and changes, even if you are dissatisfied with the prices or service.

Never agree to having your training produced using proprietary programs of any type. You will be forever shackled to the vendor, who may or may not even be in business two or three years from now when you need changes. Your initial investment becomes worthless if it needs to be updated and cannot be altered.

Today there are many excellent, easy-to-use tools on the market that are common among vendors. Insist that your vendor use a standard authoring language such as Authorware, Director, Toolbook, IconAuthor, or Quest.

• *Is the vendor using freelance developers?* It is easy for vendors to present themselves as capable of all services—video, audio, multimedia, instructional design, and Web development. Whatever you want, they do it. The truth often is that companies offers these services but do not have in-house capabilities in each particular area. Instead, they go outside the company to a freelancer.

While in theory there is nothing wrong with using freelancers, there are some pitfalls to be aware of. Freelancers can help keep costs down and bring specialized expertise to a particular job. But freelancers present a risk to you, the client. When a company uses freelancers, you really do not know who is working on your project. Neither the vendor nor you are in control of the freelance individual. What happens if the person becomes ill, moves away, or takes a job? Always make sure you ask in the RFP or follow-up meetings for the vendor to specify the exact team that will be working on your project and to tell you which ones are full-time employees and which are employed on a freelance or contract basis.

RULES FOR ESTABLISHING A GOOD VENDOR-CLIENT RELATIONSHIP

By establishing certain ground rules with your vendor prior to project kickoff, you can facilitate communications and establish your expectations about communication, progress, and service.

• *Rule 1: Maintain a single point of contact—a project manager.* Although each side typically has many team members contributing to the project, miscommunication becomes likely when several individuals are talking with different levels of each organization. For example, if the client is experiencing a technical glitch or bug, it might make sense for the client's technical support personnel to speak directly with the vendor's most advanced programmer. However, the project manager from the client and vendor should participate in this meeting or phone call to make sure that prior commitments or expectations are understood, action items agreed upon, and timetables set.

• *Rule 2: Hold frequent progress meetings.* Adhering to this simple rule helps improve communication and teamwork on a project. Ideally, once a week at a prescheduled time the vendor and client project managers should discuss the project status in person or on the phone. Topics can include new questions that have come up, answers to questions raised in the previous meeting, a review of milestones, and an update on the schedule. Even if there is little to report, a five-minute phone call confirming that everything is on schedule keeps the project moving along smoothly.

- *Rule 3: Work from detailed project schedules.* Depending on the complexity and size of your project, the schedule can be as simple as a table of items and delivery dates or as complex as GANTT charts that graphically show the overlapping tasks as bars on a timeline. Detailed schedules that are frequently updated let you see the consequences of missed deadlines or allow you to plan early for overcoming these delays.

The client's responsibility for deadlines is as important as the vendor's in meeting the final delivery date. If the original agreement and schedule is for client reviews to take place within three days and you take six, then you should be prepared to add three days to the schedule or risk sacrificing quality in order to meet the deadline.

- *Rule 4: Client project manager must be on hand for all video and audio shoots.* Most corporate training programs include a fair amount of industry jargon—technical words or phrases that might be mispronounced by a professional actor or narrator. Too often the client does not catch errors in pronunciation until the media are already incorporated into the program. At this point, correcting mistakes is expensive, requiring the rescheduling of the talent (who often charge a minimum half-day rate, even if they work for only ten minutes), the setup and possibly rental of audio or video equipment, and time to reedit and digitize the final footage.

- *Rule 5: Make all revisions to the interface in the prototype.* The first major deliverable from the vendor should be a prototype of the software. This will be a working model that includes each major section of the program: main menu, assessment questions, and several screens from the first lesson. Work with this prototype to refine the look, feel, and usability of the interface. Examine, test, change, and ultimately approve the colors, fonts, menu structure, location of navigation buttons, and interface metaphors. The interface should be approved and locked-in before significant scripting is completed so the writers will have an accurate sense of screen space when allocating text and specifying graphics.

- *Rule 6: Make all content revisions in the script.* After the prototype, the next major deliverable from the production team is the script or storyboard. This is your opportunity to review carefully the words, pictures, and sounds that will appear in the final program. Many clients give only a cursory glance at this document and then end up requesting substantial changes after the content has been implemented. It is very time-consuming and expensive to change content after it is implemented in the program. Unless there are obvious typos or mistakes in grammar, revisions to content after it is implemented should be avoided.

MILESTONES IN MANAGING THE DEVELOPMENT PROCESS

Successful project management starts with clearly defined project milestones that include client reviews and approvals at each point. These milestones or events loosely follow the instructional systems design process described in Chapter Three. Following are recommended project milestones.

- *Project kickoff.* The kick-off meeting gathers all key team members from the client and the vendor for a face-to-face review of the major project parameters. Typically, the proposal is reviewed, schedules are confirmed, and individual roles and lines of communication are clarified. If available, source materials and technical specifications are turned over to the vendor at this time.

- *Analysis, design document, and rapid prototype.* The vendor conducts a thorough needs analysis or reviews the client's analysis if one has been completed ahead of time. This step culminates in a high-level design document that reviews audience demographics, details technical specifications, provides a detailed content outline, and describes strategies for interactivity, navigation, testing, and tracking. Along with the design document, the vendor supplies a rapid prototype that is reviewed with the same technology that will be available to the students. The prototype shows the interface, structure, and performance of the software. The client carefully reviews the design document and prototype and provides written feedback to the vendor. After the vendor makes requested changes, approval is granted to continue.

- *Script or storyboard.* In this step the vendor's instructional designers produce detailed scripts or storyboards, sometimes called a detailed design document. This document describes the details of every screen, including text, audio narration, and video, and includes a description or sketch of graphics. Notes on each screen provide direction to the programmer and client about special navigation or other options (see Appendix I for a sample script). The client reviews these documents carefully and provides written feedback to the vendor. Revisions are made and approved before proceeding.

• *Development.* After final script approval, development begins on all media. Artists create graphics and illustrations while audio narration and video are recorded, edited, and digitized. When these media items are complete, programmers produce the final program. A thorough round of quality control uncovers any software bugs or other problems.

• *Pilot test or formative evaluation.* At this stage, the program is tested with members from the actual student population. This pilot test is completed with three to ten individuals in an environment that is identical to the one the actual students will use. The pilot test is designed both to uncover any technical glitches or bugs and to confirm that the instructional program is sound and achieving its objectives. Based on the results of this test, bugs are fixed and final adjustments are made to the content.

• *Delivery.* To prepare for delivery, a final round of quality control is conducted on the master CD-ROM or actual Web-site location where the program is held. After thorough testing, the vendor produces any necessary CD-ROM labels, jewel case packaging, or quick-reference user instructions. CD-ROMs are duplicated and distributed or the Web-based training program is uploaded to the server and opened for access.

• *Evaluation.* Finally, the vendor and client work together closely to evaluate the results of the program (see Chapter Three). Student evaluations and scores are tabulated and summarized, and observations of behaviors are completed. A brief memo or report describing the cost, benefit, and return on investment of the program provides both vendor and client with evidence of the effectiveness of the solution.

APPLYING IT ON THE JOB

By effectively managing your TBT vendor, you can optimize the chances for a successful project. Use the following checklist when launching your next project.

Vendor Selection

- ☐ The vendor is not just a multimedia or Web company but has experience in instructional design.
- ☐ The vendor will turn over source code for maintenance.
- ☐ The vendor will share copyright on content.
- ☐ The vendor does not use black box or engine.
- ☐ The vendor uses standard programming language such as Authorware, Director, Toolbook, IconAuthor, or Quest.
- ☐ The vendor has full-time, on-site staff for all critical project tasks.

Proposal Process

- ☐ The RFP is detailed in its specifications (see Appendix A).
- ☐ Along with prices, proposals specify the quantity and quality of media, interactivity, and content.
- ☐ The winning solution is judged on the quality of the firm's work, the strength of the company, its dedication to customer service, price, and the quality of the proposal itself.

Project Management

- ☐ The vendor is providing a single point-of-contact project manager.
- ☐ Weekly progress meetings are held.
- ☐ A detailed project schedule is created and routinely reviewed.
- ☐ A prototype is created, tested, refined, and finalized early in the development process.
- ☐ Major content changes are made in scripts and storyboards.
- ☐ The development process parallels the instructional systems design process.

Selling Your Projects Internally

Change abounds in the field of TBT. If your organization is just beginning the journey to self-paced instruction, you will find that there is significant cultural change and technology investment involved in moving out of the classroom environment. If your organization has already been using TBT, you may be transitioning from traditional multimedia CD-ROMs to Web-based training. This shift, too, comes with new investments in equipment and new expenditures for redesigning curricula. While change is necessary, not everyone will support it. Some may be personally threatened by the impact TBT will have on their own jobs. Others may fear it as a great unknown. Still others will choose to fight for limited budget dollars and a political foothold.

Despite the reasons behind the resistance, you should be prepared to become a champion for TBT and the benefits it brings to any organization. Knowing that there will be opposition to new plans and new programs—there always is—you can prepare a strategy for winning over key decision makers. This chapter will teach you how to position your projects so that senior managers and executives will see the positive value of those projects.

What You Will Learn in This Chapter

- The hot buttons of senior executives and how to translate TBT features into meaningful benefits

- How to work more productively with the information technology department

- Ways to gain support for new TBT efforts using various means of communication.

- Why solving a business problem is a more successful internal sales strategy than showcasing high-tech features

- Where to look for training case studies to bolster your TBT proposal

THE NEEDS AND LANGUAGE OF SENIOR EXECUTIVES

In any industry, the first thing a new sales professional learns is to focus on the benefits of the product or service, not on its features. A good car salesman will emphasize how safe your family will be in a new car (the benefit), because of the antilock brakes and air bags (the features). If you shop for a new mattress, you will likely be told that you will sleep better and experience less back pain (the benefits) because of special springs and firm padding (the features).

When gathering support internally for TBT efforts, remember this fundamental sales lesson. It is especially easy in TBT to fall in love with the features and mistakenly assume that others in your organization will share your passion. Remember that a CD-ROM's ability to deliver whizbang multimedia is a feature not a benefit. The Web's ability to link thousands of people and provide a vast amount of content is also a feature, not a benefit.

So what benefits should you be pitching? Figure 8.1 shows the entire TBT audience and each group's primary interest.

Students mainly want to know that the training will not be a waste of their time, and that it will not be a painful experience to complete. Traditionally, training professionals have focused on job-related competencies and have been evaluated on their ability to make a positive impact on students' knowledge, skills, and attitudes. More recently, there has been a strong shift in the training industry for trainers to become *performance-improvement consultants*. This shift aligns their goals more closely with those of business managers and broadens the range of possible solutions.

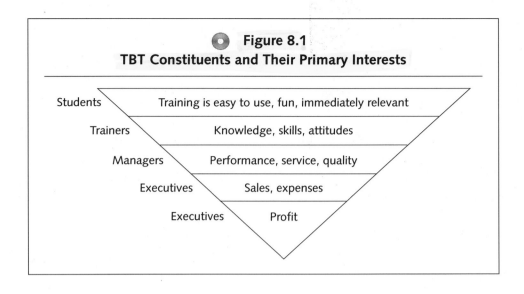

Figure 8.1
TBT Constituents and Their Primary Interests

Students	Training is easy to use, fun, immediately relevant
Trainers	Knowledge, skills, attitudes
Managers	Performance, service, quality
Executives	Sales, expenses
Executives	Profit

Midlevel managers have primary responsibility for the production or performance of the people in their department. Along with performance, excellent customer service and high quality are common objectives. These managers are also likely to have accountability for sales or managing budgets (expenses). Because of this focus on performance, managers may be opposed to training programs that require time away from the job, especially if they view the programs as having little short-term impact.

Executives at the highest levels are ultimately responsible for one thing: maximizing profit. The only ways they can increase profits are to increase sales or reduce costs. Senior executives understand that, indirectly, a sustainable and growing revenue stream is dependent on customers who are happy with the service they get and the quality of the products they buy. The production levels or performance of employees has the most direct impact on costs.

Depending on what level in the organization you are talking to, you should explain how each TBT feature would have a positive impact on that level's area of accountability. Educating your peers on the benefits an investment in TBT would have for their primary area of interest will quickly garner their support.

Will the program increase sales? Increasing sales is probably the most powerful benefit a training program can have, but few programs can claim to have a direct impact on revenue. This benefit should be pitched to senior executives if the TBT program is obviously a sales training program. Within the field of sales training, TBT can be used to teach sales professionals general selling skills, product knowledge, competitive knowledge, customer profiles, or objection handling. Other topics could include anything that would increase their efficiency, such as training on how to use their customer-contact software.

Will the program reduce expenses? The ability to save money or reduce costs is also among the highest priorities of senior executives. Chapter Six discussed how TBT can substantially reduce costs associated with student travel, lodging, and instructor fees. Reducing the number of days spent in a classroom also saves the opportunity costs associated with employees being away from their jobs.

Many training programs affect the expenses of an organization through the students' new behaviors, although this type of change is often difficult to measure. Following are some examples of how training programs can ultimately reduce costs through new skills.

- *Information technology training* can potentially reduce calls to the help desk, in turn reducing costs for the service or labor required. Additionally, increasing employees' software skills may reduce the time they spend on certain routine operations.

- *Quality improvement training* can reduce defects in product manufacturing, saving wasted materials and time while increasing customer satisfaction.

- *Safety training* can reduce accidents, medical bills, and workers' compensation fees.

- *Orientation training* can have a positive impact on new hires' morale and reduce employee turnover. This in turn reduces costs associated with recruiting and training new employees.

What are the indirect benefits? Although executives are most interested in increasing sales and reducing costs, efforts with indirect benefits that are assumed to affect either of these items will also be supported. These include anything that affects quality, service, general performance levels, or employee morale. Although the impact might be viewed as indirect, it does not mean that a certain level of outcome cannot be measured. For example, a program that teaches basic phone etiquette could actually have a measurable impact on customer satisfaction. A leadership course for frontline supervisors could have a measurable impact on employee engagement levels.

THE CONCERNS AND LANGUAGE OF INFORMATION TECHNOLOGY DEPARTMENTS

Training departments today are increasingly dependent on the cooperation and guidance of information technology (IT) departments. Previously, when almost all training was delivered by live instructors, the interaction between the two departments was almost nonexistent. With the advent of disk-based CBT and multimedia CD-ROMs, the IT department was sometimes called upon to clarify technical specifications or guarantee compatibility with existing computers. But today, with the rapid expansion of Web-based training, the IT department is becoming an equal partner in new programs. IT professionals are being called upon to maintain servers, provide remote access to the network, dictate Intranet standards, evaluate vendors, and sometimes even build or maintain Web pages. Figure 8.2 depicts this changing relationship between training professionals and IT professionals.

Many training professionals become frustrated when working with their IT colleagues. It is not uncommon to hear a training manager lament, "They can't do it" or "It will take them six months to get to us" or "They don't care." The reality is that IT professionals are just as dedicated to organizational success as any other group, but are perhaps more likely to be overworked and understaffed.

Most IT departments operate in a state of managed chaos, in which managers must evaluate and implement ever-changing hardware and software solutions while providing direct support to hundreds or even thousands of users. Special projects directly related to the information-processing needs of senior executives, or to mission-critical efforts such as ensuring Y2K compliance, can dominate limited resources. It is unfortunate but understandable when the requests of trainers are evaluated very carefully. Following are some of the more common concerns of IT.

Will it add to our workload? Overworked IT departments often just don't have the time or resources to take on any new initiatives. To win their endorsement, be very clear about what their role will be and what amount of time, if any, will be required of them. Many training departments are now hiring their own IT professional or Web-site developer to handle basic maintenance and development needs. This person, who speaks the language of technology, can also serve as the bridge between the two departments. Your ultimate goal should be to convince your IT colleagues that you will constantly communicate with them and seek their guidance but minimize day-to-day time requirements.

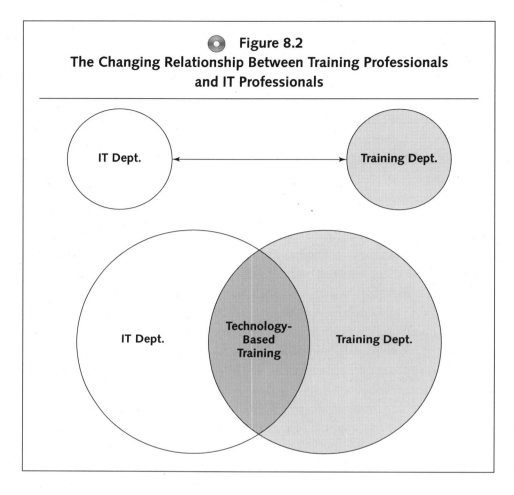

Figure 8.2
The Changing Relationship Between Training Professionals and IT Professionals

IT Dept. ⟷ Training Dept.

IT Dept.

Technology-Based Training

Training Dept.

Will it require new hardware or software? After being most protective of their time, IT departments closely guard their budget. New Web-based training programs sometimes require new servers or new server software. Make sure that any new initiatives have clear funding sources for all costs, not just costs directly related to the creation of instructional items. If possible, accept the burden for infrastructure costs as well, which could include new computer equipment, new software, or phone time to gain access to the network. In many cases, training departments invest in their own computer equipment, connections, and software in order to expedite the Web-based training process. This equipment can be located and maintained inside the training department itself, or more typically, housed with and maintained by a vendor.

Will it increase calls to the help desk? The third area of concern for IT professionals is the impact that TBT programs will have on the end-user support process. You can expect that any new training program or rollout of technology will result in at least 10 percent of the target audience encountering problems for which they need assistance. If the IT department is funding the employee help desk, they will naturally be concerned about the impact that new TBT programs will have on it.

Strategies you can use to minimize this concern include enclosing some kind of printed instructions or a quick-reference guide with the program, and thorough software testing by the IT department prior to program launch helps to minimize unexpected bugs. Additionally, the use of a simple or familiar user interface reduces questions about navigation.

Will it slow down the company Intranet? Finally, even if all other issues are addressed, the IT department will have questions about what the additional network traffic from your Web-based training program will do to the overall speed of the company's network. If your program is based on the most common technologies, such as HTML and JavaScript, it is unlikely that it will have much of an impact on the speed of the network, even if you have more than a thousand students. However, if your training program is using complex animations, audio, or video, it is likely that there will be a significant negative impact on the bandwidth of the Intranet. In effect, as your students access the multimedia over the Intranet, the speed and responsiveness of the overall network will slow down for all users. This is why many organizations that technically can deliver audio and video over their network still do not.

PRESENTING THE BUSINESS CASE

There will be a time when you will need to sell your plans for the development of a TBT program or your plans for infrastructure that will be used to support TBT efforts. Whether you are trying to get a budget approved by your supervisor or trying to gain support from another department, the guidelines presented here should help you to achieve your goals.

Focus on the business problem and solution. In all of your communications, whether a written project plan or a casual conversation with a stakeholder, make sure to focus on the business problem at hand and how your TBT program will help to solve it. If instead you focus on the features of TBT or delve into the jargon of technology, you risk losing your audience when they become confused or uninterested in the details. You should be prepared to discuss how the program will improve communication; increase performance, quality, or service; and ultimately affect sales, costs, or productivity.

Emphasize return on investment. You will get the most support when you can project real, quantifiable results using the financial terms important to top management. As discussed in Chapter Six, you should estimate your program's cost-benefit ratio, break-even point, and return on investment. Discuss in detail how you plan to control the costs and risks associated with program development, and how you will measure the results over time.

Present a clear plan of action. Even if you convince your supervisors and peers that the business problem is real and your solution is viable, they may have concerns about your ability to implement the solution. Use a detailed project approach to overcome any objections about the development of the program. Make sure to include the following:

- Description and experience of project team or vendor
- Total hardware and software budget
- Total course development budget
- Minimum hardware and software specifications
- Complete schedule or GANTT chart showing major milestones, or both
- Alpha and beta testing process
- Methods for end-user support
- Plans for program evaluation

Use case studies and research reports for proof. There is always great reluctance to try something new, especially if it will require a substantial investment. Senior executives, mindful of the relationship between expenses and profitability, tend to be conservative in this regard. They will often ask, or be thinking, "Who else has done this?" or even "What other companies has the vendor done this for?" Your cause will be helped greatly if you can point to others who have gone before you and show the results they achieved.

Fortunately, training professionals have been generous in sharing their experiences with TBT. Finding case studies, examples, and references of TBT projects should not be difficult. Often these cases come complete with return-on-investment information. Internet Web sites and publications that frequently feature case studies include the following:

- Brandon Hall Resources, headed by noted expert Brandon Hall, is the publisher of the *Multimedia and Internet Training* newsletter (www.multimediatraining.com).

- Tim Kilby maintains the Web-Based Training Information Center, an independent Web site (www.webbasedtraining.com).

- *Training* magazine has growing coverage of the field of TBT (contact Lakewood Publications at 800-328-4329).

- *Inside Technology Training* is especially strong in the area of software training (contact Ziff Davis at www.ittrain.com).

- *New Media* magazine is a general purpose multimedia publication but usually has at least one multimedia training article in each issue (contact HyperMedia Communications at 800-253-6641).

MODEL MEMO DESCRIBING NEW TBT PROJECT

There are some general guidelines to use when presenting your TBT project that apply to virtually any medium, including memos, slide-show presentations, and even one-on-one meetings. A common mistake is to lead with the capabilities of the development team, followed by the features of the project. Ideally the process should be turned around so that the major emphasis is on measurable benefits, followed by features and finally capabilities.

Figure 8.3 depicts a sample memorandum that was prepared in order to sell a new Web-based virtual university to higher management. Notice the clean memo layout using subheads to chunk the information and facilitate rapid scanning and information retrieval. Bulleted statements are used in conjunction with under-lines to draw the readers attention to key points. Also notice the order of the sections themselves:

- *Summary.* This section contains a brief description of the project and its components. It is a good idea to lead with this, even if the primary reader is familiar with the details. You never know who else the memo might get distributed to. Remember to keep this section short and to the point, so the focus turns quickly to benefits.

Figure 8.3
Sample Memorandum Prepared to Sell a New Web-Based Virtual University to Higher Management

Acme Widget Inc.

Memo

To: Jane Budget-Holder

From: Jeff WebAdvocate

CC: [All people who should be kept in the loop, especially IT department]

Date: 04/19/99

Re: Proposed Virtual University Web Site

Summary

This memo summarizes the proposed development of a new Virtual Corporate University for sales training and support. This Intranet Web site will support all 2,700 representatives and will include pages for

- Competitive information
- Weekly bulletins to the sales force
- Product knowledge tutorials
- On-line quizzes
- Threaded discussion bulletin boards to facilitate communication

Benefits

Benefits of the Virtual Sales University include

- *Information is available faster,* especially fast-breaking competitive developments.
- *Saves printing costs and paper* associated with current method of distributing weekly bulletins.
- *Saves postage and fax charges* associated with distribution of weekly bulletins.
- *Provides knowledge* database for new-hire reps that will be able to "browse" the library of previous bulletins and tutorials.
- Web-based tutorials are projected to *increase retention rates* over traditional methods, while *reducing the travel expenditures* associated with student travel.
- Online testing will automate the scoring and tracking process *saving money* over current bubble sheet scanning methodology.

Costs

I have a detailed cost analysis contained in the vendor proposal. To summarize, it will cost $85,000 to design the basic site, and to populate all "information" areas of the site, including year-to-date back issues of the weekly bulletins. Templates will also be provided so we can post new bulletins internally without additional fees.

Converting our basic product knowledge tutorials and quizzes into a Web-based format will cost an additional $175,000.

Financial Return

Working with Jane Doe in finance, I was able to calculate measurable returns for this investment. In brief, moving the weekly bulletins to a web site will yield substantial savings from elimination of printing, mail and the occasional express delivery. Based on these savings alone, the break-even point for developing the basic web site will be reached after 8 months of use.

Developing WBT for product tutorials will enable us to eliminate the one-day live "boot camp" training, thereby saving expenses related to airfare, hotel, meals, and instructor fees. The break-even point for this phase of the training is 110 students (likely to be reached within 3 months).

Total costs for all phases of development are $260,000, with savings after one year of $645,000. This yields:

- a cost-benefit ratio of 2.48
- and a one-year return on investment (ROI) of 148%.

Development Schedule

We can kick the project off within the next two weeks, and have a prototype site for evaluation in 30 days. After beta testing, we will pilot the program with a select group from our sales force. Final roll-out could take place mid-summer.

Team Experience

The vendor selection process included sending RFPs to eight vendors, and we received six responses. We asked for live presentations from three, and based on total value, we selected XYZ Company. XYZ has been in business for seven years, and they've produced very similar projects for BigCompany1 and BigCompany2. The latter project recently won awards from the ASTD and ISPI. We checked three references and their clients raved about their flexibility and service.

Next Steps

I would like to review this project with you at our department meeting, and obtain your signature on the Letter of Agreement. We will then be able to provide XYZ Training with our source content, and begin to arrange for subject matter expert interviews.

- *Benefits.* Include all benefits, especially those held most dear by the group to whom you are presenting. In this case, there are intangible benefits, such as "Information is available faster," and many tangible benefits that have an impact on the bottom line, such as "Saves printing costs."
- *Costs.* In the memo format, just provide bottom-line costs. If someone is questioning the breakdown, he or she can ask for further analysis. This tactic prevents individuals with counteragendas from focusing on the minute details and picking apart each piece of information.
- *Financial return.* This is a vital piece of the internal sales pitch and is written in clear, direct language that speaks directly to the CEO, CFO, and others responsible for profit. The financial return projections are so positive they have been bulleted to make them jump off the document page.
- *Development schedule.* Again, providing specific milestones in this type of document only provides more data to be debated. If your goal is to obtain project funding, try to leave interproject milestone dates vague to reduce objections related to conflicts with other project rollouts. Focus on major milestones like project kickoff, pilot tests, and final launch times.
- *Team experience.* The last item that should be included is the capability of the team. If the development team is internal, reference their prior experience on similar projects, academic credentials, and any other noteworthy items. If the team is an outside vendor, list previous experience, results from reference checks, and any awards or honors they have received.

APPLYING IT ON THE JOB

Following are the key points to keep in mind when selling internally:

- Focus on the benefits, not the features.
- Use the language of financial results, not technological jargon.
- Estimate cost savings, increases in revenue, impact on client satisfaction, and employee engagement.
- Allay the concerns of the IT department.
- Use case studies to present the viability of the plan.

part three

Case Studies

Increasing Sales Rep Knowledge Using CD-ROM

Cancer is the second leading cause of death in the United States, exceeded only by heart disease. According to the American Cancer Society, one out of every four deaths in this country is caused by cancer. In the battle against cancer, there have been tremendous breakthroughs recently, particularly in chemotherapy. Unfortunately, new treatments often bring with them new complications. In addition to treating the disease, oncologists, or cancer specialists, must also treat the adverse effects of the treatment itself.

Bingham-Rodway Pharmaco (BRP) is one of the companies leading the fight against cancer through development of prescription medications that treat chemotherapeutic side effects and help ease the pain of cancer patients. Pharmaceutical sales representatives are responsible for informing the oncology physicians in their territory about the benefits and appropriate use of BRP's products. Many BRP representatives found themselves wanting to engage in more meaningful dialogue with the physicians to whom they spoke. The company's manager of technology and field education was faced with the challenge of educating these sales reps to the point where they could be considered oncology consultants. The manager felt that a greater awareness of the issues involved in the rapidly evolving field of oncology would increase the reps' ability to help physicians, and not incidentally, increase BRP's sales. To give the geographically dispersed sales force the knowledge they needed to excel in the competitive market of oncology, the manager wanted a very powerful and flexible educational tool. What she eventually helped create was a single resource that does triple duty as an oncology training, reference, and marketing tool.

What You Will Learn in This Chapter

- Training concerns typical of the pharmaceutical industry
- How constructivism and classic instructional systems design can be blended for maximum results
- Ways a learning metaphor can help improve the transfer of learning to on-the-job applications
- Learner benefits of using audio and video components in TBT
- How a training investment can be leveraged by application as a marketing tool

BINGHAM-RODWAY PHARMACO

Business Background

Bingham-Rodway Pharmaco, a fictitious name we've created to discuss this real-world project, is one of the world's leading health care companies. Employing fifty thousand people worldwide, with operations in 150 countries, BRP discovers, develops, manufactures, and markets pharmaceuticals, vaccines, over-the-counter medicines, and health-related consumer products. It also provides health care services, including disease management, clinical laboratory testing, and pharmaceutical benefit management. Prescription medicines are BRP's largest business, with global sales in the billions. Their oncology division is growing, with several oncology products currently on the market. Additional indications and forms of these products are being worked on and new drugs are in development. Research and development of new solutions to existing medical problems has been the key to the division's success.

Considering Bingham-Rodway Pharmaco's research background and culture, their adoption of a radical training solution was not unexpected. Freedom of expression is highly valued at BRP and individuals are encouraged to articulate their most radical ideas. People are allowed to take risks, which can mean that occasionally they fail; indeed, it is expected that from time to time they will. This culture of risk taking facilitated the adoption of a radical approach to training. The planned multimedia product was a major undertaking and was the BRP training department's first CD-ROM.

The Challenge

The Virtual Oncology Center program, as it was eventually titled, was born out of Bingham-Rodway Pharmaco's need to solve several basic business challenges. As BRP's training manager put it, "Primarily, I felt that more education in their field would make the sales reps more helpful to the doctors they served. Ultimately, the more our reps are seen as true consultants in the area of patient management, the more likely we'll be able to educate doctors about the benefits of our products. This, of course, in turn drives sales." To enrich their sales reps, Bingham-Rodway Pharmaco decided to provide more thorough training. Foremost, the manager and the sales training department wanted to make sure that their sales reps had a detailed understanding of current cancer diagnosis and treatment practices, as well as where Bingham-Rodway Pharmaco's products fit into those practices.

Like her peers in training management, the manager was working with a tight budget and sought a training solution that could be distributed to a diverse and scattered workforce without the costs of transporting learners to seminars or trainers out to distant offices. She had investigated and was excited by the learning benefits of multimedia presentation. Because the sales force was familiar with its multimedia-equipped laptop computers, CD-ROM delivery presented itself as a solution that fulfilled needs, accommodated existing conditions, and in the long run saved money.

External Communication Tool

To leverage their investment in the educational materials they were inventing, BRP wanted a final product that could be repurposed as a marketing piece for their oncology products. The Virtual Oncology Center program would be distributed to oncologists, providing them with an informative and engaging tool to keep up with recent developments in the field. Internally, this also enabled

BRP's sales training department to obtain additional funding from the product marketing group.

ANALYSIS AND DESIGN
Training Content
The instructional designers and subject matter experts assigned to the Virtual Oncology Center worked together to define the instructional elements that would be present in the application. Their consensus was to include training on nine specific cancers, referred to medically as tumor types:

- Ovarian cancer

- Lung cancer

- Leukemia

- Head and neck cancer

- Prostate cancer

- Breast cancer

- Colon cancer

- Lymphoma

- Osteosarcoma

For each tumor type, they wanted to convey a vast amount of instruction, including background information, the latest treatment approaches, and controversial topics from the field. Each tumor type was also to have its own pretest, simulation exercises, and final assessment.

As you may recall from Chapter Four, on adult learning, specific, measurable objectives guide designers during courseware development and eventually aid students in the learning process. The instructional designers of the Virtual Oncology Center therefore created learning objectives for each tumor type. For example, the objectives created for lung cancer are provided in Figure 9.1.

Additionally, nine general cancer topics were to be discussed. The material on these topics would appear in a separate section but would relate to the materials on the specific tumor types. Assessments for these general topics would be handled through post-tests available in the same section as the tumor-type tests.

Figure 9.1
Learning Objectives for Lung Cancer Training

At the completion of the Lung Cancer training, the student should be able to

- List the staging systems used to categorize NSCLS.
- Determine which treatment modalities are used in the treatment of lung cancer.
- Determine what surgical procedures are used in stage IIB NSCLS.
- Determine what imaging techniques should be used to visualize a possible lung mass.
- Determine the standard techniques used for lung cancer screening.

Reference Content

Reference aids used to convey facts, not concepts, were planned to allow the final product to serve as a support tool for the reps as well as a value-added reference tool for the medical professionals. In the reference sections, no educational components were to be incorporated. The reference components included were as follows:

- The oncology pharmacy, a database featuring information on current cancer medications

- A U.S. centers section, detailing the standards of care at eight influential institutions. Content for this section was obtained from the vice president of patient care at each institution.

- A glossary providing listings, definitions, and audio pronunciations of key medical terms

In the final program, the databases on U.S. centers and the glossary were to be accessed from the library of the virtual clinic.

Marketing Content

It was decided that the Virtual Oncology Center would not be a traditional marketing piece. BRP's products would not be mentioned in either the program name or the introduction. Instead, the CDs would feature the use of BRP's products within their instructional scenarios and reference materials. CDs would also be made available for distribution to medical practitioners.

Media and Technology Concerns

The BRP sales force is equipped with powerful laptop computers. The specifications of the machines are listed in Figure 9.2. The multimedia capabilities of these laptops made CD-ROM delivery a viable option. Additionally, the portability of the CD-ROM made it more favorable than Web delivery for a sales force that is frequently on the road and not always able to connect to Internet servers. A desire to incorporate an abundance of rich multimedia also influenced the decision for CD-ROM delivery over Web delivery. A CD-ROM-based interactive training application accommodates the maximum number of student learning styles and creates the most realistic and engaging simulations. CD-ROM delivery enabled the team to use text, audio, video, and animation, creating a product that appeals to auditory, visual, and kinesthetic learners alike. The storage capability of CD-ROM technology, in addition to providing room for high-impact multimedia assets, provides space for extensive reference materials.

While DVD-ROM provides even greater storage potential than CD-ROM, the reps' computers did not include standard DVD players. During development it was discovered that the audio-and video-intensive product would need to be delivered on multiple CDs. The final product spans three CDs, with each disc operating independently and containing all of the reference materials but covering

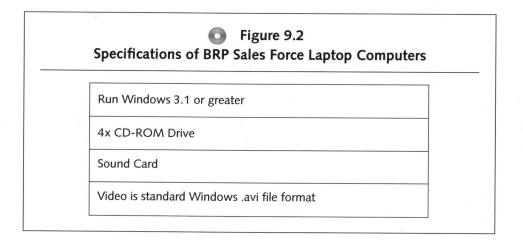

Figure 9.2
Specifications of BRP Sales Force Laptop Computers

Run Windows 3.1 or greater
4x CD-ROM Drive
Sound Card
Video is standard Windows .avi file format

only three types of cancer tumor. To increase user ease, each disc contains its own automatic installation application.

Constructivism Considered

As you may remember from Chapter Four, constructivism is a philosophical or theoretical approach to instruction that relies on discovery-learning and maintains that learners must construct their own knowledge and behaviors through undirected experiences. Most basically, constructivism asserts that learning should occur in a realistic setting and learners should choose their own path through content and activities. One of the hallmarks of contructivist approaches to learning is the use of simulation as a training tool.

Although many companies adopt TBT programs in hopes of reducing the number of on-the-job failures by simulating situations in which failure occurs, no discipline is more suited to adopting such methods than the medical profession. One of the strongest features of the software created for Bingham-Rodway Pharmaco is the opportunity for learners to misdiagnose and then be sternly warned by the expert coach that such treatment would kill their patient. An engaging event such as this in a program invokes the user's recall of past knowledge, provides negative reinforcement of a choice, and increases the chance of recall and transfer to the job. In brief, a user who "kills" a patient in the training is unlikely to suggest a similar misdiagnosis in the real world. For these sales reps, simulation affords an opportunity to see through the eyes of their customers. A vast amount of background information is needed, however, to prepare for any medical practice simulation.

Instructional System Design

Engaging simulation was not enough, however, to train the sales reps. They asked specifically for a knowledge base to make them comfortable in dealing with oncologists. The design team recognized that a straight instructional design methodology applying Gagné's events of instruction would best teach the needed medical concepts. As covered in Chapter Four, Robert Gagné laid out a nine-step process called the events of instruction that correlates to and addresses the four conditions of adult learning he had established. Grounding the instructional concepts in a real-world application was to be achieved through the simulation aspects of the training.

Theoretical Solution

The company decided to create software that would speak to both sales reps and their clients. In doing so, it understood that the resulting training product would be complex and would not also be able to serve as a tool for patients. While shortening the knowledge gap between intended audiences by focusing on professionals, the team remained aggressive in their goal. Mastery of the full Virtual Oncology Center program is comparable to the knowledge acquired by a first-year oncology fellow. To accommodate such a huge body of information while addressing the needs of both beginners and experts, the development team needed an intuitive interface.

Interface and Metaphor

The structure for this wealth of information and instruction was indeed intuitive. The interface simulates a place where people of widely ranging backgrounds and expertise often go to learn about how to practice medicine: a teaching hospital. The Virtual Cancer Center concept was created as a transparent user interface.

Instead of a typical menu-driven structure, an exploratory interface was created in which choices are made via selection of familiar hospital features. For example, to learn more about specific drugs, the user does not select pharmaceutical info from a list of topics but instead directs herself to the Virtual Cancer Center pharmacy. The center was organized to include areas for tumor-specific tutorials, presented in a grand rounds format, as well as areas for general tutorials. These sites, called the auditorium and the physicians' lounge, in keeping with the hospital metaphor, were made primarily to educate the novice sales reps through linear tutorials. Both the specific and general lessons are flexible and thorough enough to serve also as refresher or preparatory materials for doctors. The oncology pharmacy, a reference site for drug information, and the research library, a reference site containing a glossary and access to information from actual cancer centers, are primarily resources for professional users of the software but they allow inquisitive or advanced sales reps to explore the field. These reference sites are included to add value to the product but they do not contain instructional elements. The remaining rooms or areas of the center include the Halsted Conference Room, the clinic, the patient ward, and patient records.

When experienced learners no longer need the intuitive organization that the hospital metaphor provides, the program has mechanisms to skip directly to the information wanted through a content map that is always available.

The graphical approach to organizing these different areas of the hospital moves the metaphor forward; each of these sections appears to the user as a room that can be reached via the Virtual Cancer Center lobby, which appears after entering the hospital in the program. Once inside a room, students can access relevant course content and educational exercises. For example, in the patient records room, learners track their own progress throughout the course.

Media and Technology Decisions

The program was developed in Macromedia's Director. As an authoring tool optimized for CD-ROM delivery, Director was chosen primarily because of its power in handling video and audio content. The team's familiarity with this particular authoring system further influenced the choice and facilitated development. Adobe's Photoshop was employed by the project's graphic artists to create the room-specific interface graphics. The three-dimensional environment was developed using a combination of Photoshop and Strata's StudioPro. The screen resolution of the final product when running is 800 x 600.

The intensity of the role-playing scenarios is enhanced by the use of full-motion video segments. Instead of relying on text and audio to convey the emotional aspect, actors and actresses portray actual patients describing their ailments and answering questions selected by the student. The information conveyed in these video clips are summarized as text on the patient charts. To complete the charts, the patient and physician data presented in the video segments is supplemented by testing.

For example, results of a bone scan are presented to the learner as real films as well as summarized in text. This type of visual aid contextualizes the results of tests more than a simple text description or summarization. Audio is similarly employed to teach in ways that text alone cannot. The program's glossary includes audio pronunciations of all medical terms to aid the auditory learner and eliminates phonetic guides that are often misunderstood. These levels of realism and advanced learning tools are made possible only through cutting-edge technology. Still, the real marvel of the program is the result of its intuitive and flexible design.

TOUR OF THE VIRTUAL CANCER CENTER

To fully appreciate the capabilities of the Virtual Oncology Center, let's go through a sample study session, a learning structure created for use with the program. "The creation of a paper-based study guide to accompany the CDs was essential," says BRP's manager. "Also, it can be a comfort for the learners who are sometimes as intimidated by computers as they are by hospitals."

A study session for one cancer type (for this example we will use ovarian cancer) walks the learner through preparatory materials, linear tutorials, case studies, virtual diagnosis, staging, treatment, and a final assessment.

Log-In

Upon starting the program, the learner is presented with an engaging "fly-in" to the Virtual Cancer Center building, which operates as a device for capturing the learner's attention. On the next screen, featured in Figure 9.3, a security guard

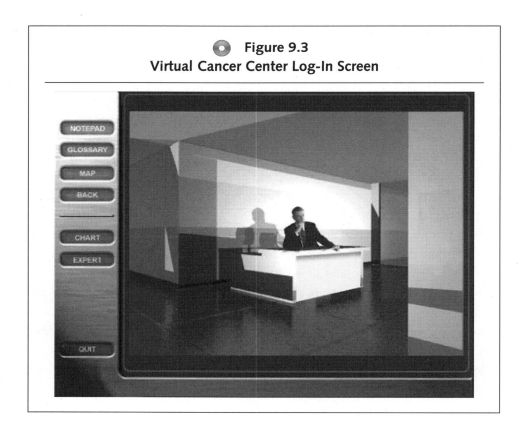

Figure 9.3
Virtual Cancer Center Log-In Screen

asks via audio for the learner's first and last names and an identification number for tracking purposes. This creative take on the log-in familiar to computer users is an example of how the program immerses the learner in role-playing.

Linear Tutorial

After learners pass the guard and enter the main lobby, text instructions guide them to select from a menu on the left side of the screen, from one on the right side of the screen, or from the elevator that appears directly in front of them. If we were to follow the paper-based study session guide, we would select the auditorium from the left menu. The selection of a choice appearing on the left or right menus causes the three-dimensional graphic environment to rotate, thus altering the user's perspective to look down the hallway to that side. The new view includes a door marked *auditorium.*

At the auditorium door the user must again interact with the program and click to enter. Within the auditorium, under the heading for ovarian cancer, a slide show is presented to the learner in the form of a straight tutorial. The learner is given control of the pace and extent of the material by chunking the whole tutorial down to sixteen individual slides. These are presented on-screen in a slide portfolio that can be used to jump to specific content within the lesson (see Figure 9.4).

Control of this sort is absolutely necessary when educating the adult learner, in order to accommodate differing learning needs, time constraints, and areas of interest. This tutorial is augmented by the extensive use of illustration and by the audio narration of the presenting doctor. Upon completion of the lesson, the user is instructed to click the *back* button to return to the hospital's lobby.

Case Studies

The Halsted Conference Room, the next site suggested by the study session, is accessed through navigation methods similar to those required to enter the auditorium. Inside the conference room, the learner reviews a patient's case and has the opportunity to pose five different questions to three members of a tumor board through an interface shown in Figure 9.5.

The Conference Room is particularly useful to students for presenting the types of conflict inherent in the field of oncology. In this portion of the program, they can get a sense that some answers will not be cut and dry.

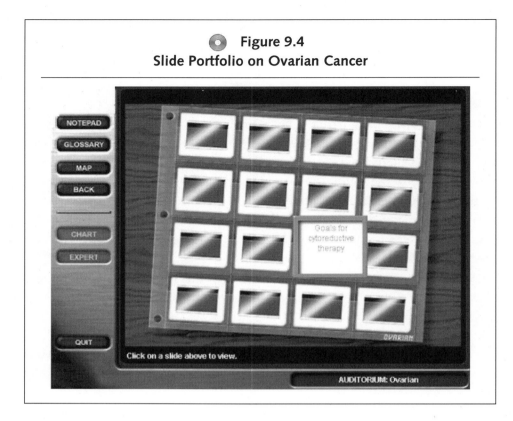

Figure 9.4
Slide Portfolio on Ovarian Cancer

Then, in the physicians' lounge, slide shows similar to those in the auditorium but centering on general cancer treatment practices, such as chemotherapy and pain management, are available.

Virtual Diagnosis

A trip to the patient ward allows learners to apply the knowledge they have been gathering in the first three legs of their journey. This room is another example of the program's creative interpretation of a common tool. The patient ward, illustrated in Figure 9.6, operates as a pretest for the learner, with questions posed by the attending doctor and immediate feedback provided, but no scoring.

After the confidence building and review in the patient ward, the learner enters the clinic via the hospital elevator. As Muzak plays in the background, the user selects the floor that corresponds to ovarian tumors. It is in the clinic that the program's instructional impact is most obvious.

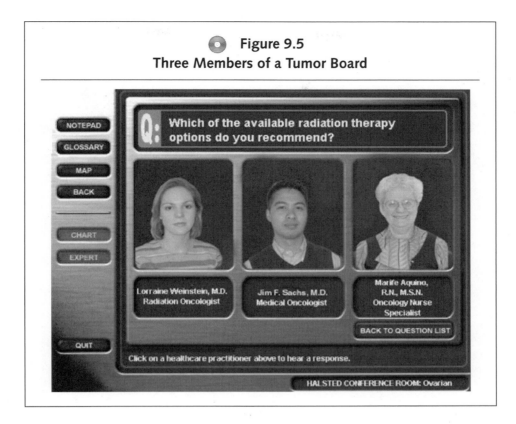

Figure 9.5
Three Members of a Tumor Board

Q: Which of the available radiation therapy options do you recommend?

Lorraine Weinstein, M.D.
Radiation Oncologist

Jim F. Sachs, M.D.
Medical Oncologist

Marife Aquino,
R.N., M.S.N.
Oncology Nurse
Specialist

BACK TO QUESTION LIST

Click on a healthcare practitioner above to hear a response.

HALSTED CONFERENCE ROOM: Ovarian

NOTEPAD
GLOSSARY
MAP
BACK
CHART
EXPERT
QUIT

Exiting the elevator, the user must select an occupied clinic room to enter. The learner finds that he or she is listed as the attending physician for the patient. After clicking the door and entering the exam room, the user watches a video of the patient describing his or her symptoms. From there the learner-doctor examines the patient employing a choice of stethoscope, hands, or eyes. A three-dimensional model of the patient's body is presented and a cursor is used to indicate what part of the body to examine. The result of the examination takes the form of an audible negative or positive. Positive findings are accompanied by text descriptions of the results (see Figure 9.7).

Staging

After further examination using tools of the medical trade, including surgeries, bone scans, MRI, and others, the learner must indicate the severity of the tumor using a process called *staging*. Again, choices are made available to the learner to

Figure 9.6
The Patient Ward

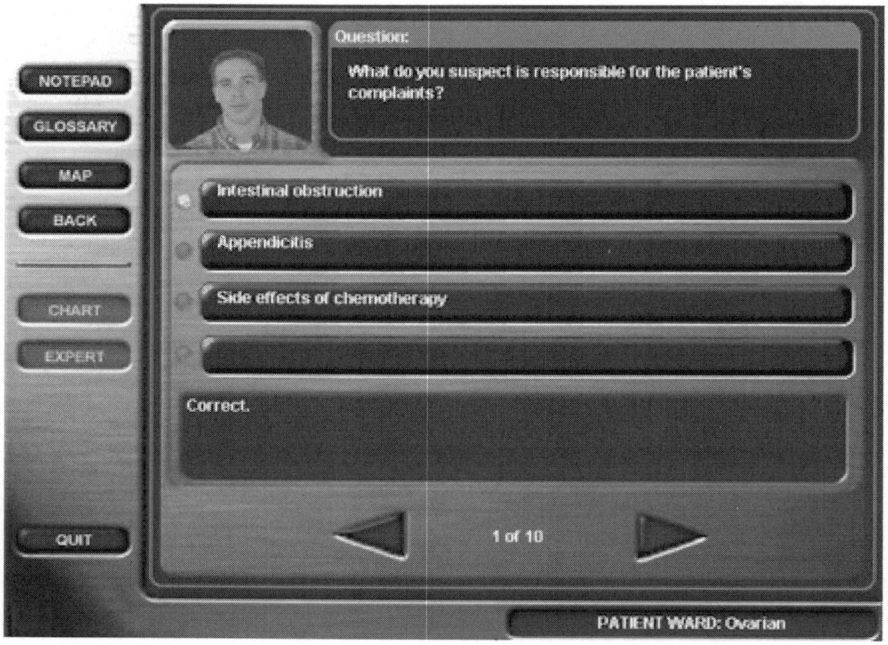
NOTEPAD
GLOSSARY
MAP
BACK
CHART
EXPERT
QUIT
Question:
What do you suspect is responsible for the patient's complaints?
Intestinal obstruction
Appendicitis
Side effects of chemotherapy
Correct.
1 of 10
PATIENT WARD: Ovarian

select proper staging, mistakes are advised against, and correct staging is accompanied by additional information.

Treatment

Finally, the learner must suggest treatment. The options for treatments are staggering and include drug choice, delivery method and dosage, timing, and number of cycles. If at any point the learner is stumped, he or she can request assistance from an expert on call. The *expert* button available at any point in the clinic section of the program provides tips and assistance that take the form of video clips of a real doctor advising what steps should be taken next. The expert function encourages learners to ask questions when they desire more oncology knowledge, a behavior the training is particularly designed to shape. The design

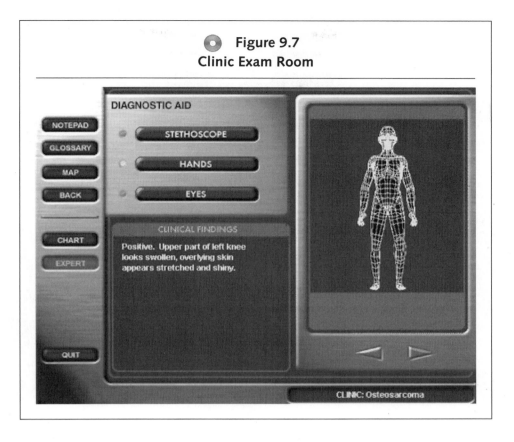

● **Figure 9.7**
Clinic Exam Room

DIAGNOSTIC AID

NOTEPAD
GLOSSARY
MAP
BACK

STETHOSCOPE
HANDS
EYES

CHART
EXPERT

CLINICAL FINDINGS

Positive. Upper part of left knee looks swollen, overlying skin appears stretched and shiny.

QUIT

CLINIC: Osteosarcoma

team understood the advantage over other media of using video when speaking directly to learners. The context-specific clips keep user confidence high and help ensure that the user will not become frustrated with the task at hand.

Final Assessment

After the full treatment of a patient, the learner may review any materials he or she would like to before going on call or taking the final assessment. To aid in review, the patient records section contains a content-tracking chart. The program uses the student log-in info to compile a complete record of visited areas. Sections that have been visited are highlighted with a V while areas still unvisited are designated with an N. When the student is confident that he or she is prepared, it's test time.

The assessment takes the form of a classic multiple-choice test, but unlike paper-based tests, both correct and incorrect answers are followed up with feedback designed to reinforce key concepts.

The final score that the student achieves is displayed and can be printed on a certificate. As part of their continuing education program, Bingham-Rodway Pharmaco intends to require grades of at least 85 percent in each of the tumor types for all of their sales representatives. The hard copies of the certificates will be included in the reps' records as proof of completion.

Instruction Events Summarized

When viewed as one lesson, the study session faithfully follows Gagné's instructional events in order to insure efficacy (see Figure 9.8).

Figure 9.8
How the Virtual Oncology Center Satisfies Gagné's Nine Events of Instruction

Instructional Event	Achieved
1. Gain attention	Initially through fly-in animation; within section through the use of audio/video
2. Inform learners of objectives	Slide shows include clear statements of objectives
3. Stimulate recall of prior learning	Patient ward asks learner to use knowledge obtained in auditorium lessons
4. Present the content	Slide shows in auditorium and physician's lounge
5. Provide learning guidance	Facts presented in text, audio, and visual forms
6. Elicit performance (practice)	Multiple-choice questions asked in patient ward; simulations presented in clinic
7. Provide feedback	Diagnoses in clinic are followed by summary screen displaying proper responses
8. Assess performance	Post-test available in patient records for each tumor type
9. Enhance retention and transfer to the job	All areas of learning grounded in familiar hospital settings

RETURN ON INVESTMENT

The Bingham-Rodway Pharmaco program has been recognized for its creative excellence. The program won the International Society for Performance Improvement's 1999 Award of Excellence for an Instructional Intervention. It also placed as a finalist in *NewMedia Magazine*'s highly prestigious and competitive Invision Award for the Best Simulation, in the Creative and Technical Excellence category. The Invision Award is considered by many to be the Oscars of the multimedia industry.

The tremendous industry recognition of the Virtual Oncology Center is accompanied by great economic benefits. The program's initial purpose is to train 125 of Bingham-Rodway's best sales consultants in the first year and an additional 125 in the following two years. The total student seat time is approximately twenty hours and it replaces a two-week training program. In addition to saving classroom time, the self-paced program eliminates the travel and lodging that would be required to bring the sales force to the home office.

The total cost of development, delivery, and maintenance of the training program has been $520,000. The direct savings in employee and instructor salaries over three years will be $1,224,200. Using the evaluation metrics detailed in Chapter Six, this training program has achieved the following:

- Total cost savings: $704,200

- Cost-benefit ratio: 1.35

- Return on investment: 35 percent

- Break-even point: 184 students

Although the cost savings only slightly justify the large investment in the program, the opportunity cost of the sales representatives' time is estimated to be $1,750,000, based on the assumption that the CD-ROM program will enable 250 representatives to spend an extra seven days in front of doctors, and each day is worth $1,000 in added company revenue.

Finally, Bingham-Rodway plans to leverage this investment by distributing CD-ROM to physicians as part of a larger marketing campaign. A positive impact on both sales and customer satisfaction is anticipated.

Orienting New Hires Using CD-ROM

Think back to the first days of any job you have held. The adjustments to a new culture, new tools, and new people were exciting but probably quite stressful, too. While formal classroom training and other orientation exercises can alleviate this stress in part, it may take weeks, even months before such classes can be scheduled. While new hires wait for training, their productivity remains below peak and their comfort levels in their new positions may be compromised. Decreasing the stress of transition to a new job would be a giant accomplishment for any company, improving employee engagement and eventually increasing retention. With these factors in mind, the BevCo Company set out to convert its office orientation to CD-ROM-formatted TBT.

The BevCo Company already had effective classroom orientation training in place. But believing that what works well can always work even better, BevCo's information services operations manager set out to decrease training costs, increase training effectiveness, and most of all provide training conveniently and immediately to new employees. When examining the extant training for clues to its success, the manager and her trainers realized that the trainer-learner relationship was a big factor in establishing student comfort. "Many of the new employees understood how to complete the computer and administrative tasks assigned to them," notes the manager. "What they needed was training to fill in the gaps in their understanding. They also wanted assurance that what they believed to be true about BevCo's office procedures was indeed correct."

The need for brief lessons on specific areas of confusion and the need to instill confidence were areas that BevCo trainers recognized could be fulfilled by a mentor. Through TBT, the company sought to provide a form of individual mentorship to each new hire. Though BevCo has one of the most recognizable brands in business, their trainers saw an opportunity to introduce new hires to their corporate imagery and set the cultural tone for each new employee's experience.

What You Will Learn in This Chapter
- Issues that must be addressed when creating software training for novice users
- The value of the human element in software training
- How an interface can be created to minimize distraction and maximize usability
- Strategies to make software training interactive rather than passive
- How a technical training investment can be leveraged by application as a corporate culture training tool
- Return on investment possible with custom-developed technology-based technical training

THE BEVCO COMPANY

Business Background

The fictional company constructed to discuss this real-world case, the BevCo Company, is a global leader in the beverage industry. Every day consumers enjoy billions of servings of BevCo's products, which are sold in more than one hundred countries around the world. A Fortune 500 company that operates on a global business scale, BevCo has maintained its commitment to ensure high standards of quality, uniformity, and exceptional service to all of its customers. BevCo's premium service has evolved from the measurable and effective training of its employees. As a result of its massive growth rate, the company needs to educate and familiarize its ever-expanding class of new associates with their office tools.

As a culture, BevCo embraces the use of technology to increase productivity. The TBT discussed in this chapter represents just one piece of a company initiative to use cutting-edge training practices. The fact that the orientation training focused largely on the application of computer practices influenced the decision to move the training to CD-ROM. BevCo's ingrained values of uniformity and consistency further contributed to the decision to use CD-ROM.

The Challenge

The manager's initial business challenge was the most primary presented to any trainer: make the corporation's training cheaper, faster, and better. BevCo searched for a training solution that could eliminate the costs of transporting learners to centralized locations for seminars or bringing trainers out to local offices. Still, the training needed to be distributed to a diverse and scattered workforce. With an associate population that is always growing and that is equipped with personal computers at their workstations, computer delivery presented itself as the most fitting solution.

The challenge faced by BevCo, then, was to convert existing paper-based and instructor-led training to a format suitable for TBT. The fact that orientation training already existed helped shape the format of the computer-based training. The program's designers needed to create interactive devices to engage learners in the training. They also needed to chunk the learning into relevant tasks and subtasks and establish mechanisms for the student to access the chunks they required. The training had to be segmented into text, audio, video, and animated presentations to accommodate different learning styles. To accomplish training goals, the designers needed to match proper presentation types with appropriate content.

An alternative solution to creating training was to purchase existing off-the-shelf TBT. Separate training programs would need to be purchased to handle each application within BevCo's curriculum. More importantly, this option had the potential drawback of a fixed per-copy cost that would indefinitely increase the total cost of training with each new hire.

In addition to financial concerns that favored a choice for custom development, there were also curriculum concerns. The most pressing concern was BevCo's desire to create training geared to their most novice associates. Custom-developed software would allow BevCo's designers to craft an experience that addressed very basic needs. Learners would receive instruction in areas that advanced programs might neglect. Moreover, the instruction they would receive would reflect BevCo's style at every level. Specific screens, such as log-ins, would exactly mirror those used by employees during their daily work, eliminating the learner's responsibility to apply abstract concepts to concrete objects. Removing such complex mental processes would leave little room for misinterpretation by the student.

BevCo's Culture

To leverage their investment in the educational materials they were inventing, BevCo wanted a final product that also introduced new employees to the corporate culture. The BEV Office Orientation program, as it was to be called, would show employees the initiatives the company had undertaken to ease their assimilation into the workplace. It would also establish behaviors in learners that reflect the company's core values. Through the training, learners would be introduced to the immediate and long-term benefits of BevCo's procedures and come to view their productivity tools with a positive attitude. Finally, the training product presented an opportunity for building brand-name recognition and a sense of the value of the brand in all new hires and for establishing images and motifs integral to the company culture.

ANALYSIS AND DESIGN
Tutorial Content

The instructional designers and subject matter experts assigned to transform BevCo's training began by examining content in the available manuals and procedure guides and attending existing classroom training. As you may recall from Chapter Four, on adult learning, measurable objectives guide designers during courseware development and eventually aid students in the learning process. The holistic objectives of the program, adapted from the existing training, are presented in Figure 10.1.

The instructional designers of BEV Office Orientation additionally created learning objectives for each lesson. This procedure was motivated by theories on adult learning that assert that properly formulated objectives provide both a goal for the learner and a mechanism for measuring whether or not the goal was achieved. The objectives created for one lesson, Introducing the Windows 95 Desktop, are provided as an example in Figure 10.2.

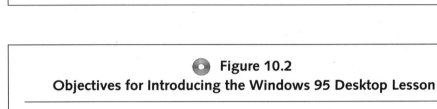

⊙ Figure 10.1
Objectives of the BEV Office Orientation Program

Upon completion of the KO Office Orientation program, users will be able to

- Identify Windows 95 desktop objects and start menu options.
- Use various methods to open and switch between multiple applications in Windows 95.
- Access Windows 95 help topics.
- Open and navigate notes databases.
- Read and manage mail documents.
- Navigate the notes Calendar.
- Navigate the Coke Machine—the company Intranet.

⊙ Figure 10.2
Objectives for Introducing the Windows 95 Desktop Lesson

Upon completion of this lesson, users will be able to

- Sign on to the KO Office system.
- Change passwords.
- Identify desktop objects.
- Identify options on the start menu.
- Shut down the computer.

Assessments for these tutorial topics would be handled through each section's final post-test. Considering how inexperienced the audience was, BevCo's trainers decided not to require that the students achieve any specific level of proficiency in order to pass the training. The post-test assessment, structured as a game, would guide the user to areas where further instruction would be valuable and leave the responsibility of acquiring full competence to the learner.

The majority of the self-assessment would be handled via exercises within the tutorials.

Exercise Content

The development team knew that after concepts were introduced, the students should be given an opportunity to apply their learning. To maintain learner engagement, the practice opportunities would be interspersed throughout the linear tutorials. BevCo's designers laid out a number of interactive exercises to include in the training, including the following:

- Multiple-choice and true-false questions to assess comprehension
- Open-ended, thought-provoking questions to establish pacing and stimulate reflection
- Simulation exercises to instruct on and assess task completion

Reference Content

Reference aids that conveyed facts, not concepts, were planned, allowing the final product also to serve as a value-added reference tool for the associates. In the reference sections, no educational components were to be incorporated. The reference information for BEV Office Systems, for example, would consist of scrolling text windows of information taken directly from the current class manuals. The reference components included were as follows:

- Selected content from appendixes of the class manual
- Voice-mail system use and features
- Computer and education services
- Information intended for some site-specific employees only, such as BEV Office applications, company services and procedures, and a map of the facility

Media and Technology Concerns

BevCo wanted to distribute the training package to many sites and employees, immediately and into the future. The intended audience population did not currently have uniform computer standards, and computers would continue to vary over time. BevCo outlined the minimum requirements of the delivery machines to reflect an assumed lowest-common-denominator system. The specifications of the computers are detailed in Figure 10.3.

The multimedia requirements of these specifications, particularly the CD-ROM drive, video application, and sound card, reflect CD-ROM delivery as the preferred option. The expressed preference for rich multimedia aspects, such as an on-screen video coach and complex full-screen simulations, influenced the choice of CD-ROM delivery over Web delivery. A CD-ROM-based interactive training application accommodates the maximum number of student learning styles and creates the most realistic and engaging simulations. CD-ROM delivery would enable the team to use text, audio, video, and animation, creating a product that appeals to auditory, visual, and kinesthetic learners alike. The storage capability of CD-ROM technology, in addition to providing room for high-impact multimedia, accommodates extensive reference materials.

The company's technology infrastructure was such that neither CD-ROM nor Intranet delivery would require additional hardware expenditures. The installation of plug-ins required to facilitate delivery would create some costs associated with Intranet delivery of the product. Even with the required plug-ins, BevCo's Intranet capabilities would limit the bandwidth of the final product, potentially eliminating video and simulation elements. While CD-ROM provides great storage potential, updating content is not as simple as with Web-based

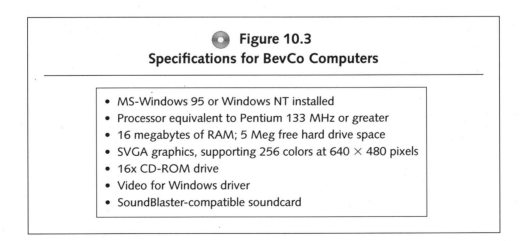

Figure 10.3
Specifications for BevCo Computers

- MS-Windows 95 or Windows NT installed
- Processor equivalent to Pentium 133 MHz or greater
- 16 megabytes of RAM; 5 Meg free hard drive space
- SVGA graphics, supporting 256 colors at 640 × 480 pixels
- 16x CD-ROM drive
- Video for Windows driver
- SoundBlaster-compatible soundcard

applications. Fortunately, however, BevCo's content was fairly static and the design team eliminated any elements from the training that might change frequently.

Theoretical Solution

Custom-designed software with a video coach was the solution selected to meet BevCo's training challenge. The coach character would serve as anchor for students' learning. Additionally, the character would provide a thread for learners to follow as they progressed through the training. Most crucially, the coach would provide the human element necessary to keep the technical training appealing to neophyte or technophobic learners.

Both instruction and remediation elements were to be handled by the coach. This consistency would allow learners to determine immediately at what point in an operation they had erred and to avoid such errors in future practice. The coach would lead the learner toward the final goal of using the BEV Office system in the field without assistance.

Instructional Systems Design Approach

It was determined that the instructional content of the training would be best addressed in linear tutorials. This decision was motivated by a desire to provide guidance to novice learners who were completely unfamiliar with BevCo's systems. The tutorial content was partitioned to allow advanced users opportunities to skip lessons where they felt mastery had already been achieved. To keep students engaged and relaxed, the designers sought ways of familiarizing them with the elements of the BEV Office system without immersing them in simulation.

The tutorial portions of the training largely reflect the influence of instructional systems design. All of the lessons in the training curriculum take a linear form in which information is presented, comprehension is tested, and concepts are reviewed. The design team recognized that such a straight instructional design methodology applying Robert Gagné's events of instruction would be best for introducing unfamiliar procedures. As covered in Chapter Four, Gagné laid out a nine-step process called the events of instruction that correlates to and addresses the four conditions of adult learning he established. The lessons are straightforward, the path to the lessons is unrestricted, and a good deal of freedom is permitted.

Behavior Modeling

Grounding the instructional concepts in real-world application was to be achieved through simulation guided by an expert character. In order for the coaching concept to succeed, the designers chose to use extensive video, which would facilitate association of the coach's instruction with learners' past experiences with live coaching. The simulation-coach system was vital to BevCo's plans to employ behavior modeling. Part of the constructivist theory to which the designers subscribed maintains that learners must construct their own knowledge and behaviors through experience. One of the hallmarks of contructivist approaches to learning is the use of simulation as a training tool. In the case of the operating system portion of BevCo's training, for example, this meant that learners should be given an opportunity to perform operations on a simulation rather than being told about the operations they should perform. If the learner makes a mistake, the coach then intervenes. The interpersonal behavior of the coach is also subject to modeling. The reinforcement instructions always congratulate accomplishments and never blame learners, providing a subtle behavioral model.

Constructivism further asserts that learning should occur in a realistic setting. Applying this tenet, the look and functionality of the BEV Office desktop are faithfully recreated.

Like many companies adopting TBT programs, BevCo hopes to reduce the number of on-the-job failures by simulating situations in which failure occurs. The realism of effective simulations increases the chance of the lesson being transferred to the job. The freedom to make mistakes outside the pressure of the workplace empowers the student to learn from failure during the training and thereby avoid failure outside of it. One of the strongest features of the BevCo software is the opportunity for learners to manipulate examples of real office software functionality while a video coach provides remediation. The concept mirrors the role of a live mentor.

Finally, constructivists avow that learners should choose their own path through content and activities. The designers of BevCo's training planned to allow freedom within the content by chunking learning into small learning objects and creating an intuitive interface for quick retrieval. With the theoretical issues addressed, the development team went to work on the specifics of the interface and programming.

Interface

"BevCo has some of the most recognizable images in business and they make up an important aspect of our corporate culture," says the manager. Starting from this perspective and considering their historic style guides, BevCo's developers crafted a program look and feel consistent with the corporate style, using logos, slogans, and a specific color palette.

The need for a simple interface to accommodate inexperienced computer users influenced the decision not to create a learning metaphor for this program. The possibility that an overly complex form would detract from the necessary function shaped a simple menu-driven interface. This menu-driven structure was enhanced by rollover effects, deliberate and consistent use of color and shape, and animation to guide users intuitively. For example, top-level menus were to be in light blue, secondary-level menus in dark blue. This consistency in visual cue coloring carried over into object placement. All top-level menus appear at the left edge of the screen and branch to the user's right.

The top level of menu structure was organized to include four areas of software and practice tutorials. These sites were made primarily to educate the associates through linear tutorials. The reference information was also made available to the student from the top level of the menu structure. The last selection on the top-level menu, self-assessment, provides learners with the option of taking a pretest in order to determine which content areas require instruction. The cumulative post-test game for the curriculum can also be accessed from this location.

To maximize screen real estate during simulation exercises, the designers took a minimalist approach. Navigational functions that should always be available to the user, such as main menu and back buttons, were presented in a consistent manner within a menu area, taking up a small portion of the screen's bottom. Menus that did not need to be viewable at all times, such as second-level menu selections on the main menu, scroll into view and withdraw from view upon user command. Text boxes and the video coach window come into and withdraw from view in a similar manner.

Media and Technology Decisions

The program was developed in Macromedia's Director. As an authoring tool optimized for CD-ROM delivery, Director was chosen primarily because of its power in handling video and audio content. The team's familiarity with this particular authoring system further influenced the choice and facilitated development. Adobe's Photoshop was employed by the project's graphic artists to create all interface graphics. The development team taped video segments in digital format, using Movie Cleaner Pro for encoding. The screen resolution of the final product when running was restricted to 640 × 480 to accommodate a maximum number of computer configurations.

The efficacy of the instruction is enhanced by the use of full-motion video segments. Instead of relying on text and audio to deliver primary instruction, actors and actresses portray experts describing processes to the student. The information conveyed in these video clips supplements text and animated illustration of practices. This type of multilayered presentation creates complex memories, aiding in recall when applying learning to work situations. To allow the video element to accompany simulation screens or textual reinforcement, the developers presented the video in a video window that occupied one-sixth of the screen. The video window appears when coaching is needed, closing for full-screen presentation of materials. The reduced size allowed the developers to present highly fluid and realistic video with a high frame rate. Creatively, the designers opted to place the video in a circular video window. This format evokes association with other BevCo circular graphical artifacts and differentiates the look of the training in the minds of users.

TOUR OF BEV OFFICE

Welcome

Upon starting the program, the learner is presented with an engaging graphic "splash screen" that operates as a device for capturing attention and placing the learner in the setting of the program. (See Figure 10.4.) The three globes in this animation, representing the three training pieces of the orientation software, coalesce into one globe, accompanied by up-tempo music. The learner is engaged and the theme of a whole-world perspective is established—an essential factor in BevCo's culture. After a few seconds, the opening ends and the main menu screen is presented to the learner.

From the main menu, the gateway to the whole of the program's content, the learner is instructed via audio narration to select the button "Introduction to the Program." A logo in the upper-left corner of the screen morphs to reveal a video window. Through video narration, the coach figure is introduced and

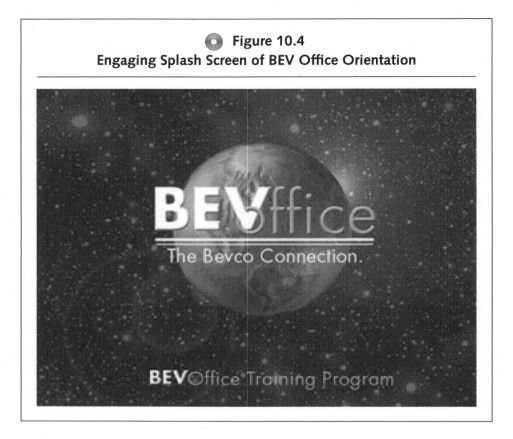

◉ **Figure 10.4**
Engaging Splash Screen of BEV Office Orientation

welcomes the student to the training. This human touch, frequently present in the training, eases the tension of technophobic users and establishes user trust. The student is instructed via narration and illustration of the navigation features, goals, and benefits of the program. The opportunity is taken to sell the user on the benefits of the training and to provide strategies for getting maximum benefit out of the lessons. From there, the employee is advised to click on a tutorial topic relevant to his job. To present a vertical slice of the functionality of the program, we will follow the selection of the Introduction to Lotus Notes course.

Introduction to Lotus Notes

Upon clicking on a first menu selection, a second-level menu animatedly branches out to reveal the associated subtopics (see Figure 10.5). Within the In-

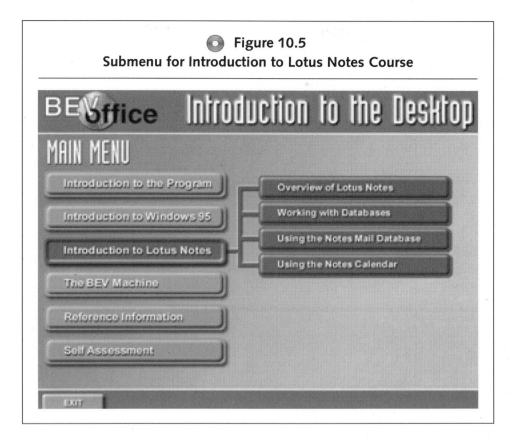

● Figure 10.5
Submenu for Introduction to Lotus Notes Course

troduction to Lotus Notes course, the user is required to complete the first lesson before moving on to subsequent lessons. To conserve screen space, users are informed of this through audio. If a selection other than the first lesson is made, a dialogue box appears to reiterate the advised course to the student.

Objectives

The first screen of all the lessons in the program lists the objectives of the lesson (see Figure 10.6). This establishes expectations for the learners to use when self-checking their mastery. The video coach appears, instructing the learner to select an objective to accomplish or use the arrow to move to the next page of content. By allowing the learner freedom to navigate with multiple processes, the program accommodates both self-directed and structure-reliant learners.

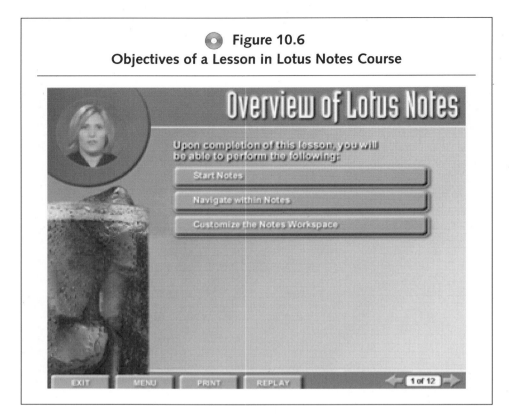

Figure 10.6
Objectives of a Lesson in Lotus Notes Course

Selecting the first objective advances the tutorial to its first page. The second and third objectives reference pages later in the progression of the tutorial.

Present Content with Simulated Screens

The first two screens of this particular lesson introduce the user to the layout of the BEV Office desktop. The learner views the desktop while hearing an audio description of its features. When points made in the narration need to be reinforced, text boxes slide out to overlay the simulated desktop (see Figure 10.7). Providing text to complement audio increases student comprehension and retention. The use of dynamic text presentation devices such as the sliding boxes allows thorough simulations while constricted to a 640 × 480 resolution.

In some cases, actual BEV Office screens are simulated but with rollover features not present in the actual software. In these cases, users can explore unfamil-

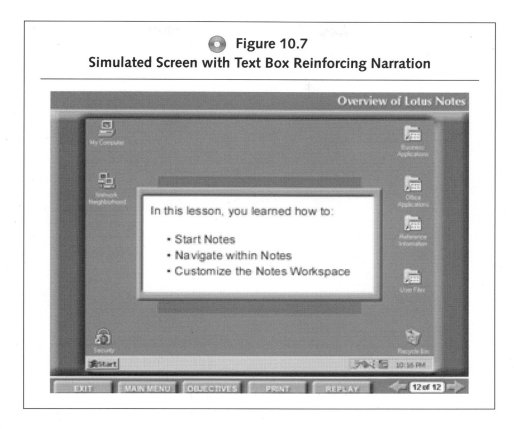

Figure 10.7
Simulated Screen with Text Box Reinforcing Narration

iar screens while screen text and audio narration help familiarize them with the contents. This common interactive strategy is illustrated in Figure 10.8.

Practice with Simulated Functionality

After discussion and illustration of some processes, the narrator asks the user to perform a simple task on the simulation software. If the user fails, text and video are provided that identify the step during which the breakdown occurred. The user must successfully complete the task in order to proceed in the tutorial. This type of interaction assures that the learner cannot passively page through the lesson without testing his own comprehension. The complexity of the interactions increases as simple tasks are strung together to make more involved operations.

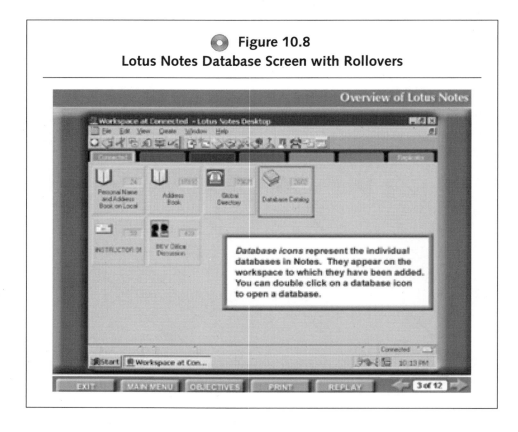

Figure 10.8
Lotus Notes Database Screen with Rollovers

The relevance of the training is immediately revealed to the user through the use of technical simulations like the one in Figure 10.9. Instead of relying solely on text and audio to convey information on the use of the computing processes, learners have the opportunity to interact with simulated applications. For example, instruction to the learner on how to toggle between Lotus Notes' active databases is presented in a display that duplicates one encountered when using the actual BEV Office system. The instruction is also summarized by the video narrator. After an on-screen arrow controlled by the computer completes a task being described in the narration, the learner is asked to duplicate the task.

This example of behavior modeling and required duplication is a simplification of the teaching mechanism used when an expert instructs a novice on a process. Although interaction with an expert may be the most beneficial training possible, training by a live expert requires that such an expert be assigned to each learner;

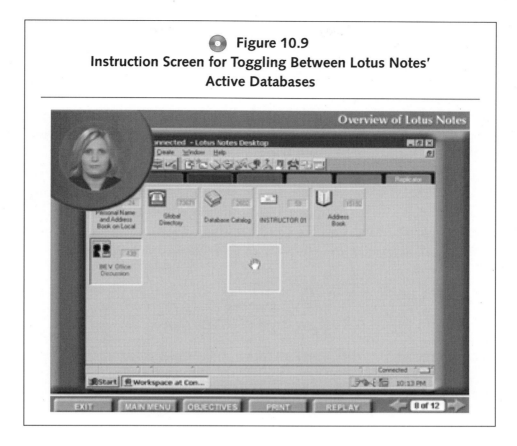

Figure 10.9
Instruction Screen for Toggling Between Lotus Notes'
Active Databases

training mediated only by text, audio, or video cannot offer this type of teaching mechanism. TBT provides the benefits of behavior modeling to students consistently and at any time without applying live trainer resources to every learner.

At any point in the tutorial, or upon completion of the lesson, the learner can exit to the objectives screen or to the main menu.

Reference Information

In addition to following the tutorial portions of the software, learners can employ the program as a reference alternative to manuals and print materials. This repackaging of materials serves those employees who prefer electronic presentation, makes the location of reference topics more efficient, and may eventually allow BevCo to reduce its cost of printing materials.

Final Assessment

After the presentation of content, confidence building, and review within the lessons, the learner is advised to move on to the final assessment. The post-test takes the form of a quiz show, with the learner competing against two computer-controlled opponents (see Figure 10.10). This positioning of the final assessment as a game is intended to engage the learner and avoid the stresses of a classic final test.

Multiple-choice, true-false, and matching questions are posed. The student responses are followed by an indication of correct or incorrect, with rationale for the correct response provided. Performance is scored on the basis of the number of correct and incorrect responses. This evaluation of the post-test exercise ensures that users have mastered the relevant learning objectives. Users do not need to achieve an acceptable score in order to pass this program. BevCo wants the

Figure 10.10
Quiz Show–Style Post-Test Game

software to be used by learners for their own benefit without the pressure that they are being judged.

In this vein, users are able to retake the post-test as many times as they desire in order to review concepts. Upon completion of the program, users are requested to complete and print out an evaluation to be returned to BevCo's information services operations department. This certification simply asserts that the training has been completed, without any indication of a grade or score.

Instructional Events Summarized

When viewed as a whole, the BEV Office training faithfully follows Gagné's instructional events in order to ensure efficacy. (The full process is detailed in Figure 10.11.)

Figure 10.11
How the BevCo Satisfies Gagné's Nine Events of Instruction

Instructional Event	Achieved
1. Gain attention	Through the use of graphics and video throughout the program
2. Inform learners of objectives	Objectives presented as lesson titles
3. Stimulate recall of prior learning	Coach calls on memory of traditional (non-computer) training experiences
4. Present the content	In learning objective chunks; through video narration, text, and illustration
5. Provide learning guidance	Video narration accompanies tutorial segments; step-by-step instruction of the topics
6. Elicit performance (practice)	Use of self-check questions throughout each lesson
7. Provide feedback	Acknowledging correct and incorrect responses and providing coaching for incorrect responses
8. Assess performance	Quiz game–style post-test scored upon completion
9. Enhance retention and transfer to the job	Training available for student review on their workstations; print manual available as a supplement

RETURN ON INVESTMENT

BevCo conservatively estimates that 3,600 employees in the home office will complete the training over three years. The BEV Office Training CD-ROM replaces a one-day orientation workshop and requires approximately three hours of user seat time to complete, thus saving approximately four hours per student trained. Additionally, the TBT will save on the salaries of instructors who would have been hired to deliver 360 classes.

The total cost of development, delivery, and maintenance of the training program has been $150,000. The direct savings in employee and instructor salaries over three years will be $541,440. Using the evaluation metrics detailed in Chapter Six, the training program achieved the following:

- Total cost savings: $391,440
- Cost-benefit ratio: 2.6
- Return on investment: 161 percent
- Break-even point: 893 students

These positive returns take into account only the home office staff. BevCo has plans to make the training available to its worldwide audience of fifty thousand employees. Additionally, the training will be available as a just-in-time resource that is likely to increase skill retention and performance further while reducing the number of calls placed to the help desk.

Strengthening Management Skills Using WBT

In today's fast-paced business environment, frontline supervisors, managers, and executives have vast and varied responsibilities. Among the business skills required are recruiting, coaching, building teams, tracking projects, formulating budgets, managing change, learning new technologies, and general leadership skills. The good news, according to *Training* magazine's 1998 "Industry Report" (Lakewood Publications, 1998), is that approximately eleven million managers and executives in the United States have received training from their employers. But how much training do they receive? On average, each U.S. manager receives less than three hours of training a month.

Despite the obvious need for and importance of management training, the challenges to offering more learning opportunities are the typical business barriers of insufficient time and money. Managers typically find themselves with too many tasks and not enough time, so they are often reluctant to dedicate the time necessary for ongoing training. Traditional workshop methods of instruction have costs associated with travel, meals, and lodging, and the "tuition" for a single seminar can be more than $500 per student per day.

Raymond Karsan Associates (RKA), a global leader in human resources consulting, saw the opportunity for the development of a Web-based management-training curriculum to overcome these obstacles. The theory was that managers with access to effective training resources would likely take advantage of such a program in the privacy and convenience of their own desks. The challenge became to build an Intranet-based solution that accommodated a wide variety of student learning styles and varied levels of experience while using the most common technologies to create a marketable off-the-shelf solution.

What You Will Learn in This Chapter

- The advantages and disadvantages of using lowest-common-denominator hardware and software standards

- How using common elements facilitates the design and development of multicourse curriculum series

- Why setting design limitations can expand potential audiences

- Learner benefits realized by integrating tutorials, simulations, and support tools

- Some media concerns unique to Web-based training

- How an assessment can be used as a multipurpose tool for pretesting, establishing learning objectives, and post-testing.

RAYMOND KARSAN ASSOCIATES

Business Background

RKA is a rapidly growing consulting firm that focuses on maximizing the potential of an organization's talent and technology. Specific service offerings include preemployment assessment, recruiting, performance improvement, and technology development.

RKA's Performance Solutions Group provides a range of instructor-led seminars and Web-based courses in a variety of topics, along with services for the custom design and development of training programs. After an analysis of market research reports and anecdotal feedback from clients, RKA decided to invest in a new Web-based product line they called the RKA Management Results series.

The Challenge

RKA's Web-based management training was designed to bridge what the organization perceived as a gap in existing products. Many of the management products available relied too heavily on media, using large graphics and extensive audio and video, and requiring special plug-ins and high-bandwidth that are not available on the majority of corporate networks. The remainder of the off-the-shelf management training products, while Web-friendly, lacked interactivity and failed to involve the reader, simply providing on-line references or guidebooks.

RKA designers wanted to encourage learning through interactivity but remain mindful that, as an off-the-shelf product, it would need to be capable of running well on the most common corporate networks. To maximize the number of clients to whom this product would be useful, RKA chose to develop the training to the hardware and software standards of a lowest-common-denominator user. That meant when they created graphics, animations, and interactive elements, they had to engage learners with less technology than was available in order not to exceed the limitations of the specifications RKA had chosen as boundaries.

Target Customers

Just like any off-the-shelf training product, RKA Management Results is necessarily geared to a broad audience of users, including medium and large companies in a variety of industries. It was designed to meet the needs of companies that have numerous offices and wish to offer training for their supervisors and managers who are dispersed throughout the country. The Web-based solution replaces on-site training sessions that take employees away from their desks and that can be expensive, especially when travel, hotels, and meals are factored into the cost.

ANALYSIS AND DESIGN

Curriculum Content

Market analysis performed by RKA determined the subjects most in demand by management trainers. Based on requests from those polled and replies from advertisements in industry publications, RKA selected twelve initial topics that the training would cover. These areas represented an initial curriculum to be expanded on as new lessons were demanded and created. Following are the initial twelve topics:

- *Coaching.* Employee coaching helps to improve both work processes and performance. This course teaches managers specific coaching skills and techniques required in a competitive work environment.

- *Communication.* Strong communication skills are key competencies for managers. This course provides tools and techniques to help managers develop essential skills in active listening, speaking, and persuasion.

- *Conflict resolution.* Successful managers know how to turn unavoidable conflicts into opportunities. This course provides practical strategies and tactics for managing work-related conflicts.

- *Effective meetings.* This course teaches the fundamental skills required to schedule, plan, and facilitate meetings effectively in today's collaborative work environment.

- *Financial fundamentals.* Even today's nonfinancial managers must be fluent in basic financial fundamentals. This course teaches the basics of business finance to enable managers to make effective decisions.

- *Interviewing.* A well-planned and executed interview reveals vital candidate information. This course provides the knowledge and tools necessary to interview and hire quality employees.

- *Leadership.* All managers need to develop their own leadership behaviors. This course teaches steps necessary to develop and communicate an effective vision and motivate colleagues, and how to coach direct reports to obtain their own peak performance levels.

- *Performance appraisals.* Peak performance is obtained with the objective and accurate review of performance. The skills necessary to prepare and provide effective performance appraisals are addressed in this course.

- *Problem solving:* As today's business has become more competitive, effective analyzing and problem solving have emerged as key success factors. This course provides a step-by-step approach to improving business problem solving.

- *Project management.* Today's multifaceted managers require a diverse skill set to oversee their projects and resources successfully. This course provides knowledge and tools for improving the management process.

- *Successful presentations.* Effective presentation skills allow today's managers to increase the likelihood of business success. This course focuses on skills and strategies to help managers sell their ideas to internal and external clients alike.
- *Team building.* A team-driven workplace increases motivation, quality, and overall performance results. This course covers the basics concepts, skills and tactics required to build an effective and efficient work team.

Course Features

To provide continuity among courses in the series, instructional designers decided that each course would contain the following common elements:

Overview. This introduction to the course content also provides instruction on navigating the program.

Assessment. This tool is used as preassessment to generate a personalized study plan of learning objectives. Once the course is completed, the postassessment generates a completion certificate.

Instruction. The actual training elements of the program use a variety of learning strategies:

- Linear tutorials, designed using classic instructional systems design (ISD), provide explanations and examples of key concepts and fundamental principles of management.

- Discovery-learning simulations, based on theories of constructivism, provide opportunities for learners to practice and apply the key concepts introduced in the tutorial section.

- Skill wizards provide electronic job aids or performance support tools that can be used on-line or printed out.

Resources. This section provides links to bibliographic references, on-line articles, and Internet sites.

Collaboration. This section allows subject matter experts access to on-line communication areas, such as bulletin boards, threaded discussions, chat rooms, lists of frequently asked questions, and e-mail, to extend on-the-job application of the training.

Technology and Media Issues

Technology concerns are at the heart of every TBT solution and were particularly relevant in this instance. From the project's outset, RKA was committed to using the Web to deliver the product. Among the factors driving the decision to deliver via the Web was the advantage that the training would be available anywhere, anytime. The lack of quality solutions on the market made the Web even more desirable—and challenging.

The RKA team decided on technical specifications that balanced desired functionality with the most commonly available delivery platform. Choosing advanced or special technologies would enable greater use of audio and video and interactivity, but would limit the number of available users. Choosing too low minimum requirements would enable the largest possible audience but would prevent the delivery of anything other than straight text.

The final minimum specifications decided on for the first version of the training program were as follows:

- Connection to corporate Intranet or the Internet is required.

- Low bandwidth dial-up connections are acceptable.

- Allowed browsers include Microsoft Internet Explorer (version 4 or higher) and Netscape Navigator or Communicator (version 4 or higher).

- No plug-ins are necessary.

- No audio or video capability is needed.

The decisions to require no plug-ins and no audio-video capabilities particularly expanded the potential participating audience, because most corporate students still don't have access to the high-bandwidth networks required for this type of delivery. However, selecting browsers of version 4.0 or later would enable certain interactivity and animations that use the built-in Flash technology.

What these decisions meant in practice was that the designers were limited in their use of complex animation, but rollover effects (the changing of text and graphics when rolled over by the cursor) and simple interactive elements were available. Although audio and video would enable students to model soft skills behaviors better, few users would be able to access them. Instead, still photographs, text boxes, and animations were used to indicate proper behaviors. RKA anticipates that advances in technology will make high-quality video and audio a common occurrence on corporate Intranets over the next couple of years, so future versions of the product will incorporate the media.

Tutorials

The performance consultants at RKA began with a traditional ISD approach, which meant they wanted more than a passive reading experience for the learner. There already was a glut of Web-based management skills references, but these lacked effective teaching elements. Putting management training information on a computer screen doesn't qualify as a training course. The developers agreed that information would be there, but the tutorial portions would be the heart of the instruction.

To provide interactivity and learner practice, RKA devised a series of *interactivity objects* to be attached to the content. For example, after being presented with information about the value of hiring and maintaining good retention, the student would be encouraged to click a "facts and stats" icon. Charts and data showing average turnover rates and costs for each new hire would then be presented. The facts and stats icon, while linked to specific content, would be made available at various points throughout the course, and consistently throughout the entire curriculum.

By making the instruction content specific to the concepts at hand but the interaction vehicle part of a bank of interactions, the learner would become familiar with the interactions while realizing the new learning value of each particular instance. The consistent use of interactions also allowed RKA's development team to create templates for each interaction type, streamlining that part of the development process.

Simulations

After examining the content, the designers realized that simulations would serve the learner best if they were integrated into the tutorials. The communications skills, it was determined, could best be transferred to the student when modeled rather than simply explained. Sample conversations would be presented to the learner, with important choices affecting the exchange decided from among three alternatives. In addition to simulations of interpersonal communications, simulations of business practices, such as filling out reports, were planned. Within these practices, sample documents would be presented to the learner. The transfer of learning to the job could be significantly increased if the forms used in training closely resembled those used in day-to-day practice.

Skill Wizards

Despite the advantages of Web-based instruction, many managers may still find themselves in need of a just-in-time performance support tool. Imagine that you have to check a job candidate's references or conduct a formal coaching session and you have neither the time nor the experience in formal training. With a sophisticated electronic job aid, you could access a blank reference-checking form, complete with sample questions, or gain access to coaching worksheets that help you to analyze the root of the performance problem. To meet these kind of practical business needs, RKA created "skill wizards" specifically for the management-training curriculum. (As noted in Chapter Four, wizards are step-by-step instructions for completing complex tasks.)

Like other performance support tools, skill wizards are goal-oriented. For example, if the goal of a manager is to properly document a meeting, that goal could be realized through training, retention, and application of skills. Performance support theories claim that if an electronic assistant exists to prompt each of the proper steps toward documentation, little or no other training is necessary. RKA's skill wizards combine the theory of electronic performance support systems with instructional design through their integration in the training curriculum. Learners are trained on the tools they will bring back to the work environment, but they are also given the opportunity to be assisted in using these tools as the situation arises and where they are needed on the job.

Theoretical Solution

The RKA Management Results series was the integrated solution borne out of RKA's development and following the ISD model. New content would be presented in the tutorial's static elements and comprehension would be increased by way of its interactive elements. Simulations would elicit performance and present feedback. The skill wizards would augment retention and job transfer. The need of the adult learner to have clear learning objectives would be addressed specifically within each topic in a lesson but holistically by the assessment tool's pretest function. The post-test would present the learner with final certification and confidence.

The development concerns were handled by top-down designing. Before any courses were designed, script, graphic, and interface templates were agreed on. One course was fully designed and programmed to be used as a model for the subsequent ones. With the script templates well defined, simultaneous writing, graphic design, and programming of discrete parts of the whole were enabled. Reiteration of the course design process was simplified by the multiple uses of script, graphic, and program code elements.

Interface

Simplicity was the universal design solution to many of RKA's challenges: an icon-driven structure was the key to useful simplicity. First, the use of iconic representations throughout the course established an elegant look and feel that separated RKA Management Results from competitors' training products. Further, the choice to go with icon simplicity eliminated the photo-realistic elements present in early interface and graphic treatments. This greatly enhanced performance on the Web by decreasing loading and refresh times. The use of icons also aids the user in navigating the interfaces intuitively, which in turn eliminates the need for extensive text instruction, again adding to the elegance of the interface.

To further increase ease of use while adding interactivity, the designers planned for rollover effects. By using the full potential of the programming languages selected, the team's programmers were able to achieve the effects desired without the use of plug-ins or downloaded additions.

TOUR OF RKA MANAGEMENT RESULTS

An organization implementing the RKA Management Results courseware has great flexibility in its setup, and setup decisions are typically made by the director of training or the vice president of human resources. Some organizations will provide open and instant access to anyone in their company. Others will choose to distribute an access password in advance to certain students. This selected group may consist of all managers, managers within a certain department, or all employees at a certain location. Tracking options are abundant as well, from no student tracking to complete integration with third-party tracking databases.

Log-On and Course Selection

Upon connecting to the program, the learner is presented with a clean and organized home page that provides an area for students to log on to the RKA Management Results training program. The visual tone of the entire curriculum is set here. The use of a consistent look and feel throughout RKA Management Results keeps the interface transparent to learners, allowing them to focus on the instruction.

Course selection is handled through an iconic menu, shown in Figure 11.1. The circular arrangement of the icon selections eliminates the hierarchy inherent in a vertical or horizontal menu and presents a unique look to the user, focusing attention on the center area of the screen. This center of attention is taken full advantage of and all of the information a user needs to make a selection is presented within the center text area.

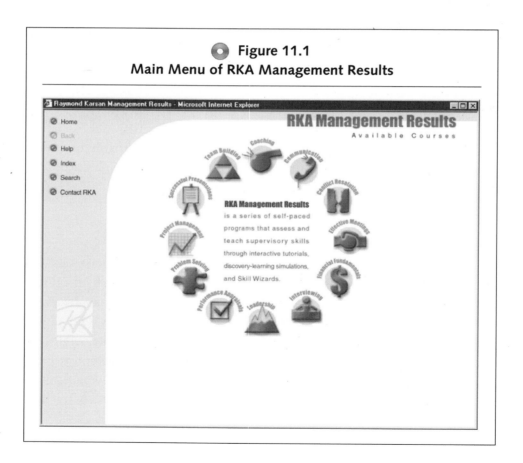

Figure 11.1
Main Menu of RKA Management Results

RKA Interviewing Course

For the sake of this sample program tour we will assume that you selected the interviewing course. Clicking on the icon brings up the main menu page of the course, shown in Figure 11.2. Worth noting is the interviewing course icon present in the corner of the screen. This type of threading of symbols and other graphic elements helps to continually and intuitively orient the learner.

The objectives of the interviewing course are clearly stated to the learner onscreen, providing the learner with an opportunity to gauge how much of the content is familiar and how much is unfamiliar or of particular interest. As per classic ISD, the objectives also provide a model for self-check as the learner progresses through study. RKA Management Results goes one step further in providing the student with a personalized study guide generated from within the assessment section.

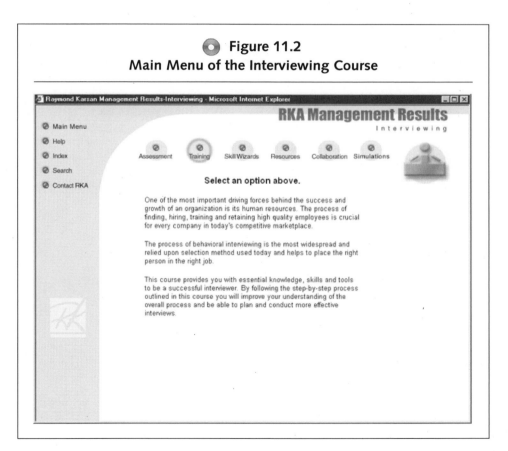

Figure 11.2
Main Menu of the Interviewing Course

Assessment as a Pretest

Though assessment has connotations of final test, this function in RKA Management Results also acts as a pretest to define learner proficiencies and needs. By answering multiple-choice questions centered on the content of the interviewing course, the learner gets a preview of what is to come. The program grades the test and uses the results to create a personalized course guide. The learner now has an explicit structure to complement their internal processes. This hyperlinked guide can be used directly to navigate the lesson or as a suggested course of study.

Guided Tutorials

Each tutorial is structured around Gagné's events of instruction (see Chapter Four). In the "Conducting the Interview" portion of the course, shown in Figure 11.3, questions and self-reflection are used to first gain students'

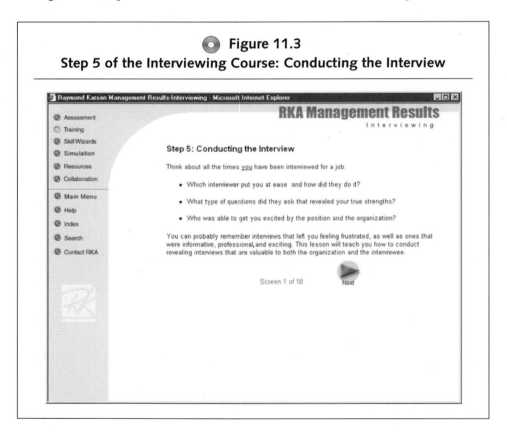

Figure 11.3
Step 5 of the Interviewing Course: Conducting the Interview

attention and then stimulate their memory-retrieval process. Learning objectives, illustrated in Figure 11.4, are then presented to provide guidance and create instructional expectations.

The actual tutorial content presented in this lesson, along with a series of interaction icons, is shown in Figure 11.5. When the icons are clicked on, interactive objects provide additional depth of content in a pop-up window. This is useful for new users and learners who need additional information. Other interactive objects deliver questions and exercises that are used to facilitate practice and feedback.

An example of a Pop Quiz is shown in Figure 11.6. After being presented with tutorial content on appropriate forms of small talk in an interview, learners are asked to use this information to judge four statements.

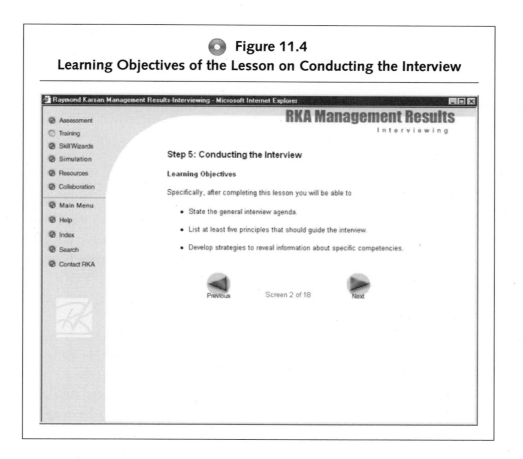

● Figure 11.4
Learning Objectives of the Lesson on Conducting the Interview

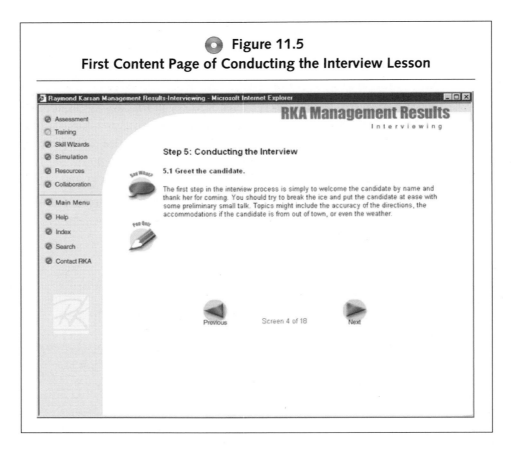

Figure 11.5
First Content Page of Conducting the Interview Lesson

The object-oriented exercise is one of the key design elements in RKA Management Results. These exercises singularly represent the three major ways the project succeeds—through its simplicity, interactivity, and modularity. Four examples of such exercises are shown in Figure 11.7.

Simulation

After completing each tutorial, students are invited to practice their newly gained knowledge and skills in a realistic simulation. In the example shown in Figure 11.8, on-screen text and graphics are used to simulate an actual candidate interview. For each step in the interview process, the manager is asked to choose a statement. The manager says something to the candidate by dragging

Figure 11.6
Pop Quiz Used to Assess Learner Comprehension

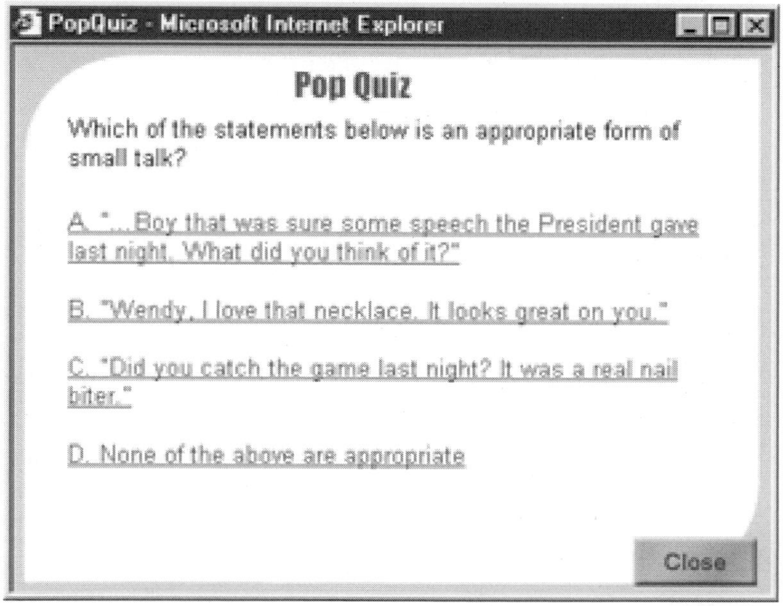

> **PopQuiz - Microsoft Internet Explorer**
>
> ## Pop Quiz
>
> Which of the statements below is an appropriate form of small talk?
>
> A. "...Boy that was sure some speech the President gave last night. What did you think of it?"
>
> B. "Wendy, I love that necklace. It looks great on you."
>
> C. "Did you catch the game last night? It was a real nail biter."
>
> D. None of the above are appropriate
>
> Close

the desired statement onto the graphic of the candidate. The candidate responds in a cartoon-style text bubble, followed by some feedback from the on-line coach.

Skill Wizards

The skill wizards in the interviewing course provide access to worksheets, forms, and databases that help generate job descriptions and competency-based questions, and that aid in the completion of candidate evaluations and reference checks. Figure 11.9 shows a blank worksheet that can be used during an actual candidate interview. It provides areas in which to jot notes about the candidate's answers as well as grading of the answers. The form can be printed directly from the browser and can be downloaded as an Adobe Acrobat or Microsoft Word file.

Figure 11.7
Types of Object-Oriented Exercises

Icon	Name	Interactivity	Advantage
	Self Check	Written answer to question followed by example response	Provides reinforcement of concepts and builds confidence
	Pop Quiz!	Multiple choice, true or false, or fill-in question with immediate feedback	Clarifies distinctions, focuses attention, and builds confidence
	Say What?	Selection from sample conversation in business environment	Contextualizes abstract concepts and provides model for behaviors
	Facts and Stats	Additional information accompanied by charts and graphs	Represents information both textually and graphically, serving the needs of users with diverse learning styles

Return to Assessment

Upon completion and review of the lessons, a final assessment is administered to the student. This assessment presents forty questions, including multiple choice, true or false, drag and drop, matching, and fill-in. When the assessment is com-

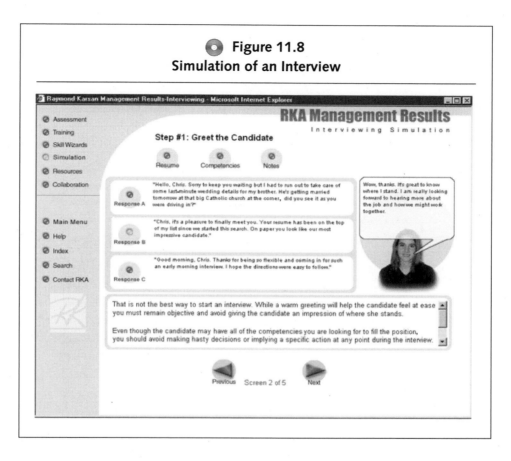

Figure 11.8
Simulation of an Interview

pleted, it is automatically graded. With an 80 percent or better score, the system generates a completion certificate that can be printed, e-mailed to a supervisor, or simply logged in a student-tracking system.

Resources

The resources section of the interviewing course provides students with hyperlinks to Web contents outside those provided by the program. Due to its connected nature, the Web excels at providing supplemental information for the learner almost immediately upon request. Non-Web resources are also suggested for additional reinforcement of concepts when the learner is away from the program. Figure 11.10 shows the books and Internet links that provide more information to those interested in recruiting and interviewing.

Figure 11.9
Interview Skill Wizard

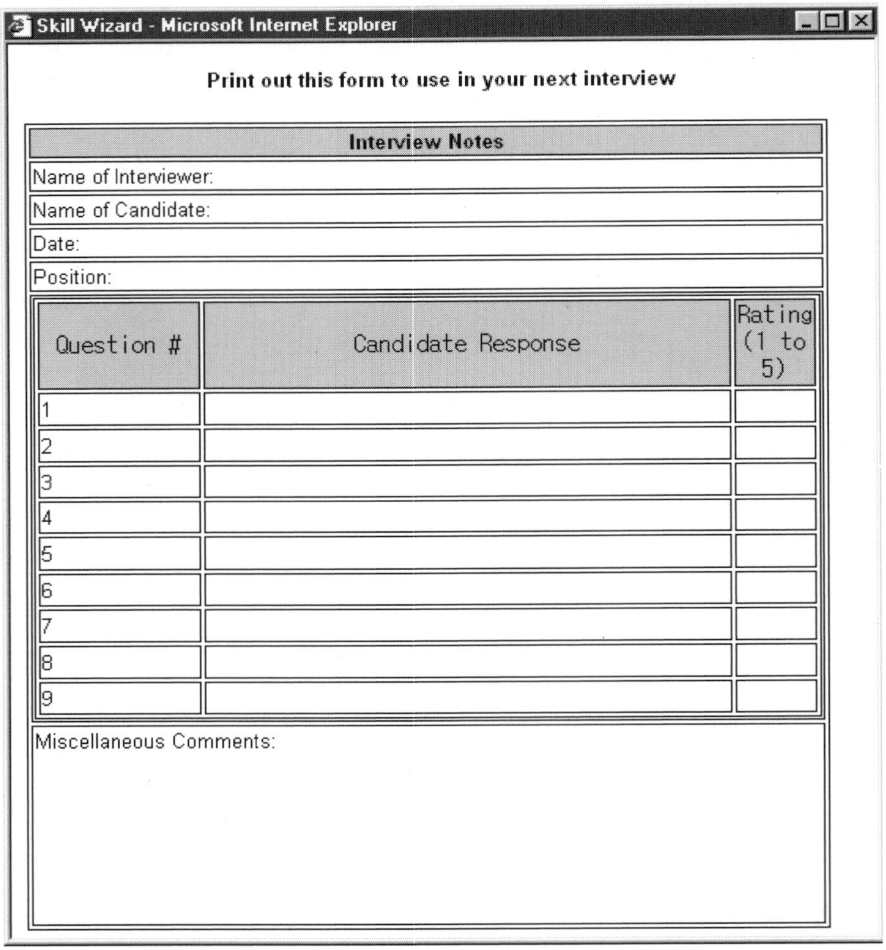

Skill Wizard - Microsoft Internet Explorer

Print out this form to use in your next interview

Interview Notes		
Name of Interviewer:		
Name of Candidate:		
Date:		
Position:		

Question #	Candidate Response	Rating (1 to 5)
1		
2		
3		
4		
5		
6		
7		
8		
9		

Miscellaneous Comments:

Collaboration

Most theories of collaborative training assert that learning can be improved through peer interaction. Certain theories go as far as to state that types of knowledge, such as cultural knowledge, are created and learned only by collabo-

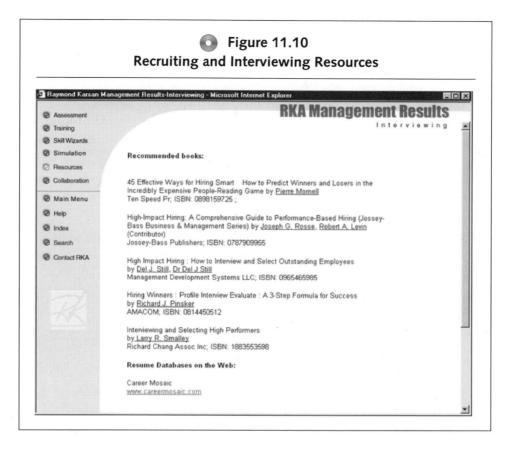

Figure 11.10
Recruiting and Interviewing Resources

Raymond Karsan Management Results-Interviewing - Microsoft Internet Explorer

RKA Management Results
Interviewing

- Assessment
- Training
- Skill Wizards
- Simulation
- Resources
- Collaboration

- Main Menu
- Help
- Index
- Search
- Contact RKA

Recommended books:

45 Effective Ways for Hiring Smart   How to Predict Winners and Losers in the Incredibly Expensive People-Reading Game by Pierre Mornell
Ten Speed Pr; ISBN: 0898159725 ;

High-Impact Hiring: A Comprehensive Guide to Performance-Based Hiring (Jossey-Bass Business & Management Series) by Joseph G. Rosse, Robert A. Levin (Contributor)
Jossey-Bass Publishers; ISBN: 0787909955

High Impact Hiring : How to Interview and Select Outstanding Employees by Del J. Still, Dr Del J Still
Management Development Systems LLC; ISBN: 0965465985

Hiring Winners : Profile Interview Evaluate : A 3-Step Formula for Success by Richard J. Pinsker
AMACOM; ISBN: 0814450512

Interviewing and Selecting High Performers by Larry R. Smalley
Richard Chang Assoc Inc; ISBN: 1883553598

Resume Databases on the Web:

Career Mosaic
www.careermosaic.com

ration. RKA Management Results addresses the needs of either theory type by providing e-mail capabilities and electronic bulletin boards, also known as threaded discussions.

Students can employ the electronic communications provided in the collaboration section of courses to look outside the content for assistance from peers and experts. By asking questions about factual material, learners can improve their understanding of concepts and fill in areas of confusion that could not be anticipated by the course designers. Discussions initiated about company practices and the application of the training shared by the learners can simultaneously define and teach aspects of a company's culture.

USER BENEFITS

At the time of this writing, RKA had just launched the RKA Management Results Web-based curriculum. The company believes that the product will be particularly useful to large companies, such as those comprising the Fortune 1000. Many of these companies have literally thousands of managers located around the world. RKA Management Results will enable a large number of new managers each year to complete a "digital boot camp" in supervisory skills. More senior managers will take advantage of the search capabilities and learning object structure to refresh themselves in select areas. All managers would find the step-by-step forms and wizards useful on almost a daily basis.

RKA has plans under way to add new titles to the curriculum and to develop higher-bandwidth multimedia add-ons. More importantly, RKA is working to integrate this performance improvement tool with on-line assessments. The next generation of the product will include the means for managers to generate custom learning plans from their superior's Web-based performance reviews or from "upward feedback" results from their direct reports.

chapter
TWELVE

Introducing New Work Processes Using WBT

The seasoned business traveler and the casual vacationer alike know of the pressures and difficulties of boarding a departing flight. The crowded, hectic environment; the noise of the travelers, intercoms, and equipment; and the tension of meeting a scheduled departure time all contribute to make a potentially nerve-wracking experience. The customer, however, is not the only individual experiencing pressures when traveling. Anyone who has tried to gather five friends or family members into a car can appreciate the challenges an airline gate agent faces when attempting to seat several hundred passengers properly aboard a commercial jet. Eliminating the stress of boarding for both the customer and the agent might be the single most important stride a commercial airline could make toward improving customer satisfaction, with the ultimate goal of retaining and increasing market share. With these factors in mind, Global Air (a fictitious name) set out to introduce its new Nexus system of gate-boarding hardware, software, and practices.

These new tools were designed to provide more efficient and effective gate and boarding processes, reduce the burden currently endured by the agents, and improve the accuracy and timeliness of information to both agents and customers. Even with all of the advantages of the new Nexus system, "Global Air's employee's are just like all people. Change, even when it's required, even when it is requested, is very difficult," asserts Global's vice president in charge of multimedia training. As part of Global Air's information technology transformation, the vice president and his department needed to provide training to the agent community on the new Nexus software and gate-boarding process. To complicate their training challenge, Global's staff needed to create the training concurrently with the development of Nexus.

In each of the case studies we have looked at so far, some form of training on the subject covered has existed prior to the new TBT. But what challenges are presented when the hardware, software, and practices on which the learners are to be trained are developed simultaneously with the training itself? Global Air faced exactly this question when creating training for their new Nexus boarding hardware and software. The benefits promised would not fully be realized if the employees were not properly trained. Ineffective or hard-to-use training could turn off gate agents to Nexus before it was even implemented. If the training was successful, however, Nexus could be successful. If the training was inviting, the gate agents would welcome Nexus and their anxiety would be eased. The vice president knew that in great part the success of Nexus depended on the success of Nexus training.

What You Will Learn in This Chapter

- Why a highly collaborative work process is required to develop effective multimedia training

- Advantages realized and challenges faced when employing hybrid CD-ROM/ Web delivery

- Ways in which a learning metaphor can engage the learner's interest

- Learner and designer benefits of using a virtual guide

- How a training investment can be leveraged by application as an internal marketing tool

- Return on investment possible with technology-based technical training

GLOBAL AIR
Business Background

Global Air, the fictional corporation created to illustrate this real-world scenario, is a major air carrier that provides scheduled air transportation for passengers, freight, and mail. Global Air currently serves one hundred domestic cities in thirty states, and fifty cities in twenty-five foreign countries. Global Air flies more than 103 million people yearly, which reflects its capacity and its excellence in providing customers with world-class service. Global Air is investing in its employees by replacing outdated equipment and providing them with updated and improved tools with which to do their jobs. Global Air asked agents what they needed to make their jobs easier and the improved Nexus system was the result of a design process centered on the agents. Nexus will help agents spend more time on customer service and less time on keyboarding, as well as helping Global Air achieve higher levels of on-time performance for its flights.

Within Global Air's background and culture, multimedia training has become part of the norm. Global Air has had success with several creative-metaphor computer-based training projects and the development team considered these previous approaches when creating the Nexus training.

The Challenge

The primary challenge faced by Global Air was to create technical training for the set of new Nexus devices, applications, and procedures. It was decided from the outset that this training would take a technologically mediated form. Global Air's past success with TBT, coupled with the fact that the Nexus processes themselves relied on computer interaction, influenced this decision. Given that the Nexus system was still under development while the training was being created, the work process needed to accommodate frequent revisions easily.

Like his peers in training management, the vice president was working with tight budgets and sought a training solution that could be distributed to a diverse and scattered workforce without the costs of transporting learners to seminars or trainers to distant offices. He and his students had experience with the learning benefits of multimedia presentation through prior training initiatives. With a gate-agent community numbering in the thousands already trained on existing terminals, computer delivery presented itself as the most fitting solution.

Confidence Builder

To leverage their investment in the educational materials they were inventing, Global Air wanted a final product that would also serve as a marketing piece for their new Nexus procedures that was targeted to the employees who would be using them. The program Nexus: Taking Flight into the Future, as it was to be called, would provide the agents with confidence in the initiative undertaken by their employer. The program would also establish the primary scope and functionality of Nexus's initial release so agents could understand the immediate and long-term benefits and view this improved flight management process with a positive attitude. Finally, the program would give the gate agents an informative and engaging tool for keeping up with alterations made to a system that was still in the early phases of implementation. Internally, this marketing purpose enabled Global Air's sales training department to justify its budget for the training product.

ANALYSIS AND DESIGN
Tutorial Content

The instructional designers and subject matter experts assigned to Nexus: Taking Flight into the Future began by defining the necessary tutorial elements. Their consensus was to include training in four areas:

- Business needs and overall goals of Nexus
- Benefits of Nexus to the agents
- Software orientation
- Ticket reader (hardware) orientation

It was further decided that these content areas would be best addressed in straightforward, linear tutorials because the materials contained within these sections were entirely new to students. The designers sought ways of familiarizing the learners with elements of the Nexus system before immersing them in simulation.

As you may recall from Chapter Four, on adult learning, the segmenting of complex concepts into their discrete simple elements, called *chunking*, aids students in the learning process. To take advantage of this, the instructional designers of the Nexus training chunked the software and hardware orientations into manageable sections. The chunks created for the software orientation module are provided in Figure 12.1. Assessments of these tutorial topics would be handled through the simulation exercises planned for inclusion later in the software.

Practice Content

The development team knew that after concepts were introduced students should be given an opportunity to apply their learning. To engage the learner, the practice opportunities would take the form of games. This positioning of the tasks associated with their jobs as entertaining exercises was meant to shape gate agent behaviors relative to their duties. The practice games to be included were as follows:

- A question-and-answer game to increase knowledge of the hardware and software
- A drill-and-practice game to increase proficiency in using Nexus's functions

Figure 12.1
Chunked Tutorial Content for the
Nexus Software Orientation Module

Chunk	Content
Seat Maps	Discover how the Seat Map can help you when assigning seats.
Lists window	Learn how to access passenger PNRs using the Lists window.
Flight summary window	Explore the use of the Flight Summary window for continually updated flight information.
FIDS	Examine the FIDS window to request and view arriving and departing flight informaiton.
Interaction between Nexus windows	See how the Nexus windows work together to give maximum data quickly.

Simulation Content

The final training piece was to be simulation experiences mirroring the events of a typical day. The designers hoped that the progression through the training would move the learner logically from abstract concepts to concrete applications. The tutorials would introduce Nexus, the practice games would place the concepts of the functioning of the system into the context of the system's actual use, and then the simulation adventures would position the use of the system in the context of gate agents' day-to-day work environment. As learners moved from being told about Nexus to being shown Nexus to using a simulation of Nexus, they would incrementally build proficiencies. By ultimately using a simulation of Nexus within simulated work situations, learners would realize where these proficiencies could be applied to improving their own work efficiency.

These training simulations would be chunked into individual challenges to be overcome. A sample breakdown of one full scenario follows:

- Sign on, input password, read the briefing materials for the flight.
- Complete flight and gate setup procedures and establish yourself as primary agent.
- Print reports, examine summary window in Nexus software, exit and log off from system.
- Log on at gate.
- Assign a seat and issue a boarding document.
- Process standby passengers.
- Minimize the Nexus display window.

The chunking of these associated topics would improve learner retention along with allowing learners to return for refreshers on specific trouble spots after a first pass through the training.

Media and Technology Concerns

Global Air began by outlining the requirements of the delivery machines based on the computers they had in place. The specifications of the machines are provided in Figure 12.2.

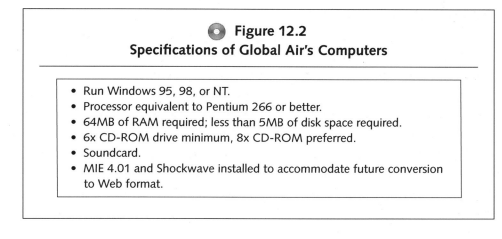

Figure 12.2
Specifications of Global Air's Computers

- Run Windows 95, 98, or NT.
- Processor equivalent to Pentium 266 or better.
- 64MB of RAM required; less than 5MB of disk space required.
- 6x CD-ROM drive minimum, 8x CD-ROM preferred.
- Soundcard.
- MIE 4.01 and Shockwave installed to accommodate future conversion to Web format.

The multimedia capabilities of these machines made CD-ROM delivery a viable option. A desire to incorporate an abundance of rich multimedia also influenced the decision for CD-ROM delivery as opposed to Web delivery. A CD-ROM-based interactive training application accommodates the maximum number of student learning styles and allows realistic and engaging simulations. Further, CD-ROM delivery would enable the designers to use text, audio, video, and animation, creating a product that appeals to auditory, visual, and kinesthetic learners alike. The storage capability of CD-ROM technology provides sufficient room for high-impact multimedia assets.

Although CD-ROM provides great storage potential, updating content is not as simple as with Web-based applications. Considering the changing nature of the content (Global Air plans to refine Nexus up to and after the training launch), the team needed a method for content updating. Additionally, initiatives within the company to move all training onto the corporate Intranet influenced a desire for a product that would be easily transferred to the Web. During development it was decided that the initial launch would be handled with CDs equipped to search for updated content on Global Air's Intranet. To increase user ease, the disc application would contain its own automatic Web-search function. Further, the team decided to incorporate audio and animation elements but avoid video elements to ease the eventual conversion to Web format.

Instructional System Design Elements

The tutorial portions of the training largely reflect the influence of instructional system design. The earliest lessons in the training curriculum take a linear form, where information is presented, comprehension is tested, and concepts are reviewed. This approach was adopted to provide the learner with maximum structure and guidance. As the learner's comfort level with the new material increases, the structure is loosened and more freedom is permitted. The design team recognized that a straight instructional design methodology, applying Robert Gagné's events of instruction (see Chapter Four) would be the best way to introduce the new equipment and procedures. Gagné laid out his nine-step process, which correlates to and addresses the four conditions of adult learning he had established. Instructing the gate agents on the application of the new processes would be accomplished through tutorials.

Constructivist Elements

Grounding of the instructional concepts in real-world application was to be achieved through the simulation aspects of the training. Constructivist theories most basically assert that learning should occur in a realistic setting and learners should choose their own path through content and activities. One of the hallmarks of constructivist approaches to learning is the use of simulation as a training tool. Global Air's designers wanted to apply pieces of constructivist theory, specifically simulation, but felt that learners would be engaged by a metaphor that transported them out of a realistic setting. (The designers eventually chose an outer-space theme, which is discussed in greater detail later in the chapter.) They also believed that learners needed guidance to make their learning experience most beneficial.

Like many companies adopting TBT programs, Global Air hopes to reduce the number of on-the-job failures by simulating situations where failure occurs. The realism of effective simulations increases the chance of transfer to the job. The freedom to make mistakes outside of the pressure of the workplace empowers the student to learn from failure in order to avoid failure outside of the training. One of the strongest features of Global Air's software is the opportunity for learners to manipulate examples of real Nexus functionality while a computer coach provides remediation. The concept mirrors the role of a live mentor without having to devote the time of an expert to every learner. For the coaching concept to succeed, the designers needed to create a coach.

Theoretical Solution

Globulus was created to introduce gate agents to the Nexus processes. This character from the future would serve as an anchor for students' learning. Additionally, the character would provide a thread for learners to follow as they progressed through the training. It was decided that Globulus's guidance would be extensive early in the program and would gradually be reduced as the program continued. In this way the learner could become comfortable at his own pace and move toward the final goal of using the Nexus system in the field without assistance.

To overcome the difficulties of creating training for Nexus while simultaneously developing Nexus itself, the team put a highly iterative work process in place. The look and feel of the work was finalized early in the process and prototypes were made frequently for review. Scripts were written modularly to allow for frequent revisions. Most important, constant contact was maintained between the training design team and the system designers. Changes made in the Nexus system were noted immediately and reflective changes in the scripts and programming of the training were made immediately. The final safety net was provided by the Web functionality of the CD. After the CDs were distributed, changes to the training could be made and placed on the company Intranet. When a user attempted to access a training section, the training program would check the Intranet site for updates. If new materials were present, they would be used instead of the outdated CD content. With the general challenges overcome, the development team went on to develop the specifics of the program's interface and content.

Interface and Metaphor

"For Global Air agents, work may feel a lot like a never-ending journey of discovery into the unknown," says Global's vice president. "If things go well, the experience is a combination of hard work, accomplishment, and fun. If things go poorly, you can end up feeling lost in space." Starting from this perspective and considering the approaches of previous training products, Global Air decided on a space exploration metaphor to organize its training. In the fantasy future the learner is transported to a universe where advanced beings use Nexus. In fact, a whole solar system exists devoted to manufacturing, studying, and using the Nexus gate-boarding system. Even the sport in this future centers on the use of Nexus.

Instead of a typical menu-driven structure, an exploratory interface was created in which choices are made via selection of destinations on a starmap. The graphical approach to organizing these different areas moves the metaphor forward; each section appears to the user as a planet that can be reached via the starmap. Once on a planet, students can access relevant course content and educational exercises. For example, to learn more about gate-reading hardware, the user does not select hardware info from a list of topics but rather directs himself or herself to the planet Technos.

The fictional solar system was organized to include areas for both hardware- and software-specific tutorials. These sites, the planets Technos and Academia, were made primarily to educate the gate agents through linear tutorials. The Asteroid Challenge, a game testing Nexus knowledge, and the Tournament Palace, a game testing speed and skill in manipulating Nexus software, reinforce concepts, build gate agent confidence, and encourage agents to embrace their work activities with a sense of excitement. The remaining planets of New Atlanta, Andromeda, and Ventrusca provide the simulations that serve as both training and assessment.

As learners gain experience and no longer need the organization that the Globulus mentor provides, the program provides greater opportunity to skip directly to the information wanted through a fully revealed and functioning starmap.

Media and Technology Decisions

The program was developed in Macromedia's Authorware. An authoring tool optimized for CD-ROM delivery, Authorware was chosen primarily because of its power in handling animation and audio content. Global Air also selected this authoring tool over Macromedia's Director because of Authorware's advanced student-tracking capabilities and to leverage an existing investment in the software. The team's familiarity with this particular authoring system further influenced the choice and facilitated development. Adobe's Photoshop was employed by the project's graphic artists to create the bulk of the program's graphics.

Macromedia's Flash was used to create animations, due to its easy integration with Authorware and its Web-delivery advantages. The minimum screen resolution of the final product when running is 1,024 × 768 pixels.

The choice to create a hybrid application eliminated the use of video. The intensity of the role-playing scenarios remained intact through the use of technical simulations. Instead of relying solely on text and audio to convey teaching on the use of the Nexus processes, learners have the opportunity to interact with simulated applications. For example, instruction on how to toggle between Nexus's active windows is presented in a display that duplicates one encountered when using a Nexus terminal, and is also summarized in text.

This type of concrete illustration contextualizes the learning more than a simple text description or summarization. The fact that these processes are not played out against a realistic backdrop does not detract from the learner's experience. It is hoped that the juxtaposition of the familiar practices against the fantastic setting improves retention by giving the learner additional associative paths to access their learning from memory.

Audio is similarly used to provide an additional layer of depth to the learner's experience. These levels of realism and advanced learning tools are made possible only through cutting-edge technology.

TOUR OF THE NEXUS TRAINING

Before embarking on a tour of the Nexus training, examine the flow chart in Figure 12.3 to gain a better understanding of how the program is organized. Notice that the early portion of the program is entirely linear, but further along in the flow the learner has several branching options.

Log-In and Meet Globulus

Upon starting the program, the learner is presented with an engaging "fly-in" to the space station, which operates as a device for capturing attention and placing the learner in the setting of the program. An airlock requires that the learner's name, proper identification, and password be supplied before entering the program, as illustrated in Figure 12.4.

After the airlock slides open, the user enters the space station to encounter his or her guide, Globulus, for the first time. Through audio narration, the animated

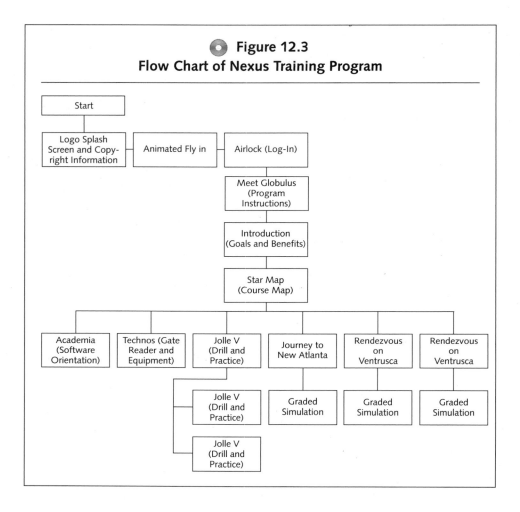

Figure 12.3
Flow Chart of Nexus Training Program

android figure introduces himself as "the gate agent of the future," establishing a relationship as both peer and mentor to the learner. As his first duty, Globulus asks the student if instruction is needed in the use of the program. If the yes button is clicked, details on the use of the navigation features of the program are provided in both audio and text forms.

Aboard the Space Station

Globulus prompts the user to "step inside my head" to learn about the training program's functions and the benefits and goals of the Nexus system before

🔵 **Figure 12.4**
Log-In Screen for Nexus Program

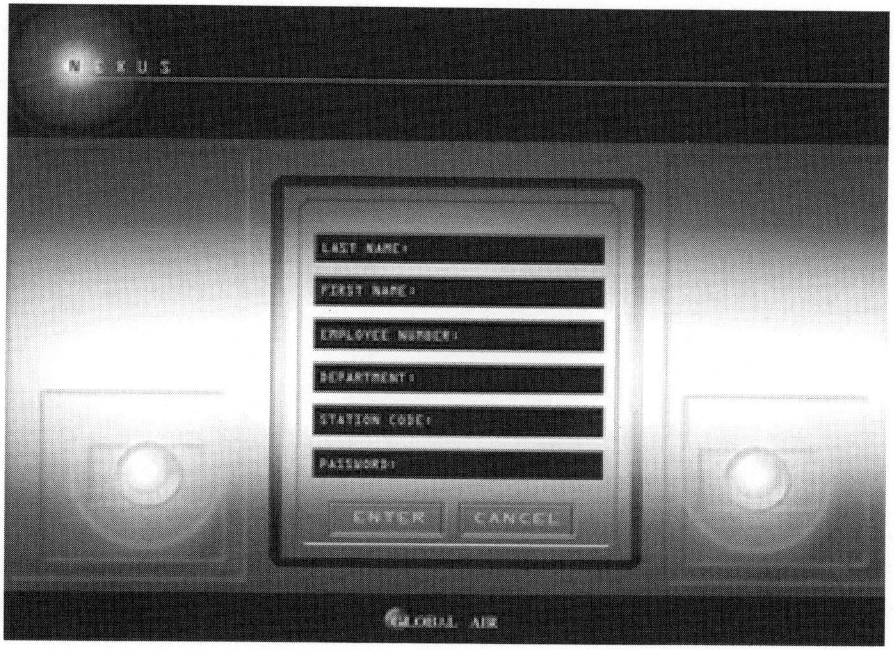

embarking on the learning journey. The menu created around the metaphor of Globulus's brain is presented in Figure 12.5.

Clicking on one of the buttons accesses a tutorial in the form of text screen accompanied by Globulus's narration. A text prompt informs the learner that all of the brochure materials must be examined before the starmap can be accessed. After the learner has finished examining all of the goals and benefits documents, the starmap button on the program's navigation bar becomes active. Globulus's narration instructs the user to continue on to the starmap.

Starmap

Completion of the guided instructions and benefits tour is required for any first-time user logging on to the program. After its completion, and upon subsequent

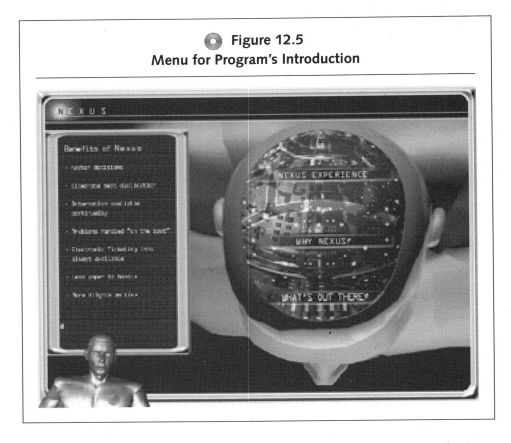

Figure 12.5
Menu for Program's Introduction

uses of the program, the user is introduced to the starmap view. This map of planets, shown in Figure 12.6, is the main navigation device for the entire program. The six planets visible on the map correspond to the six modules that make up the Nexus training. The first three, Academia, Technos, and Jolle V, appear to the user in vibrant hues to designate that they are accessible. The cluster of the three outer planets, New Atlanta, Andromeda, and Ventrusca, all appear muted to signify to the learner that these selections are not yet available to them.

Globulus advises the user to "travel" to a planet by clicking upon it. If the learner asks Globulus for help by clicking on his figure or the help button, a dotted line between the planets is revealed to suggest a course of instruction. This is one example of how the program uses the mentor character to streamline the interface and make interaction more intuitive. The narration advises the user to select Academia from the map. The selection of a choice causes the map's graphic

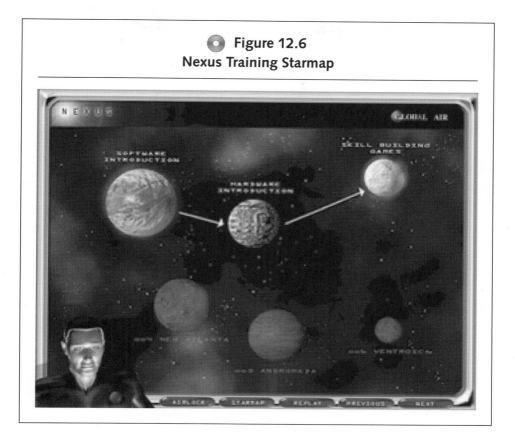

Figure 12.6
Nexus Training Starmap

environment to blur, representing the learner's journey through hyperspace to her selected destination. Following Globulus's advice, the first destination for the learner is Academia.

Academia

The view with which the learner is presented after exiting hyperspace details the surface of Academia. This screen, which is essentially a submenu, presents the cities on the surface of the planet (see Figure 12.7). By rolling over the cities the user calls up text boxes that describe the lesson contained within each site. By clicking on a city, the user initiates a tutorial on one of the features of the Nexus software.

The tutorial sections contained on Academia are paginated, moving logically and linearly forward. As Globulus describes aspects of the Nexus software, simulations of the screens from the actual application are presented. After discussion

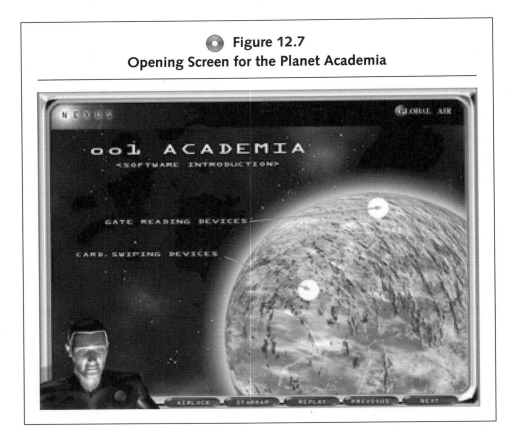

Figure 12.7
Opening Screen for the Planet Academia

and illustration, the narrator asks the user to perform a simple task using the simulation software. If the user fails, both text and audio are provided that break down the task into step-by-step elements. The user must successfully complete the task in order to proceed in the tutorial. This type of interaction ensures that the learner cannot page through the lesson without testing his own comprehension. The complexity of the interactions increases as simple tasks are strung together to make complex operations. At any point in the tutorial the learner can exit to the world view and from there to the starmap.

Technos

The next suggested stop is the planet Technos. As Globulus narrates, "It is on this rugged world that the gatereaders and cardswipers that are required for efficient flight boarding are manufactured." The worldview the student is provided with features locations on the planet's surface corresponding to different lessons on the devices the agents will use in their daily activities. The lesson structure presents the user with tutorials driven by the audio narration and supplemented by screen text.

The simulation interactions here include photos of the gate boarding equipment, such as the one in Figure 12.8. Within these lessons the freedom of the student is increased. The student can click on parts of the equipment to access information about the function and proper practices of the machine. In this way the learner is given control of the pace and extent of the material by chunking the whole tutorial down and relating it to parts of the equipment. Control of this sort is absolutely necessary when educating the adult learner in order to accommodate differing learning needs, time constraints, and areas of interest.

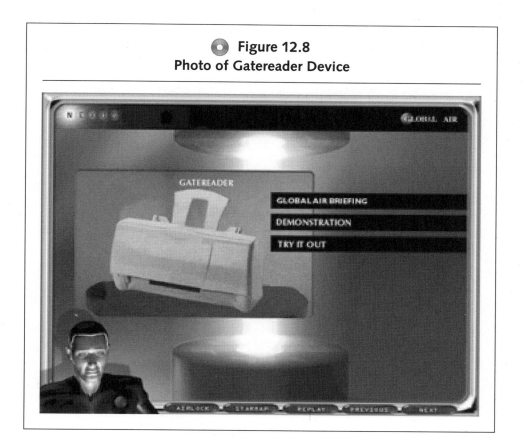

Figure 12.8
Photo of Gatereader Device

Jolle V

On the game planet of Jolle V, the learner has an opportunity to test the knowledge and practice the skills learned on Academia and Technos. The two selections presented on the worldview of Jolle V—Asteroid Challenge and Tournament Palace—represent the game choices available to the learner.

Within Asteroid Challenge, illustrated in Figure 12.9, the learner is asked a variety of questions about the Nexus software, its functions, and best practices. Each time the learner answers incorrectly, an asteroid gets a little closer. When a correct answer is provided, an asteroid is destroyed.

The Tournament Palace places the learner in an arena where masters of Nexus proficiency come to compete. Alien competitors, like the one in

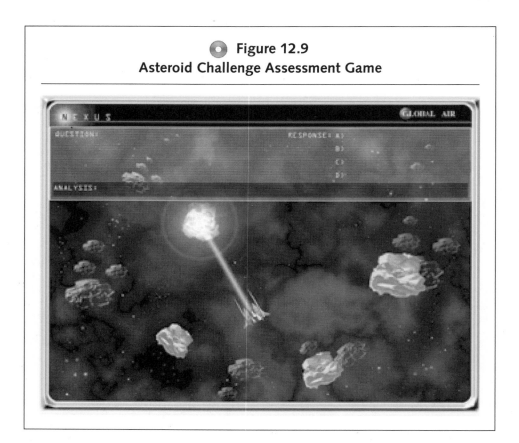

Figure 12.9
Asteroid Challenge Assessment Game

Figure 12.10, challenge the learner to complete operations on a mock-up of the Nexus software within a given time limit. If the user can beat the clock and the competitor, he moves on to subsequently more difficult opponents. These areas provide a good example of the program's creative interpretation of a common tool. Both Asteroid Challenge and the Tournament Palace operate as pretests for the learner, with questions and operations providing immediate feedback and scoring.

The Outer Planets

After the presentation of content, confidence building, and review of the inner planets are completed, the learner gains access to the outer planets. Upon

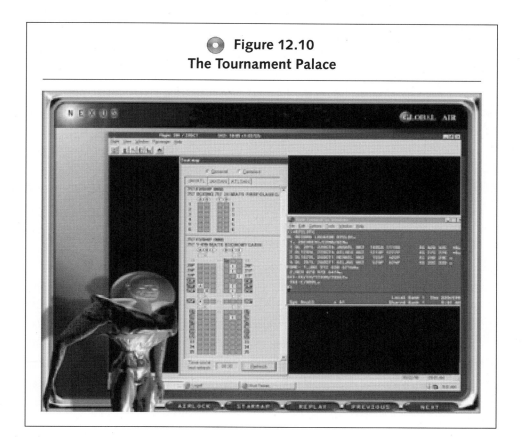

Figure 12.10
The Tournament Palace

returning to the starmap after visits to the first three planets, the next three planets appear in active color. Selecting one of these planets now transports the user back into the space station. It is by sending passenger flights to the outer planets that the relevance of the program's instruction becomes fully apparent. New Atlanta, the first of the outer planets, will be discussed for the purpose of this program tour.

After entering the space station, the user comes to a menu unlike the worldviews of the inner planets. The selection lists flights being sent out to distant destinations, and Globulus's audio prompts the user to select a flight to work. Upon choosing an assignment, the learner is presented with a narrated introduction and graphic screen introducing the work scenario in which he will be engaged. The next menu presents specific responsibilities of the gate agent in a sequential order. These selections represent challenges taken directly from the daily responsibilities of a gate agent. For example, the learner is asked to establish herself as the primary gate agent for the departing flight to New Atlanta. By selecting and presenting scenarios taken directly from agent experience, the realism and relevance of the scenarios remains inherent even within the exotic metaphor. From there the learner must demonstrate proficiency in completing the task using the new Nexus processes.

The simulation exercises of Nexus: Taking Flight into the Future are unique in that they also function as the program's final assessments. The skill with which the user completes challenges is recorded as a form of score. If mistakes are made or at any point the learner is stumped, he or she can request assistance from Globulus. Globulus's tips and assistance take the form of audio coaching and on-screen illustration of what steps should be taken next. The context-specific assistance keeps user confidence high and helps ensure that the user will not become frustrated with the learning at hand.

While Globulus can be consulted during the training program, the goal of the training is to enable gate agents to function without assistance in the real world. Thus points are deducted from an agent's score when Globulus appears in the testing sections of the program. The final score the student achieves is displayed on screen and is stored in a database for review by supervisory personnel. These results are tied directly to the competencies outlined at the scenario's start. The learner is informed of what specific areas of Nexus's operation they had trouble with and given an opportunity to jump directly to review content and exercises. Global Air intends to require successful completion of the training program by all of its domestic gate agents.

Instructional Events Summarized

When viewed as a whole, the Nexus training faithfully follows Gagné's instructional events to ensure efficacy (see Figure 12.11).

Figure 12.11
How Global Air Satisfies Gagné's Nine Events of Instruction

Instructional Event	Achieved
1. Gain attention	Primarily through metaphor; within sections through the use of audio/animation
2. Inform learners of objectives	Planet maps chunked into objective associated tasks
3. Stimulate recall of prior learning	Simulations on outer planets ask learner to use knowledge obtained in tutorials
4. Present the content	Tutorials available on Technos and Academia
5. Provide "learning guidance"	Narrator offers tips and memory aids
6. Elicit performance (practice)	Practice games on Jolle V; simulations presented on outer planets
7. Provide feedback	Successful operations in games rewarded; improper operations remediated with text, narration, and illustration of proper practices
8. Assess performance	Simulation exercises on outer planets scored
9. Enhance retention and transfer to the job	Training available for student review at terminals within their work area

RETURN ON INVESTMENT

Global Air released the Nexus training initially to their 2,000 ticketing agents in the United States, who are located at 140 different airports. This will be followed by a global rollout that will double the total number of students. The complete Web-based training takes approximately three hours of seat time, and replaces a seven-hour course. Additionally, the TBT will eliminate the need to hire contract instructors for approximately 200 classes.

The total cost of development was $120,000. The direct savings in student salaries will be $260,000 and the elimination of contract instructors will save $280,000 (assuming $1,400 per class-day). Because Global Air instructors and students would normally fly free of charge on company planes, the TBT solution does not yield additional savings in travel. Total projected savings for the U.S. rollout alone is $540,000.

Using the evaluation formulas detailed in Chapter Six, the Global Air Web-based training achieved the following:

- Total net cost savings: $420,000

- Cost-benefit ratio: 4.5

- Return on investment: 350%

These impressive returns will double once the training is used on a global basis, and the program will have additional value as an ongoing training device for new hires.

APPENDIX A: MODEL REQUEST FOR PROPOSAL

This request for proposal (RFP) template can be used when soliciting bids from vendors for the development of CD-ROM and Web-based training programs. After completing this RFP template, you will have a document that provides thorough and consistent information to each vendor, and you are guaranteed to get back all the information you need to make an informed decision.

DATE:

TO: [Sales rep's name]
          [Vendor's Name]
          [Address]
          [City, State, Zip]

FROM: [Client's name]
          [Title]

SUBJECT: Request for proposal [Type CD-ROM or WBT]

I am pleased to send you the attached Request for Proposal for [company name] [project, product, initiative, etc.]

I would ask that you submit the proposal to me no later than [specified date, typically four weeks after the date the RFP is mailed].

Please forward your proposal to:

> [Client's name]
> [Title]
> [Company name]
> [Address]
> [City, State, Zip Code]

I. BACKGROUND

[Company name] is an international, industry-leading provider of [describe mission of company or department, etc.].

The purpose of this project is to create a [number]-hour interactive, multimedia CD-ROM-delivered training [or Web-based training] for the purpose of [goal, type of content, etc.].

II. SCOPE OF WORK

Target Audience

The target audience will consist of approximately [number] users.

- [Level of computer experience]
- [Their titles]
- [Their geographic location]

Content

Without respect to the specific organization of the information or the method of presentation (such as video, audio, animation, and so on), the training program will provide approximately [number] hours of training on the following topics:

1. [Topic 1]
   - [subtopic a]
   - [subtopic b]
2. [Topic 2]
3. [Topic 3]

This program will also include a post-test automatically graded by the computer.

Deliverables

This program will exist on [CD-ROM or Web] and will include video, audio, text, graphics, and animation.

The final deliverable of the program must meet the following criteria:

- It will run on [Windows 3.1, Windows 95, NT, Macintosh].
- It will be developed using commercially available tools.
- All source code and working files will become the property of [client].
- [If Web-based training, indicate high or low bandwidth connection.]
- [If Web-based training, indicate type of browser and version.]
- [If Web-based training, indicate ability to use plug-ins.]
- [If Web-based training, indicate whether or not Java is allowed.]

III. WORKING RELATIONSHIP

The work described here will be accomplished in a team context with team members having professional expertise in the areas cited above. The general working relationship is described here. Any additional responsibilities will be detailed in a specific contract.

- Project managers will be assigned by both [client] and the vendor and will act as single points of contact.
- [Client] has immediate needs and aggressive time frames. These time frames are dictated by client demands and vendors are expected to meet all deadlines.
- It is understood that selected vendors will need to interface with [client] teams. Vendors may need to travel to the [client] site for reviews or meetings. Vendors will submit a detailed project plan and schedule with key project milestones.

- Vendors will submit weekly status reports and participate in weekly status meetings, if required.

IV. VENDOR RESPONSE

To establish your qualifications, please provide the following in your response:

1. A well-defined project approach for scope of work including a description of interactivity and media treatments.
2. A project schedule and a work plan that depicts intermediate tasks and milestone events.
3. A description of your courseware development process.
4. A summary of corporate experience in successful completion of multimedia or Web-based courseware projects. (If experienced in more than one delivery method, please include examples of each.)
5. A list of clients.
6. A description of quality control processes.
7. A description of your organization:
   - Number of employees
   - Locations
   - Years in business
   - Awards and honors
8. Project costs in a firm, fixed price.
9. Which project functions, if any, are outsourced to contractors.
10. Three professional references (key contact names, titles, and telephone numbers). [Client] would like to speak with people who have direct knowledge of your ability to provide these services for similar projects.

V. EVALUATION CRITERIA

Proposals will be reviewed with the following criteria in mind:

- *Performance capability:* the extent to which the vendor demonstrates the ability to provide the depth and breadth of experience, skills, and knowledge generally required by this work. This will include a review of professional references.
- *Cost:* the total cost to [Client] of the proposed preferred vendor relationship.
- *Completeness and quality of bid response:* the thoroughness and concern for quality in the vendor's response

  Vendor responses must be received at [Client] by [time] on [date].

APPENDIX B:
SAMPLE VENDOR PROPOSAL

This sample proposal is a good example of the types of proposals you should receive from vendors who are bidding on a project. Note that the solution is clearly laid out, the budget is specific, and vendor background information is detailed.

CLINICAL RESEARCH NETWORK

Web-Based Training and Tracking System

Prepared for:

_____

NAME

TITLE

CLIENT NAME Inc.

Prepared on March 19, 1999 by:

_____

Kevin Kruse,

Principal

Jason Keil,

Instructional Designer

Raymond Karsan Associates

I. EXECUTIVE SUMMARY

Background

CLIENT NAME Inc. is a research-based, global pharmaceutical company. They discover and develop innovative, value-added products that improve the quality of life of people around the world and help them enjoy longer, healthier, and more productive lives. The company has three business segments: health care, animal health, and consumer health care. CLIENT NAME's products are available in more than 150 countries.

Challenge and Opportunity

CLIENT NAME Pharmaceuticals Group provides training to Clinical Research Associates across North America and worldwide in its standard operating procedures. A curriculum for teaching standard operating procedures exists but needs to be unified, clarified, and put into the proper form for Web delivery.

Additionally, interactive exercises and assessments must be created in order to transform the information that exists into true instruction. Upon the advice of CLIENT NAME Pharmaceuticals, Raymond Karsan Associates (RKA) is prepared to deliver a Web-based virtual university to be used as an initial training tool and learner supplement for review of the procedures.

The program we are proposing will consist of the following:

- *A dual site design* to meet the needs of U.S. and international employees
- *Log-on and tracking features* for use by students and supervisors
- *Engaging tutorials* to cover concepts
- *Instructional interactive exercises* to provide practice and reinforcement
- *Post-tests* to provide certification of standard procedures competency

II. DESIGN AND TREATMENT

CLIENT NAME Clinical Research Network

Raymond Karsan Associates is proposing the development of a Web-based corporate university to meet the needs of CLIENT NAME's diverse employee base. This virtual university will be called the CLIENT NAME Clinical Research Network and it will enable employees to complete all required training and assessment remotely, using standard Web browsers and Intranet access.

This system will be private, secure, and accessible by CLIENT NAME students with access to CLIENT NAME's Intranet. The system will include features for

- Courses (tutorials)

- Assessment, certification, and tracking

- Communication between students and CLIENT NAME

Site Features

Log-In and Custom Content. This tool will permit students to log in and specify whether they are with U.S. Pharmaceuticals or CLIENT NAME Pharmaceuticals Group. Based on this information, different content can be delivered to the home page as well as in the tutorials.

Overview to Clinical Research Division. This section will introduce employees to CLIENT NAME's Clinical Research division as well as provide an overview of the site's functions, goals, and capabilities. This top level of structure will correspond to the site's home page.

Assessment Center. Learner will access this section to check their current status in the curriculum. This report will indicate

- Which courses they are certified in (flagged by achieving an 80 percent or better score on the module's post-test)

- The scores for each exam that was taken but for which mastery was not achieved

- Which courses they have begun but not yet completed

- Which courses have not yet been accessed

The student will be able to print this report for submission to a supervisor or for personal tracking purposes.

Courses. This is the primary gateway into the coursework contained in the Clinical Research site. These courses will be effectively organized following the tenets of instructional system design and will contain tutorials, interactive exercises, case studies, testing, and remediation. Students will be given the opportunity to test out of modules and will be automatically prompted to contact appropriate Clinical Research personnel whenever repeated errors occur.

Site Map. This section will provide a visual map of the site domains and learning modules.

Instructional Strategies and Tactics

Each specific lesson will be highly interactive and engaging. Lessons will be chunked into learning objective segments that will have the following structure:

- Introduce the topic and provide the benefit or relevance to the job (captures students' attention and increases retention)
- Specific instructions including document examples will teach the learner the specific procedure (such as how to conduct a prestudy visit and properly fill out the Prestudy Site Selection Report)
- Provide content (text-based) and ask the learner to perform an interactive exercise to improve comprehension and retention (such as by matching form purposes with proper form names)
- Provide feedback in the form of textual remediation and suggest additional practice if necessary

Standard Features

The interactive training site will include the following navigational options:

- Student log-in for score reporting, tracking, and certification
- Move back to the previous screen
- Move forward to the next screen
- Jump to the menu
- Exit on any page

Media

The software will use

- On-screen text and document recreation to emphasize key points
- Simple graphics, animation, and photos where appropriate

Student Time Estimate

The Web-based Clinical Monitoring course will consist of eight learning objectives as described in the provided source material. RKA estimates that each learning objective will include approximately fifteen screens of information and take approximately fifteen minutes of a student's time to complete. This brings the total learning time to complete the Clinical Monitoring course to two hours, including assessments.

III. TECHNICAL SPECIFICATIONS

Computers

The CLIENT NAME Clinical Research Network will be available via the CLIENT NAME Intranet. RKA assumes the following minimum server specifications:

- Windows NT, IIS
- Active Server Page technology
- Access database

  RKA also assumes that client computers will be equipped with the following:

- IE 4.0 or later
- Flash and Shockwave

Development Language

RKA has extensive experience with all of the major authoring tools and programming languages and can work with a specific tool upon client request.

It is likely that Dreamweaver will be used to generate the required code using HTML, DHTML, JavaScript, Flash, and Shockwave.

IV. COURSE SPECIFICATIONS

The following table provides specifications for the Clinical Monitoring module. RKA assumes that all other modules will have the same scope.

Item	Specification
# of lessons or modules	8 learning objectives
Screens/time per learning objective	15 screens/15 minutes
Total audio production	0
Total video production	0
Total screens/time in tutorial	120 screens/2 hours
Total # stock images and simple art	40
Total # on-line forms	Provided by CLIENT NAME
Music tracks, licenses	0

Preliminary learning objectives of this course are as follows:

- Explain the responsibilities of CLIENT NAME personnel and their agents during the monitoring of clinical trials.

- Describe prestudy activities used by CLIENT NAME to initiate clinical trial sites.

- State the purpose and requirements of the prestudy visit.

- Describe the activities of the site sign-up process.

- Outline the requirements for study initiation.

- Describe the key activities that should occur before, during, and after monitoring visits.

- Outline end-of-study close-out activities.

- Define the contents of trial master-study file and terms of archiving documents at the conclusion of a study.

V. WORK PROCESS

Overview

At RKA we pride ourselves on delivering projects on time, on budget, and at a level of quality that exceeds our client's expectations.

We consistently meet this goal by working within a carefully crafted project development framework. This framework is based on the classic ADDIE model in instructional systems design:

- Analysis
- Design
- Rapid prototype
- Development
- Implementation
- Evaluation (using Kirkpatrick's model)

RKA follows the classic steps for instructional systems design. A final list of project milestones will be developed prior to project launch. An overview of anticipated steps is as follows:

1. Project launch meeting
   - Confirm resources and schedule
   - Sign agreements
   - Identify roles and responsibilities
   - Review project bible

2. Design document
   - Create user interface and style guide
   - Develop detailed content outlines
   - Determine voice talent
   - Develop rapid prototype
   - Client sign-off required

3. Program development
   - Write scripts (client sign-off required)
   - Create artwork (client sign-off required)
   - Shoot and produce video (client presence required)
   - Record and produce audio (client presence required)
   - Programming

4. Review, quality control, revise
   - CLIENT NAME Pharmaceuticals Group will review and provide a single set of consolidated feedback.

- RKA will use Quality Assurance methodology to check for programming bugs and usability.
- RKA will revise all materials to reflect CLIENT NAME Pharmaceuticals Group feedback

5. Final draft delivery
  - Camera-ready duplication masters are delivered
  - Source code and raw media files delivered
  - Master CD-ROM delivered

6. Duplication and distribution
  - RKA will assist CLIENT NAME Pharmaceuticals Group with the packaging, duplication, and distribution of all materials if necessary.

7. Program Evaluation (RKA will assist with Kirpatrick's four levels)
  - Reaction (simple student satisfaction survey)
  - Learning (analysis of post-tests)
  - Transfer (observation sheet for managers)
  - Return on investment (analyze over instructor-led activities or projected versus actual sales results)

VI. SCHEDULE

A complete and detailed schedule will be developed during the analysis phase of the work process. A preliminary estimate is that the first module will require two months to complete.

The RKA project development process is highly collaborative with the client and there will be frequent project status and review meetings throughout the schedule.

VII. DELIVERABLES AND INVESTMENT ANALYSIS

RKA is making the following assumptions in order to estimate the scope of this project:
- Creation of the CLIENT NAME Clinical Research Network home page
- *2 hours* of training content for the Clinical Monitoring course

- Text and interactive exercises will drive the primary sequences
- Post-test corresponding to each course
- Printable score report or diploma upon completion

The following budget is based on the assumption that there will be a total of nine Web-based tutorials, all of similar size and scope as Clinical Monitoring.

Item	Fee
Clinical Monitoring WBT • Instructional design and writing • Graphic art • Programming • Quality control • Project management	$20,500
Clinical Research Network Home Page • Log-in • Overview • Assessment center • Course menu • Site map	$7,500

VIII. WHY CHOOSE RKA?

Overview

RKA's focus is innovative human resource solutions. We have twenty-two offices and more than four hundred employees. With an annual growth rate of 42.5 percent, RKA has placed on *Inc.*'s 500 list three years in a row (1994–1997), and RKA's CEO Rudy Karsan was named Entrepreneur of the Year (1997) by *Inc.* magazine.

RKA's TBT team is Princeton, New Jersey-based and is a nationally recognized leader in the development of interactive multimedia for training and education.

RKA's Awards and Distinctions

As a company we've been named for four consecutive years, most recently in October 1998, to the Inc. 500, a yearly list compiled by *Inc.* magazine of the fastest-growing private companies in the nation. RKA joins the prestigious company of Microsoft, Timberland, and Domino's Pizza, all of whom have been previously included on the list.

We're a two-time recipient of the **International Society for Performance Improvement's Award of Excellence.** Our most recent honor comes in the form of the 1998 Award of Excellence for an Instructional Intervention for our work on Bingham-Rodway Pharmaco's Virtual Oncology Center.

RKA's performance support team is proud of being a finalist in *Newmedia* magazine's **Invision Awards,** the TBT field's equivalent of an Oscar. Nominated for our work with Bingham-Rodway Pharmaco's in creating the Virtual Oncology Center, a CD-ROM-based training resource for sales representatives, we were finalists in the category of Best Simulation.

Further, we were a winner of the **American Society of Training and Development's Blue Ribbon Award for Instructional Technology** for our work on technical training for DuPont Pharma.

Publications

RKA and our clients are frequently showcased in leading industry publications. These have included the following:

- *CBT Solutions*
- *Corporate University Review*
- *Multimedia and Internet-Based Training*
- *Newspost*
- *Selling Power*
- *Training*
- *Training and Development*

Client List

RKA has more than one hundred clients worldwide. Satisfied clients include

- American Management Association
- Delta Airlines
- Du Pont Pharmaceuticals

- Glaxo Wellcome
- Merck
- Merrill Lynch
- Johnson & Johnson
- PR Newswire
- SmithKline Beecham
- The Coca-Cola Company

References

We strongly urge CLIENT NAME Pharmaceuticals Group to contact our references to hear firsthand about our dedication to customer service and our ability to exceed client expectations.

Reference 1

Contact info

Reference 2

Contact info

Reference 3

Contact info

APPENDIX C: MODEL POWERPOINT PRESENTATION

This PowerPoint slide show provides an overview of Web-based training (WBT). These slides, used selectively or as an entire presentation, can be used to educate senior executives about using the corporate Intranet to deliver training. You can use this presentation to educate your peers in training and information technology, too. It reviews the basics of the Internet and Web technology, discusses the rapid growth in WBT, and outlines some of the major issues to be considered when rolling out a WBT program.

Web-Based Training

An Overview

What Is the Internet?

- Worldwide network of thousands of computers operated by businesses, government, universities
- Started as DOD ARPA project in 1969
- Secure communications for war
- 1980s funding from National Science Foundation (NSF)
- Now commercially funded; Internic

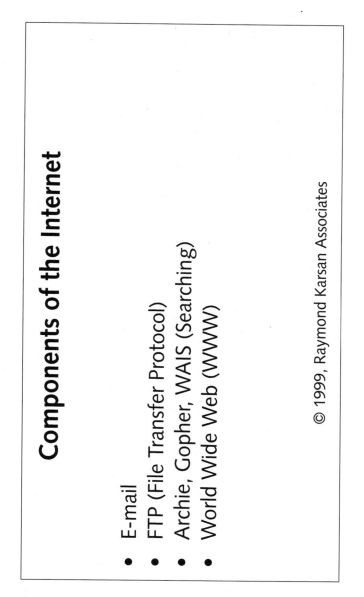

Components of the Internet

- E-mail
- FTP (File Transfer Protocol)
- Archie, Gopher, WAIS (Searching)
- World Wide Web (WWW)

© 1999, Raymond Karsan Associates

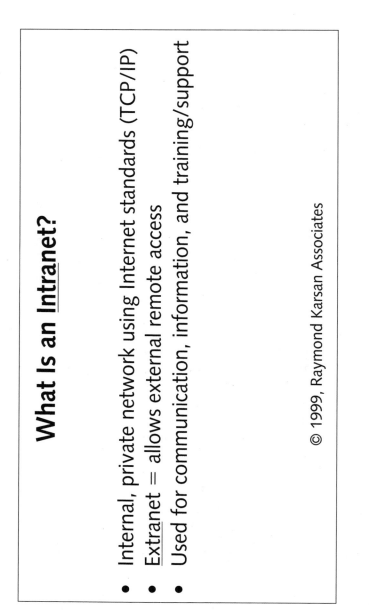

What Is an Intranet?

- Internal, private network using Internet standards (TCP/IP)
- Extranet = allows external remote access
- Used for communication, information, and training/support

© 1999, Raymond Karsan Associates

Bandwidth

- 9600, 14.4, 28.8, 33.6, 56 Kbps modems
- ISDN (128 Kbps)
- T1 (1.5 Mbps)
- T3 (45 Mbps)
- Cable Modems (10 Mbps)
- ADSL (1.5–9 Mbps receive)
- Satellite: DirecPC, Teledesic (400 Kbps–3 Mbps)

© 1999, Raymond Karsan Associates

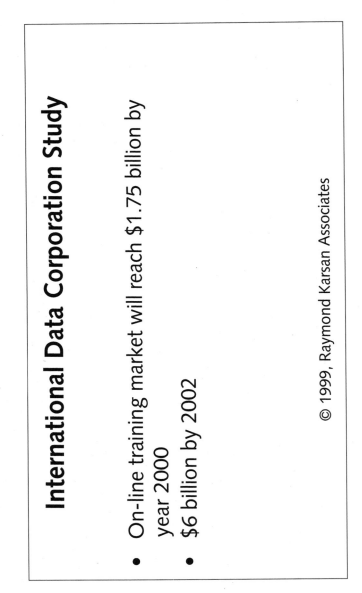

International Data Corporation Study

- On-line training market will reach $1.75 billion by year 2000
- $6 billion by 2002

© 1999, Raymond Karsan Associates

Benefits of WBT

Benefits over instructor-led training:

- Students view anytime, at own pace
- Reduces costs for travel, lodging, instructors
- Consistent presentation
- Reduces learning time
- Increases retention

© 1999, Raymond Karsan Associates

Benefits of WBT

Benefits over CBT/CD-ROM:

- Accessible 24 hours a day, worldwide
- Easy development languages
- Universal platforms (MAC, Windows)
- Easy setup (modem, browser)
- Content is easily updated; JIT
- Affordable

© 1999, Raymond Karsan Associates

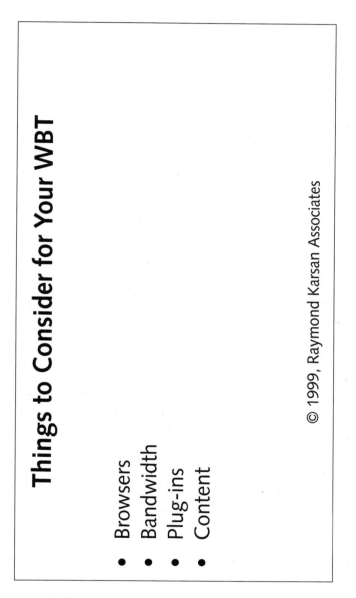

Things to Consider for Your WBT

- Browsers
- Bandwidth
- Plug-ins
- Content

© 1999, Raymond Karsan Associates

295

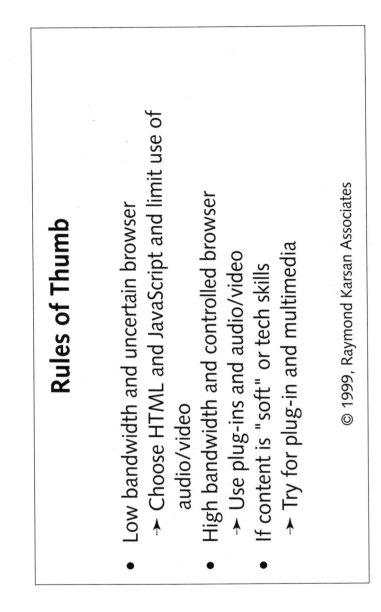

Rules of Thumb

- Low bandwidth and uncertain browser
  - ↗ Choose HTML and JavaScript and limit use of audio/video
- High bandwidth and controlled browser
  - ↗ Use plug-ins and audio/video
- If content is "soft" or tech skills
  - ↗ Try for plug-in and multimedia

© 1999, Raymond Karsan Associates

Sales Training Intranet

What is it?

- Browser-based access to information
- Sales support network sits on a "server" computer
- Private Intranet, not public Internet

© 1999, Raymond Karsan Associates

Sales Training Intranets

How are they used?

- Provide communication among representatives, managers, trainers, and others
- Provide on-line reference materials
- Provide tutorials
- Provide automated testing and assessment and tracking

© 1999, Raymond Karsan Associates

Is It Training?

- Interactivity is the key to learning results!
- Are you on-line publishing or on-line training? There are different types of WBT applications.....

© 1999, Raymond Karsan Associates

The Five Levels of WBT

- Level 1: Communication
- Level 2: Reference
- Level 3: Testing and assessment
- Level 4: Distribution of tutorials
- Level 5: Delivery of tutorials

© 1999, Raymond Karsan Associates

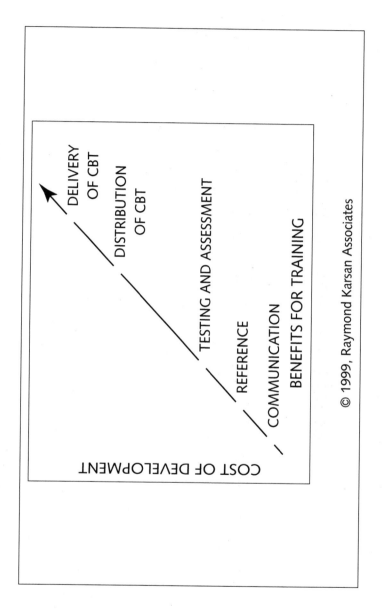

© 1999, Raymond Karsan Associates

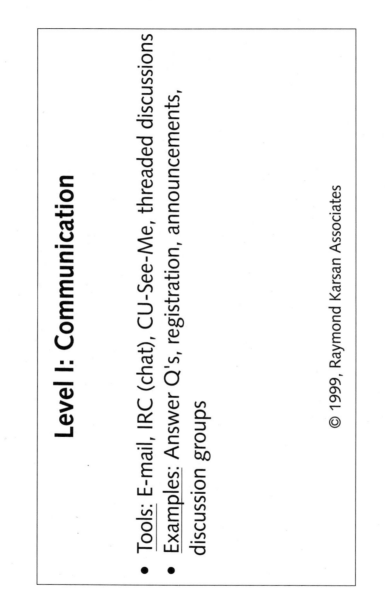

Level I: Communication

- <u>Tools:</u> E-mail, IRC (chat), CU-See-Me, threaded discussions
- <u>Examples:</u> Answer Q's, registration, announcements, discussion groups

© 1999, Raymond Karsan Associates

Level II: **Reference**

- <u>Tools</u>: HTML, FrontPage, PageMill, NetObjects
- <u>Examples</u>: Course catalogs, schedules, workbooks, manuals

© 1999, Raymond Karsan Associates

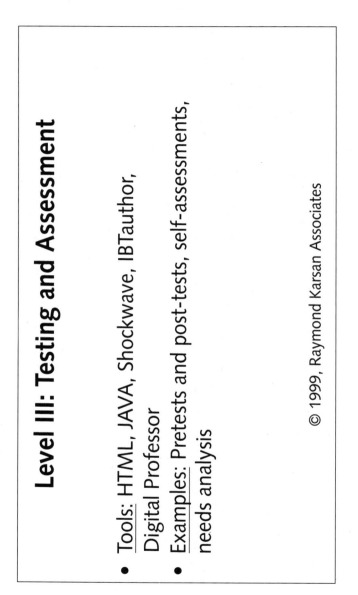

Level III: Testing and Assessment

- <u>Tools</u>: HTML, JAVA, Shockwave, IBTauthor, Digital Professor
- <u>Examples</u>: Pretests and post-tests, self-assessments, needs analysis

© 1999, Raymond Karsan Associates

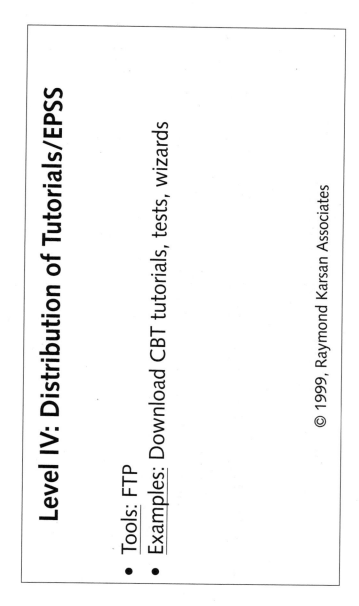

Level IV: Distribution of Tutorials/EPSS

- Tools: FTP
- Examples: Download CBT tutorials, tests, wizards

© 1999, Raymond Karsan Associates

305

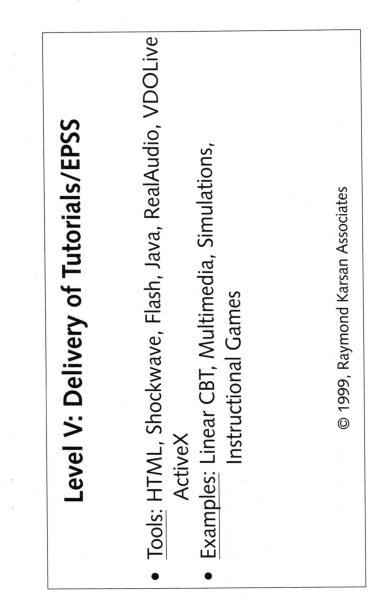

Level V: Delivery of Tutorials/EPSS

- Tools: HTML, Shockwave, Flash, Java, RealAudio, VDOLive ActiveX

- Examples: Linear CBT, Multimedia, Simulations, Instructional Games

© 1999, Raymond Karsan Associates

Instructional Design Challenge

- Old design applied to new media
- The power of the Web and Web databases
- Think of learning moments, not course hours!

© 1999, Raymond Karsan Associates

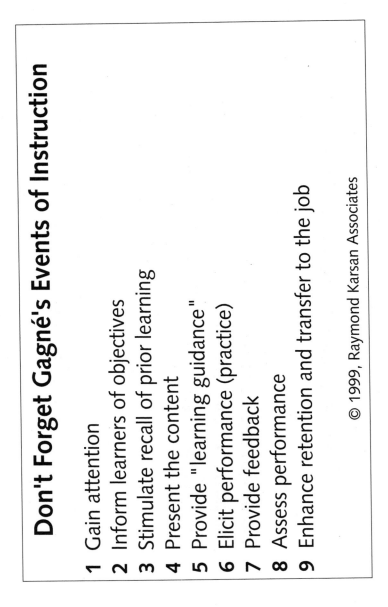

Don't Forget Gagné's Events of Instruction

1 Gain attention
2 Inform learners of objectives
3 Stimulate recall of prior learning
4 Present the content
5 Provide "learning guidance"
6 Elicit performance (practice)
7 Provide feedback
8 Assess performance
9 Enhance retention and transfer to the job

© 1999, Raymond Karsan Associates

Lessons Learned in the Real World

1 Information (on-line publishing) is *not* an effective method for adult learning. Instruction *is* (remember Gagné's events of learning).

2 Video and audio *still* don't play well on low-bandwidth connections—don't try it if you have no control over student computers.

3 Plug-ins (such as Shockwave and Flash) are great tools, *if* you can control student computers.

4 Threaded discussions seem to work better than chat rooms.

5 Assessment, tracking, and flexible objects are the wave of the future.

© 1999, Raymond Karsan Associates

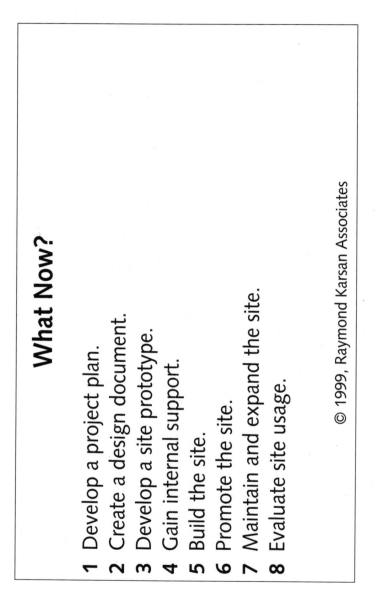

What Now?

1 Develop a project plan.
2 Create a design document.
3 Develop a site prototype.
4 Gain internal support.
5 Build the site.
6 Promote the site.
7 Maintain and expand the site.
8 Evaluate site usage.

© 1999, Raymond Karsan Associates

For more info on the Web...

- www.masie.com
- www.multimediatraining.com
- www.tbtsupersite.com
- www.webbasedtraining.com

© 1999, Raymond Karsan Associates

311

APPENDIX D: COST-BENEFIT WORKSHEETS

These blank worksheets can be photocopied and used to measure the costs and benefits of a proposed or completed TBT program. Measurements include cost savings of TBT versus instructor-led training, break-even analysis, cost-benefit ratio, and return on investment. Chapter Six provides step-by-step instructions and a detailed example for completing these forms.

Phase One: Assumptions	
Item	Assumptions
1.1 Life span of course	
1.2 Total # of students over life of course	
1.3 Total hours of training, measured in ILT	
1.4 Estimated reduction in seat-time for TBT	
1.5 Burdened compensation for one instructor	
1.6 Burdened compensation for one student	

Phase Two: Design and Development		
Item	Instructor-Led Training (ILT)	Technology-Based Training (TBT)
2.1 Create courseware		
2.2 Train the Trainer		
Phase 2 Total		

Phase Three: Delivery		
Item	**Instructor-Led Training (ILT)**	**Technology-Based Training (TBT)**
3.1 # of ILT sessions		

3.2   Instructor costs
     • Prep and travel time
     • Time delivering training
     • Travel costs		

3.3   Student costs
     • Time in training
     • Opportunity cost
     • Travel costs		

3.4   Location fees
     • Room rentals
     • Shipping
     • Storage		

3.5   Equipment fees
     • Projectors
     • Shipping
     • Storage		

3.6   Student materials
     • Workshop handouts
     • CD's
     • Miscellaneous		

Delivery Total		

Phase Four: Administration and Maintenance

Item	Instructor-Led Training (ILT)	Technology-Based Training (TBT)
4.1 Tracking • Student registration • Testing • Certificates		
4.2 Technical support		
4.3 Updates to content		
4.4 Updates to technology		
Final Administration Total		

Phase Five: Summary

Item	Instructor-Led Training (ILT)	Technology-Based Training (TBT)
Design and development		
Delivery		
Administration and maintenance		
Final Total		

Total Cost Savings of TBT

Item
Instructor-led Costs − Technology Training Costs = Total Cost Savings
Total Savings =

Break-Even Analysis for Technology-Based Training	
Step 1	Per-Student Delivery Cost of Technology-Based Training (TBT) = Total TBT Delivery Costs ÷ Total Number of Students
Step 2	Per-Student Delivery Cost of Instructor-Led Training (ILT) = Total ILT Delivery Costs ÷ Total Number of Students
Step 3	Break-Even Point = $$\frac{\text{Total TBT Development Costs} - \text{Total ILT Development Costs}}{\text{Per-Student ILT Costs} - \text{Per-Student TBT Costs}}$$
Step 1	Per-Student TBT =
Step 2	Per-Student ILT =
Step 3	**Break Even =**

Cost-Benefit Ratio
Financial Benefits ÷ Total Cost of Training = Cost-Benefit Ratio
Cost-Benefit Ratio =

Return on Investment
(Total Benefits − Total Costs) ÷ Total Costs × 100
ROI =

APPENDIX E: TRAINING AND MULTIMEDIA ASSOCIATIONS

Technology-based training is a field the fuses the disciplines of multimedia and Internet technologies with training and adult learning. The following organizations are excellent resources for learning more about both sides of this industry.

American Society for Training and Development (ASTD)

1640 King Street
Box 1443
Alexandria, VA 22313-2043 USA
Phone: 703-683-8100
Web: www.astd.org

British Interactive Multimedia Association (BIMA)

5–6 Clipstone Street
London, England W1P 7EB
Phone: 44 (0) 171 436 8250
Web: www.bima.co.uk

EDUCAUSE

1112 16th Street NW, Suite 600
Washington, DC 20036-4822 USA
Phone: 202-872-4200
Web: www.educause.edu

International Society for Performance Improvement (ISPI)

1300 L Street NW, no. 1250
Washington, DC 20005 USA
Phone: 202-408-7969
Web: www.ispi.org

Society for Applied Learning Technology (SALT)

50 Culpepper Street
Warrenton, VA 20186 USA
Phone: 540-347-0055
Web: www.salt.org

APPENDIX F: INTERNET RESOURCES FOR TRAINERS

The Internet is the best place to obtain up-to-date, detailed information on technology-based training. In addition to the Web sites of the training and multimedia associations listed in Appendix E, the following Web sites are excellent sources for current information.

Brandon Hall Resources

www.brandon-hall.com

This Web site is an excellent companion site to the *Multimedia and Internet-Based Training* newsletter published by industry guru Brandon Hall. The Web site provides independent information and reviews of the latest trends and developments in the field of TBT.

Masie Center

www.masie.com

The Masie Center is an international think tank dedicated to exploring the intersection of learning and technology. This Web site provides a wealth of articles, resources, and information about upcoming industry events.

TBT Supersite (Raymond Karsan Associates)

www.tbtsupersite.com

This site, sponsored by Raymond Karsan Associates, provides a vast amount of tutorials, tools, demos, and information on the use of educational CD-ROMs and Web-based training.

Training Supersite (Lakewood Publications)

www.trainingsupersite.com

Lakewood Publications and dozens of other companies have partnered to create this virtual mall for general training topics. Topic domains include publications, job banks, a speakers bureau, and vendor directories.

Web-Based Training Information Center

www.webbasedtraining.com

This site is a nonprofit resource for those interested in developing and delivering Web-based training, on-line learning, or distance education. You will find a WBT primer, surveys, discussion forums, and resource links.

APPENDIX G:
SAMPLES OF WEB-BASED TRAINING

Perhaps the best way to learn about options in Web-based training, and to see examples (both good and bad) of on-line instructional design, is to access many of the free demonstrations available on the Internet. Following is a list of some of the more popular WBT programs.

Arthur Andersen Virtual Learning Network	www.aavln.com
Digital Think	www.digitalthink.com
Learn2	www.learn2.com
McGraw Hill Online Learning	www.mhonlinelearning.com
RKA Online Learning Center	www.raymondkarsan.com
UOL Publishing	www.uol.com
Ziff Davis University	www.zdu.com

This sample design document is an example of a brief blueprint for a CD-ROM-based training program. Note that the instructional designer describes clearly the goals of the program and the intended audience. Both the creative metaphor and the structure of the content are reviewed. Technical requirements are laid out in great detail, which will reduce the likelihood of technology problems later in the process.

NEW PHARMACEUTICAL PRODUCT LEARNING SYSTEM

Design Document

March 15, 1999

Version 1.0

Prepared for:

_____

NAME

Product Manager

COMPANY

Prepared by:

_____

Michael Boudreau,

Instructional Designer

Andy Howe,
Project Manager

Raymond Karsan Associates

TABLE OF CONTENTS

I. WHAT IS A DESIGN DOCUMENT?

This report is the design document for the PRODUCT® Learning System.

The design document serves as the blueprint for a project. It specifies the content, look and feel, and instructional design elements of the program. It includes the following sections:

- Program overview

- Intended audience

- Instructional design

- Program navigation and visual treatment

- Program content

- Program features

Decisions about these elements should be made in the design document phase.

II. PROGRAM OVERVIEW

Description

The PRODUCT® Learning System is a self-administered CD-ROM-based program for training COMPANY field sales representatives in selling PRODUCT® for the treatment of DISEASE. The program consists of the following elements:

- Interactive multimedia tutorials

- Case studies

- Sales call simulation

- Self-assessment Jeopardy-style game

- Glossary

- Final assessment (post-test)

The program will be implemented on one CD-ROM and will require one to two hours for a trainee to complete.

Goals

The goal of the PRODUCT® Learning System is to prepare COMPANY sales representative with a solid background in

- DISEASE, including its biological basis, its prevalence, and how it differs from other disorders
- Treatment of DISEASE, including diagnosis and psychotherapeutic and pharmacological interventions
- Clinical studies supporting the safety and efficacy of PRODUCT® for the treatment of DISEASE
- Selling PRODUCT® for the treatment of DISEASE, including the sales environment, key targets for sales promotion, and issue handling

The marketing imperatives of creating the market and convincing the market are to be stressed throughout.

Audience

The PRODUCT® Learning System is intended for COMPANY field sales representatives and other personnel who may require background on this new indication for PRODUCT®.

Content

Content of the CD-ROM PRODUCT® Learning System will be based on the print-based PRODUCT training manual and other materials supplied by COMPANY.

III. CREATIVE DESIGN

User Interface

The theme of the program is "COMPANY Mental Health Clinic," and the user interface will incorporate elements of a typical mental health care facility.

The program will begin with an engaging "splash screen" using sound and animation to capture the user's attention. Next, an animated fly-in sequence will show the mental health clinic as if seen from an airplane. The fly-in will bring users to the clinic entrance.

From the entrance, users will enter the clinic lobby. The lobby guide will serve as the program's main menu. Six doorways will lead off from the lobby to the various parts of the clinic where users can access the program information and take part in the interactive exercises. The doorways will be labeled as follows:

- Auditorium: accesses information about DISEASE and its treatment
- Library: accesses the glossary
- Patient ward: accesses the patient case studies
- Physicians' offices: accesses the simulated sales call
- Physicians' lounge: accesses the Jeopardy game
- Test center: accesses the final assessment

The basic structure of the program is summarized in the flow chart in Figure H.1.

IV. SCREEN DESIGN AND VISUAL TREATMENT

The program is implemented with a number of screen designs. [Author's note: These screens have been omitted for space and confidentiality reasons.]

V. INSTRUCTIONAL DESIGN

A variety of instructional techniques and interactive devices will be integrated into the PRODUCT® Learning System CD-ROM. Through the following combination of tutorials and exercises, the learner will gain an overall understanding of the content and will increase his ability to anticipate objections and handle real-world situations.

Multimedia Tutorials

Multimedia tutorials presenting key content information and instructions on the use of PRODUCT® in the treatment of DISEASE will be found in the clinic's auditorium. The information will be presented using a classic instructional systems design approach of linear interactive tutorials and will make maximum use of

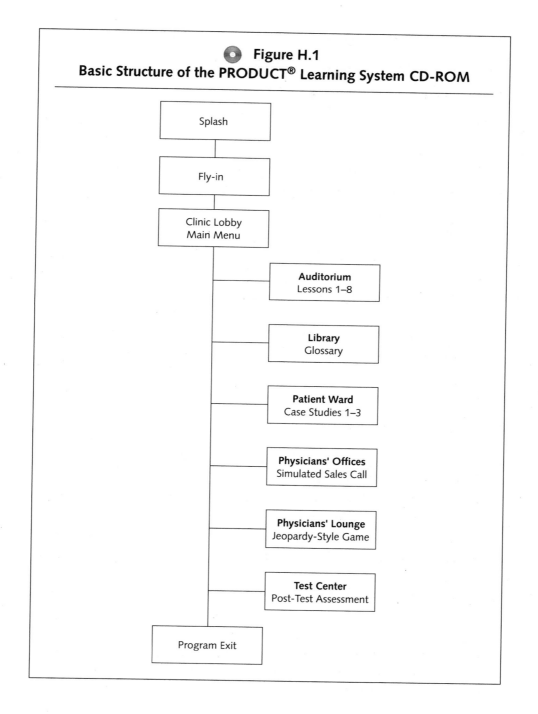

Figure H.1
Basic Structure of the PRODUCT® Learning System CD-ROM

Splash

Fly-in

Clinic Lobby
Main Menu

Auditorium
Lessons 1–8

Library
Glossary

Patient Ward
Case Studies 1–3

Physicians' Offices
Simulated Sales Call

Physicians' Lounge
Jeopardy-Style Game

Test Center
Post-Test Assessment

Program Exit

multimedia, including the following:

- On-screen text for key points
- Audio narration as the primary learning modality
- Graphics, animation, and photographs where appropriate
- High-end, three-dimensional animations for mechanism of action

The tutorials will be structured as a series of lessons, each including learning objectives, interactive presentation screens, and review questions.

Case Studies

Patient case studies will be accessed in the patient ward. The ward will contain three exam rooms, each with a different case, where the user can explore treatment from three perspectives: patient, physician, and the significance of the case to PRODUCT® sales. The case studies will use video segments of the patients and doctor, and voice-over narration to emphasize and expand on key points. All patient and physician video will be taken from the existing case studies CD-ROM.

Simulations

The sales call simulation will occur in the doctor's office and will be used to reinforce product knowledge and objection handling. The simulation will be designed to address and overcome the most common resistance issues physicians have about prescribing PRODUCT® for DISEASE. The sales call will use video to show the interaction between the physician and the sales representative.

Each time the physician raises an issue, three responses will be presented in text for the user to choose from. When the user selects a response, a sales coach will appear on video. If the user does not choose the most appropriate response, feedback will be provided instructing the user to try again. When the user chooses the most appropriate response, the sales coach will confirm the correct choice and explain why it is the most appropriate response. A representative demonstrating the response will then be shown on video. After seeing the most appropriate response, the learner may choose the other responses to see the feedback associated with them or may go on to the next issue.

Glossary

Users will be able to access an interactive glossary in the clinic library. The glossary will provide definitions and pronunciations of as many as 150 key terms. The glossary screen will contain the following:

- Word list
- Pronunciation button
- Alphabet menu
- Search field
- Definition box
- Close button

Clicking on a word in the word list will give the definition in the text box. Clicking on the letters in the alphabet menu will scroll the word list to words beginning with that letter. Clicking on the pronunciation button will give an audio pronunciation of a word selected in the word list. Clicking in the search field will allow the learner to search the word list for a particular term. Clicking the close button will takes the learner back to the screen from which the glossary was accessed.

The glossary will also be accessed via hyperlinks in the text of the lessons. In this case, the glossary screen will open with the term selected in the word list and defined in the definition box.

Review Game

The Jeopardy review game will take place in the physicians' lounge. The game will provide a fun and engaging way for users to assess their mastery of the program material before taking the final exam. Game features will include the following:

- A Jeopardy-style game set with players and host
- Animated player characters
- Two rounds of play, twenty questions per round
- Questions such as multiple choice, true or false, and fill-in
- Support for one, two, or three players
- Final score, which may be printed or saved to disk

Final Assessment

The user will take the final assessment exam in the clinic's test center. The exam will include twenty-five multiple-choice questions and a certificate that the user can print upon successful completion. This exam will serve as a self-assessment for the user.

VI. PROGRAM NAVIGATION

The PRODUCT® Learning System will include the following navigation devices and features.

The basic navigation buttons will be

- *Back.* This will take the user back to the previous screen, where previous is defined as the previous screen in the tutorial or the previous review question.

- *Exit.* This button will display a dialog box confirming the user's decision to quit the program. If the user clicks on yes, the program will exit. Clicking on no will close the dialog box.

- *Glossary.* Clicking on this button will accesses the glossary screen.

Buttons that may be on some screens include

- *Replay.* Clicking on this button will replay the audio or video associated with the window or screen.

- *Close.* This button will close a pop-up window.

VII. PROGRAM CONTENT

Content Outline by Lesson

Lesson 1: Anxiety Disorders
Definition of anxiety disorders
Anxiety symptoms:

- Motor tension

- Autonomic hyperactivity

- Vigilance and scanning

Lesson 2: Disease Overview
American Psychiatric Association DSM-IV criteria for diagnosis of DISEASE
Hallmark symptoms:

- Fear of scrutiny by others
- Persistent fear of performance situations in which humiliation may occur
- Avoidance of feared situations

Common situations that precipitate DISEASE
Somatic symptoms

- Palpitations, sweating, muscle tension, trembling, dry mouth, and so on

Lesson 3: Prevalence of DISEASE

Lesson 4: Biological Basis of DISEASE (pathophysiology)
Innate anxiety network (IAN)

- Amygdala
- Periqueductal grey area
- Dorsal raphe
- Locus coeruleus
- Hypothalamus

Corticosteroids
Autonomic system
Neurotransmitter systems

- Adrenergic
- Serotonergic
- Dopaminergic

Dysregulation Hypothesis

Lesson 5: Epidemiology
Genetic predisposition
Early developmental stessors
Traumatic experiences

Cultural influences

Comorbidity

Lesson 6: Emotional and Societal Impact

DISEASE sufferers tend to be single and socially isolated

Early onset of DISEASE contributes to many long-term consequences

Detrimental effect on job performance

DISEASE patients have a higher incidence of health care utilization than non-DISEASE patient

High incidence of comorbid conditions

Quality of life issues

Lesson 7: Diagnosing DISEASE

Poorly diagnosed

- Under recognition by primary care physicians (PCPs)

- Lack of patient awareness that DISEASE is disease with biological origin

Keys to improved diagnosis

- Inform patients that DISEASE is biologically based disease

- Educate PCPs and psychiatrists to recognize DISEASE as medical illness

- Inform PCPs and patients that DISEASE can be effectively treated

Diagnostic assessment tools

- Structured diagnostic interview

- Behavioral assessment

- Cognitive assessment

- Self-rating questionnaires

  Social Phobia Inventory (SPIN)

  Mini International Neuropsychiatric Interview (MINI)

  Brief Social Phobia Scale (BSPS)

  Social Phobia and Anxiety Inventory (SPAI)

Clinical Rating Scales/Severity Assessment Tools

- Liebowitz Social Anxiety Scale (LSAS)

- Clinical Global Impression Scale (CGI)

Physician cues

- "Does being the center of attention make you uncomfortable?"
- "When you're around people, do you feel nervous, self-conscious, or uncomfortable?"

Lesson 8: Treatment Options
Psychotherapeutic interventions

- Exposure procedures (EP)
- Social effectiveness therapy (SET)
- Cognitive-behavior therapy (CBT)
- Cognitive-behavior group therapy (CBGT)

Pharmacologic interventions

- Monoamine oxidase inhibitors (MAOIs)
- Benzodiazepines
- Adrenergic blockers
- Buspirone
- Selective serotonin reuptake inhibitors

Pivotal PRODUCT clinical studies

- Other SSRI study findings

VIII. TECHNICAL SPECIFICATIONS

Computers

Based on information provided by COMPANY, the PRODUCT Learning System program will be developed to operate within the following minimum technical specifications:

- Pentium 200 MHz
- Windows NT 4.0 operating system

- Video for Windows driver
- SoundBlaster-compatible soundcard
- 64 MB RAM
- 800 × 600 screen resolution, 16–bit color
- 20x CD-ROM drive
- 5 MG free hard-drive space

Development Tools and Acquisition Formats

The following development tools will be used to create all elements for the program.

Macromedia Director 7.0 will be the primary authoring tool for combining the media assets into a 32–bit Windows application. PrintOmatic, a third-party extra, will likely be used for printing completion certificates.

Adobe PhotoShop will be the primary graphics creation tool. Graphics will be exported from layered photoshop files into PICT files for use within director.

Media 100, a nonlinear video system, will be used to digitize and edit all video and audio to ensure the highest quality.

Media Cleaner Pro 3.1 will be used to encode all digital video.

Sound Forge will be used to process audio.

DVC Pro, digital videotape and recording equipment, will be used for all video and audio acquisition.

Setup Factory will be used to create the install program.

Miscellaneous Technical Notes

The vast majority of program content will reside on the CD-ROM, but a small executable, some director extras, and database components will reside on the user's hard drive.

Video will be compressed using the Video for Windows (AVI) format and optimized to run smoothly on the delivery platforms.

APPENDIX I: SAMPLE SCRIPT

This partial script is an example taken from a much larger script for a satellite communications Web-based training program. The header information includes client and project information, as well as script page numbers.

The *screen* parameter indicates the numerical label given to this particular screen, or frame, of the program. Generally the numbering of screens is in increments of ten, so future screen additions can be added easily without having to renumber the entire document.

The *graphics* parameter is a text description of any required graphical images. In a storyboard format, a sketch or stock image might be included to provide a visual example.

The *screen text* parameter indicates specifically the words that will appear on this particular screen.

The *notes* parameter provides direction to the entire development team about any special animation, navigation, or other special instructions.

If this were a script for a multimedia CD-ROM, additional parameters would include *audio voice-over* and *video.*

SCREEN: **0010**

Graphics: Montage of satellite images

Screen Text:

> **Module 3: The Satellite Value Proposition**
> *(Approximate time needed to complete this module: 15 minutes)*
>
> INTRODUCTION:
>
> More than any other event of the space age, satellite communications has probably had the greatest effect on the average person.
>
> By gaining a clearer picture of satellite communications you will have a better understanding of how the CLIENT system works, its value to our customers, and its advantages over our competitors in the GMPS industry.
>
> *Click the forward arrow to begin* ➤

Notes: Bold words appear in the glossary.

SCREEN: **0020**

Graphics: No images, but use graphical check boxes for objectives

Screen Text:

Module 3: The Satellite Value Proposition

LEARNING OBJECTIVES:

After completing this module, you should be able to:

☐ **Give a brief history of mobile satellite communications**   —0030
☐ **Define Mobile Satellite Services (MSS) and describe its uses**   —0040
☐ **Describe the main components of an MSS**   —0050

Click on each learning objective to go directly to that section.

Objectives that you have already completed are indicated by a check mark ✓.

When you have completed all of the objectives, you can test your knowledge by taking this quiz.

☐ **Module 3 Quiz**

Notes:

SCREEN: **0030**

Graphics: CLIENT's logo and satellite photos? Some kind of graphic representing the CLIENT system

Screen Text:

> **A BRIEF HISTORY OF SATELLITE COMMUNICATIONS:**
> Page 1 of 4
>
> CLIENT's global communication service uses satellite technology to provide cost-effective global communications. A satellite is defined as a man-made body put into orbit around the earth. Communication satellites act as relay stations that circle the earth, receiving and transmitting signals.

Notes:

SCREEN: **0031**

Graphics: Possible NASA logo, picture of Sputnik, COMSAT logo? Create a
time line with rollovers showing Sputnik launch in 1957,
communications acts.

Screen Text:

A BRIEF HISTORY OF SATELLITE COMMUNICATIONS:
Page 2 of 4

NASA and several telecommunications companies including AT&T and Hughes
Aircraft Corporation helped develop satellite communication technology during the
early 1960s. The Communications Satellite Corporation (COMSAT) and the
International Telecommunications Satellite Service (INTELSAT) used this technology
to create the first global satellite communications network in 1969.

Early satellite communications included distribution of television signals, telephone
circuits, and government use.

Notes:

SCREEN: **0032**

Graphics: Picture montage of INMARSAT

Screen Text:

> **A BRIEF HISTORY OF SATELLITE COMMUNICATIONS:**
> Page 3 of 4
>
> Over time, the technology improved and equipment became smaller and more powerful, which allowed for the development of mobile satellite services that didn't rely on giant earth stations with 100-foot reflector dishes.
>
> In 1979, the UN International Maritime Organization sponsored the establishment of the International Maritime Satellite Organization (INMARSAT) to provide telephone service to ships at sea. INMARSAT was the world's first global mobile satellite operator.
>
> INMARSAT would eventually form CLIENT in 1995 to help meet the growing need for mobile global telecommunications services.

Notes:

SCREEN: **0034**

Graphics: Question mark and check mark graphic

Screen Text:

> **A BRIEF HISTORY OF SATELLITE COMMUNICATIONS:**
> Page 4 of 4
>
> *Self-Check!*
>
> Which organization was the first to provide global <u>mobile</u> satellite communications?
> A) NASA
> B) COMSAT
> C) INMARSAT
> D) INTELSAT
> E) AT&T
> *(Click the best answer)*

> *Correct Feedback:*
>
> That's correct: INMARSAT began providing maritime service in 1979.

> *Incorrect Feedback:*
>
> Although that organization was involved in early satellite communications,
> that's not the correct answer. Try again.

Notes: Clicking next from the feedback screen returns you to screen 0020.

GLOSSARY

adaptive

Adaptive training programs adapt themselves to the skill level or preferences of the learner.

ADDIE model

Classic model of an instructional system design process that includes the steps analysis, design, development, implementation, and evaluation, from which the acronym is taken.

adult learning theory

Principles and practices of providing instruction to the adult learner. Primarily concerned with an adult's well-defined learning goals, wealth of experience, and ability and desire to direct his or her own learning. See ANDRAGOGY.

AI

See ARTIFICIAL INTELLIGENCE.

alpha version

An alpha version of a program, also known as a *pilot version,* can be tested for over-all usability and training effectiveness.

analysis

The first step in the classic ADDIE model of instructional system design. In the analysis phase the audience is defined and performance improvement needs are identified.

andragogy

The opposite of PEDAGOGY. A European term introduced into the English vocabulary by Malcolm Knowles, it is the art and science of helping adults learn. A prime contributor to most theories of adult learning, andragogy as set out by Knowles emphasizes adults' capabilities to direct and motivate themselves, utilize past knowledge to assist learning, and evaluate the contents of training for relevance and quality.

animation

The rapid sequential presentation of slightly differing graphics to create the illusion of motion. Animation can have greater purpose than a static visual in illustrating a process, but it requires more information to be processed by the computer and thus higher bandwidth. Compare to AUDIO, VIDEO, TEXT, and GRAPHIC.

applet

A small program that runs on the Internet or an Intranet, written in the programming language known as *Java*.

application

Any stand-alone computer program.

ARCS model

A theory of adult learner motivation developed by Kellar that details four criteria to be met by a training product: gain learner *attention,* describe the training's *relevance,* instill *confidence* in the learner that the training can be successfully completed, and leave the learner *satisfied* after a learning goal has been achieved.

artificial intelligence

The range of technologies that allow computer systems to perform complex functions mirroring the workings of the human mind. Gathering and structuring knowledge, problem solving, and processing a natural language are activities that can be carried out by an artificially intelligent system.

asynchronous training

Training that is self-paced. A learning program that does not require the student and instructor to participate at the same time.

attitude

A disposition toward a certain behavior. Psychological theories hold that attitudes are revealed by examining behaviors, and shaping attitudes can in turn influence behaviors.

audience

The intended end-user population of a training product. Careful consideration of audience factors such as learning styles, level of education, preferences, background, and job responsibilities helps create more successful TBT.

audio

The medium of delivering information to be processed by a learner's ears. Compare to TEXT, VIDEO, GRAPHIC, and ANIMATION.

authoring

Similar to *programming*, developers assemble discrete media components using a tool called an AUTHORING SYSTEM.

authoring system

A program, such as Macromedia Authorware, designed for use by a noncomputer expert to create training products. An authoring system does not require programming knowledge or skill to operate. Selection of an authoring system largely influences and is influenced by the intended features of a training product.

bandwidth

The measure of the amount of information that can flow through an information channel. Commonly measured in bits per second. Modem connection to an Internet server is a typical example of a low-bandwidth connection; an Ethernet connection within a LAN is an example of a high-bandwidth connection.

baud

A measure of the quantity of information transmitted on a communication line; largely replaced by the use of bits-per-second.

BBS

See BULLETIN BOARD SYSTEM.

behavior

An action or set of actions performed by a person under specified circumstances that reveals some skill, knowledge, or attitude. Training seeks to increase desirable behaviors and eliminate undesirable ones. Also, one of the three components of a proper learning objective as outlined by Robert Mager.

benchmark

A standard of reference used for comparison. The performance of a learner is measured against a benchmark such as the performance of an expert. The performance of a TBT product is measured against a benchmark such as the training procedures it replaces.

beta test

An important function of quality control and one of the last steps before release of a software product. Beta testing involves the use of a product by selected users to create a formal documentation of content errors, software bugs, usability, level of engagement, and other factors.

binary

Data made up of only two values, 0 or 1, is considered binary. Files such as pictures or programs are binary files. To send such a binary file via e-mail, it must be coded into text by the sender and decoded back into a binary form by the receiver.

bit

The elementary constituent of digital information, the value of which can take only the forms 0 or 1. Bits are often measured by adding prefixes to signify a value. One kilobit contains approximately a thousand bits; one megabit contains approximately a million bits; one gigabit contains approximately one billion bits.

bits-per-second (bps)

A measure of the speed of the transmission of information over a communication line; often confused with BAUD.

Bloom's Taxonomy

A hierarchical ordering of affective and cognitive learning outcomes developed by Benjamin Bloom.

branching

A tutorial structure that progresses through material in a path that depends on the learner's response to questions.

browser

Also called a Web browser. A program used to access the text, graphic, audio, video, and animation elements of the Internet and Intranets. Netscape Navigator and Microsoft Internet Explorer are the most commonly used browsers.

bulletin board system

Also known as BBS. The computer equivalent of a public note board, messages can be posted to a BBS for viewing by other users and other computers. A BBS is often called a *threaded discussion.*

byte

A word made up of eight bits of information. One byte is the amount of information required to represent one character.

CBE

See COMPUTER-BASED EDUCATION.

CBL

See COMPUTER-BASED LEARNING.

CBT

See COMPUTER-BASED TRAINING.

CD-ROM

Compact disc–read only memory. An optical disc recorded on and read by a laser; used to store large quantities of information. One CD-ROM has 650 megabytes of storage capacity.

chunking

The process of separating learning materials into brief sections in order to improve learner comprehension and retention.

clip media

Preexisting pictures, audio files, or videos clips that can be "clipped" out and pasted directly into a computer program.

CMI

See COMPUTER-MANAGED INSTRUCTION.

cognitive loading

The process of placing elements into a person's short-term memory.

collaborative learning

Learning through the exchange and sharing of information and opinions among a peer group. Computers excel in mediating collaborative learning for geographically dispersed groups.

compression

A technique used to encode information so that it fits into a smaller package for easy storage or transmission.

computer-based education

A generic term for a computer program used by a learner to acquire knowledge or skills. See TECHNOLOGY-BASED TRAINING.

computer-based learning

A generic term for a computer program used by a learner to acquire knowledge or skills. See TECHNOLOGY-BASED TRAINING.

computer-based training

A generic term for a computer program used by a learner to acquire knowledge or skills. See TECHNOLOGY-BASED TRAINING.

computer-managed instruction

The components of TBT that provide assessment, student tracking, and personalized lesson plans.

computer-supported learning resources (CSLR)

The parts of a TBT product other than those that instruct, test, or track progress. These include glossaries, bulletin boards and chats, bibliographies, databases, and so forth.

condition statement

One of the three required parts of a properly composed learning objective. Circumstances under which the performance will be tested and materials that will be provided to the student are described in the condition statement.

cost avoidance

Component of analyzing competing business alternatives based on reducing or eliminating costs. Return-on-investment studies take account of cost avoidance in calculating final returns.

cost-benefit analysis

Method of analyzing competing business alternatives based on comparing total costs to total benefits. A proper cost-benefit analysis takes into account all benefits, including productivity, savings, and motivation, and weighs them against all costs, including expenditures, overheads, and lost opportunities.

course

Term used to describe the collection of elements that make up training on a given subject. Usually a course is broken up into lessons, sections, or modules; but *course* is sometimes used interchangeably with these terms.

course map

Usually a flowchart or other illustration, a course map details all of the component elements of a course.

criterion statement

One of the three required parts of a properly composed learning objective. The performance level that must be achieved by the student along with a concrete measurement for the performance level are described in the criterion statement.

criterion-referenced instruction

A system of instruction developed by Bob Mager. Synonym for *performance-based instruction*. Instruction whose value is measured by the ability of the end user to meet specified criteria after completion.

curriculum

A series of related courses.

delivery method

Term describing the way in which training is distributed to learners. Print, classroom, video, CD-ROM, and the Internet are all sample delivery methods.

design

The second step in the classic ADDIE model of instructional system design. The design phase builds on the analysis information and includes the formulation of a detailed plan for the instruction.

designer

Any member of a training project team, usually creators such as writers, graphic artists, and programmers.

developer

A member of a training project team involved in development activities, or the project team as a whole.

development

The third step in the classic ADDIE model of instructional system design. The development phase follows the plans created in the design phase to create materials ready for several iterations of testing and refinement.

digital

Computer signals, the information manipulated by a computer and transferred on the Internet, are digital. A digital signal varies by discrete values only; that is, any point defined within a digital signal will have the value of either 1 or 0.

domains of learning

Three divisions used to classify types of learning: psychomotor (physical), cognitive (mental), and affective (emotional).

drill and practice

An interactive exercise used to develop basic skills such as keyboard operation. Involves the repetition of short sequences of practice, chained together to make up more complex processes.

DVD-ROM

Digital video disc–read only memory. Like a CD-ROM, an optical disc recorded on and read by a laser, but used to store even larger quantities of information, specifically 8.5 gigabytes.

electronic performance support system (EPSS)

A program that provides on-demand assistance on a discrete task. Considered to be a support tool or job aid. A good example of an EPSS is the built-in help functions of many software programs.

E-mail

Short for *electronic mail.* The process of one user employing a computer to send a text message to an electronic mailbox to be retrieved and viewed by another user. Also, the message itself.

embedded instruction

Instruction available to a learner during a training challenge or immediately following the presentation of content. This style of presentation combines instruction and testing for maximum learner benefit.

entry behavior

The prior knowledge, skill, or attitude that is a prerequisite to a given course.

EPSS

See ELECTRONIC PERFORMANCE SUPPORT SYSTEM.

Ethernet

A means of connecting computers in a local area network with high-bandwidth coaxial or optical cable connections. Sometimes called *10baseT*.

evaluation

The final step in the classic ADDIE model of instructional system design. The evaluation phase involves formative evaluations, evaluations of the product during development, and a summative evaluation, the final evaluation of the effectiveness of the training in solving the instructional problem.

events of instruction

The nine steps outlined by Robert Gagné that correlate with and address the conditions of adult learning.

expert system

An artificial intelligence program in which a decision tree is created based on an expert's decision criteria.

FAQ

See FREQUENTLY-ASKED QUESTIONS.

feedback

Information provided to a learner, caused by and referencing either a specific action or a set of actions. Feedback can be positive or negative, is used to shape behaviors, and should closely follow an action for maximum result.

file transfer protocol

Generally called FTP. One method of transferring files over Intranets or the Internet.

firewall

An application that isolates part of a network, like a company's private Intranet, from access to or by other parts of the network, such as the public Internet.

formative evaluation

An evaluation performed during development, used to revise and improve a product before launch.

frequently-asked questions

A Web document made up of questions commonly asked about a particular subject or in a particular forum, and the associated answers.

FTP

See FILE TRANSFER PROTOCOL.

generic (off-the-shelf) courseware

TBT products developed for a broad audience, not for a specific organization.

graphic

The medium of delivering static images to be interpreted visually by the learner. Compare to audio, video, text, and animation.

graphical user interface (GUI)

A way of representing the functions, features, and contents of a program to a user by way of visual elements, such as icons, as opposed to textual elements, such as words and character strings. The Microsoft Windows operating system is the classic example of a program with a GUI.

GUI

Pronounced "gooey." See GRAPHICAL USER INTERFACE.

hardware

Physical equipment such as computers, printers, and scanners. Compare to SOFTWARE.

help desk

A group that can be contacted by end users for assistance with hardware and software problems.

high bandwidth

A high-bandwidth connection, such as a cable modem, will allow transmission rates in the range of gigabits per second and allow the use of data-intensive information like video, audio, and complex animation.

HTML

See Hypertext Markup Language.

hypermedia

Hypermedia link text, graphics, video, audio, and animation and leaves the control of navigation through its elements in the hands of the user.

hypertext

Text elements within multimedia documents, classically underlined and in colored font, that can be clicked on by the user to follow a path to a new location in a document, supplemental material such as a graphic, or another page on the net.

Hypertext Markup Language

More commonly referred to as HTML. The standard programming language for Web documents meant to be accessed by browsers.

icon

A simple symbol representing a complex object, process, or function. Icon-based user interfaces have the user click on on-screen buttons instead of typing commands.

ILT

See Instructor-led Training.

implementation

The fourth step in the classic ADDIE model of instructional system design. The implementation phase involves the delivery of the training to the intended audience and its use by that audience.

individual instruction

Technique in which a learner follows a specific curriculum that covers only the material not already known, as opposed to working through a generic curriculum designed for a whole class of learners. Does not refer to a learner working without regard to the activities of other learners while still in a shared curriculum.

instructional systems design

Term describing the systematic use of principles of instruction to ensure that learners acquire the skills and knowledge essential for successful completion of overtly specified performance goals.

instructor-led training

Training mediated by a live instructor, such as classroom training or live workshops.

interaction

A two-way exchange of information between two parties. In TBT, interactions break up presentation of content to make sure that content is being mastered. Communication between the user and technology that does not contribute to enhanced understanding, such as advancing a page, does not count as interaction.

interactivity

A term whose use is frequently debated and misused by trainers and learners but is the agreed-upon key to successful training. An interactive training product challenges and engages the learner. The final goal of interactivity is to maintain learner interest, provide a means of practice, and ultimately increase learner understanding of the training content.

Internet

The modern network of tens of thousands of interlinked computers, evolved from the U.S. government's ARPANET project of the 1960s. The public Internet encompasses the World Wide Web, the popular multimedia portion, as well as E-mail, FTP, gopher, and other services.

Intranet

A network owned by an organization that functions like the public Internet but is secure from outsider access and regulated by representatives of the organization, often called *system administrators.*

ISD

See INSTRUCTIONAL SYSTEMS DESIGN.

job aid

A tool that can exist in paper form or on the computer that provides on-the-job instruction for a specific task.

LAN

See LOCAL AREA NETWORK.

learning objective

The clear and measurable statement of the behavior that must be observed after training is concluded in order to consider the training a success. According to Robert Mager's work, a learning objective contains a condition statement, a performance statement, and a criterion statement.

learning style

An individual's unique approach to learning based on strengths, weaknesses, and preferences. Though experts do not agree how to categorize learning styles, an example of a categorization system is one that separates learners into auditory learners, visual learners, and kinesthetic learners.

lesson

A unit of learning concerned with a specific skill. This term is sometimes interchanged with the terms *section* and *module.*

local area network (LAN)

A network of computers in a confined area, such as a room or a building. A LAN accessed with Internet technologies can be considered an Intranet.

log-in

Procedure performed by a user to declare that a specific system or application is going to be used. Log-in information is used by the computer to mark and track information specific to the user. It can also be used to declare to other users that an individual is presently active on a network.

low bandwidth

A low-bandwidth connection, such as a telephone line, will allow transmission rates in the range of kilobits per second and restrict the use of data-intensive information such as video and photo-quality graphics.

mastery learning

Also known as CRITERION-REFERENCED INSTRUCTION, in which students are evaluated as having mastered or not mastered specific criteria or learning objectives.

menu driven

Generally refers to a simple, text-based organization. A menu-driven program structure relies on lists of sections divided into lists of subsections used in the navigation through content.

metaphor

A creative interpretation of the contents of a program as elements of something fantastic or familiar in order to improve accessibility by the user. Placing the learner in the role of knight and figuring the contents of a lesson as the contents of a room in a dungeon is an example of the use of a learning metaphor.

mixed media

The combination in one curriculum of different delivery media such as books, audiotapes, videotapes, and computer programs. Not to be confused with MULTIMEDIA, in which different media are integrated into one product.

model

A representation of an object, process, behavior, or attitude used by a learner for comparison or contrast and duplication or avoidance. Both positive and negative examples can serve as models.

modeling

The activity of recreating the functions and aspects of a model. When a novice salesperson watches an expert make a sales call and then mimics the expert's tone and wording, he or she is exhibiting a modeling process.

modem

A piece of hardware used by computers to transfer and receive information. The term is taken from the full title *MOdulator-DEModulator*.

multimedia

The integration of different media, including text, graphics, audio, video, and animation, into one program. Also referred to as new media.

negative reinforcement

Encouraging a behavior by punishing any behaviors other than it. An example is taking away a child's television privileges after he or she throws a tantrum in order to encourage behaviors alternate to throwing tantrums. Negative reinforcement is not recommended for most adult learning situations.

network

A collection of computers that can exchange information and share resources.

newsgroup

An electronic bulletin board reserved for discussion of a specific topic.

off-line

Operation of a computer while not connected to a network.

on-line

Operation of a computer while connected to a network.

operating system

A computer program that controls the components of a computer system and facilitates the operation of applications. Windows 98, Windows NT, UNIX, and MacOS are common operating systems.

pedagogy

Opposite of ANDRAGOGY. The art and science of helping children learn.

performance statement

One of the three required parts of a properly composed learning objective. Observable and measurable actions that should be demonstrated by the learner after the completion of training are detailed in the performance statement.

performance objective

The performance capability the learner should acquire by completing a given training course. Synonymous with LEARNING OBJECTIVE.

performance-based instruction

Learning activities centered more fundamentally on the acquisition of skills than on the acquisition of knowledge. Performance-based instruction, also called CRITERION-REFERENCED INSTRUCTION, relies on learning objectives to communicate what is expected to be achieved, and evaluation of task completion to determine success.

pilot test

Also known as an *alpha test* or FORMATIVE EVALUATION. A version of the training program is delivered to a subset of the target audience for an evaluation of its instructional effectiveness.

pixel

Term created by joining the words *picture* and *cell,* a pixel is the basic unit of measurement for picture displays. Computer screen size is often measured in pixels, with 640 × 480 and 800 × 600 being common measurements.

plug-in

A small piece of software that works in conjunction with a Web browsers to add additional functionality, such as streaming audio or video.

positive reinforcement

Encouraging a behavior by rewarding that behavior after it is exhibited. An example is buying a child a toy after they do well on a test. An example in adult education is congratulating a learner after a question is answered correctly.

prerequisite

A basic requirement or step in a process that must be fulfilled before moving on to an advanced step. Being able to stand is a prerequisite to being able to walk. In computer training, being able to turn on a computer may be a prerequisite to being able to use the computer.

PRM

See PROGRAMMER-READY MATERIALS.

processor

The chip or chip set that performs the operations central to a computer's functioning.

program

A detailed set of instructions that make a computer able to perform some function. A program can be written by the user but the term is commonly used to refer to a specific precreated software package, such as a word processor or spreadsheet.

programmer-ready materials (PRMs)

The individual components that are ready for assembly by a programmer or multimedia developer. Typically, PRMs include scripts, graphics, and audio and video files.

prototype

A working model created to demonstrate crucial aspects of a program without creating a fully detailed program. Adding details and content incrementally to advancing stages of prototypes is one process for creating successful applications.

real time

Instantaneous response to external events. A real-time simulation, such as a driving simulator, follows the pace of events in reality. In simulated time one compresses or distorts time for instructional effect, as in a financial model.

repurpose

To revise preexisting training material for a different delivery format. For example, instructor guides and student manuals are often repurposed into Web-based training.

search engine

The two types of search engines, the catalog and the crawler, both locate requested information on a Web site or on the whole World Wide Web. A catalog engine compares the user's request with a collection of data on Web sites. A crawler engine scours the contents of sites themselves to find a match to a word or string of words.

section

A division of training concerned with one topic. Several sections commonly make up a lesson, but the term is sometimes used interchangeably with the term LESSON or *module*.

self-paced instruction

Any instruction in which the learner dictates the speed of progress through content. Self-paced instruction lets the novice work through difficult challenges and the expert speed through basic materials.

server

A networked computer that is shared by many other computers on the network. Intranets use servers to hold, or host, Web pages.

simulation

A mode of instruction that relies on a representation in realistic form of the relevant aspects of a device, process, or situation.

software

Programs that allow a user to complete tasks with computers, such as word processing and graphics programs. Compare to APPLICATION.

SME

See SUBJECT MATTER EXPERT.

storyboard

A collection of frames created by a developer that detail the sequence of scenes that will be represented to the user; a visual script.

subject matter expert (SME)

The member of a project team who is most knowledgeable about the content of the instruction. Frequently the SME is an expert contracted or assigned by an organization to consult on the training being created.

subordinate objective

A task or objective that must first be mastered in order to complete a terminal objective.

summative evaluation

An evaluation performed after development, used to measure the efficacy and return on investment of a training program.

synchronous training

A training program in which the student and instructor participate at the same time. For example, an instructor-led chat session is a form of synchronous training.

target population

The audience defined in age, background, ability, and preferences, among other things, for which a given course of instruction is intended.

task analysis

A process of examining a given job to define the discrete steps (tasks) that ensure effective and efficient performance of the job's requirements.

TBL

Technology-based learning. Synonymous with TBT, or TECHNOLOGY-BASED TRAINING.

TBT

See TECHNOLOGY-BASED TRAINING.

TCP/IP

Transmission control protocol/Internet protocol. The set of rules and formats used when transmitting data between servers and clients over the Internet.

technology-based training (TBT)

The term encompassing all uses of a computer in support of learning, including but not limited to tutorials, simulations, collaborative learning environments, and performance support tools. Synonyms include CBL (computer-based learning), TBL (technology-based learning), CBE (computer-based education), CBT (computer-based training), and any number of other variations.

terminal objective

A learning objective the student should be able to master after completing a specific lesson or part of a lesson.

text

The medium of delivering information via words to be read and interpreted by the learner. Compare to AUDIO, VIDEO, GRAPHIC, and ANIMATION.

tutorial

A mode of instruction that presents content, checks understanding or performance, and continues on to the next relevant selection of content. Tutorials may be linear or branched.

uniform resource locator

More commonly referred to as URL. The standard address for a Web page on the Internet or an Intranet.

URL

See UNIFORM RESOURCE LOCATOR.

usability

An evaluation and measurement of a computer program's overall ease of use.

user interface

The components of a computer system employed by a user to communicate with the computer. These include the equipment, such as a keyboard or mouse, and the software environment, such as the desktop of Windows or the program lines of DOS.

vertical slice

A program prototype that includes the development of one section, usually a complete lesson, for the course.

video

The medium of delivering information created from the recording of real events to be processed simultaneously by a learner's eyes and ears. Compare to AUDIO, TEXT, GRAPHICS, and ANIMATION.

World Wide Web

The most popular component of the Internet, which can be accessed with browser software. Offers interconnected screens containing text, graphics, and occasionally other types of media.

WWW

See WORLD WIDE WEB.

BIBLIOGRAPHY

This bibliography includes works cited in this text as well as those that would be a valuable addition to any TBT professional's library.

American Society for Training and Development (1997). National HRD executive survey. In *Measurement and evaluation*. Alexandria, VA: American Society for Training and Development.

American Society for Training and Development (1998). *1998/1999 buyer's guide.* Alexandria, VA: American Society for Training and Development.

Booker, E. (1997, July 21). Drug company anticipates that proposed Intranet will save $1M a day. *WebWeek.*

Boyle, T. (1997). *Design for multimedia learning.* Englewood Cliffs, NJ: Prentice Hall.

Bruner, J. (1961). The acts of discovery. *Harvard Educational Review, 31*(1), 21–32.

Burns, H., Parlett, J. W., & Redfield, C. (1991). *Intelligent tutoring systems: Evolutions in design.* Hillsdale, NJ: Erlbaum.

Cooper, A. (1995). *About face: The essentials of user interface design.* Foster City: IDG Books Worldwide.

Dick, W., & Carey, L. (1996). *The systematic design of instruction.* New York: Harper-Collins.

Driscoll, M. (1998). *Web-based training: Using technology to design adult learning experiences.* San Francisco: Jossey-Bass Pfeiffer.

Duffy, T. M., & Jonassen, D. H. (1992). *Constructivism and the technology of instruction: A conversation.* Hillsdale, NJ: Erlbaum.

Ely, D. P., & Plomp, T. (1996). *Classic writings of instructional technology.* Englewood Cliffs, NJ: Libraries Unlimited.

Fickel, L. (1998, July 15). Working smart. *CIO Magazine.*

Fletcher, J. D. (1991, Spring). *Multimedia Review,* pp. 33–42.

Gagné, R. M. (1965). *The conditions of learning and theory of instruction.* Austin, TX: Holt, Rinehart and Winston.

Gagné, R. M., Briggs, L. J., & Wager, W. W. (1992). *Principles of instructional design.* Orlando: Harcourt Brace.

Gagné, R. M., & Medsker, K. L. (1996). *The conditions of learning: Training applications.* Orlando: Harcourt Brace.

Gery, G. J. (1991). *Electronic performance support systems.* Boston: Weingarten.

Gordon, J. (1998). Who gets trained? Where the money goes. *Training the human side of business* (pp. 55–76). Minneapolis: Lakewood.

Hall, B. (1997). *Web-based training cookbook.* New York: Wiley.

Hills, M. (1997). *Intranet business strategies.* New York: Wiley.

International Data Corporation (1998). *The emerging market for web-based training, 1996–2002.* International Data Corporation.

Jerram, P. (1994, October). Who's using multimedia? *NewMedia.*

Keller, J. M., & Kopp, T. W. (1987). *Instructional Theories in Action.* Hillsdale: Erlbaum.

Kirkpatrick, D. L. (1975). Techniques for evaluating training programs. *Evaluating Training Programs* (pp. 1–17). Alexandria, VA: American Society for Training and Development.

Knowles, M. (1970). *The Modern Practice of Adult Education: Andragogy Versus Pedagogy.*

Lakewood Publications (1998, October). Industry report 1998. *Training,* pp. 43–76.

Mager, R. (1962). *Preparing instructional objectives.* Atlanta, GA: Center for Effective Performance.

Mandel, T. (1994). *The GUI-OOUI war: Windows versus OS/2—The designer's guide to human-computer interfaces.* New York: Van Nostrand Reinhold.

Phillips, J., Pulliam, P., & Wurtz, W. (1998, May). Level 5 evaluation: ROI. In *Info-line.* Alexandria, VA: American Society for Training and Development.

Ravet, S., & Layte, M. (1997). *Technology-based training.* Houston: Gulf.

Reeves, B., & Nass, C. (1996). *The media equation: How people treat computers, television, and new media like real people and places.* Stanford, CA: Center for Study of Language and Information Publications.

Reynolds, A., & Iwinski, T. (1996). *Multimedia training: Developing technology-based systems.* New York: McGraw-Hill.

Roberts, B. (1998, August). Training via the desktop. *HR Magazine,* pp. 99–104.

Rothwell, W. J., & Cookson, P. S. (1997). *Beyond instruction: Comprehensive program planning for business and education.* San Francisco: Jossey-Bass.

Rothwell, W. J., & Kazanas, H. C. (1998). *Mastering the instructional design process: A systematic approach.* San Francisco: Jossey-Bass.

Schank, R. (1997). *Virtual learning: A revolutionary approach to building a highly skilled workforce.* New York: McGraw-Hill.

Webb, W. (1996). *A trainer's guide to the World Wide Web and Intranets.* Minneapolis: Lakewood.

Weiss, E. (1993). *Making computers people-literate.* San Francisco: Jossey-Bass.

Zemke, R. (1998, June). Wake up! (and reclaim instructional design). *Training,* pp. 36–42.

INDEX

A

Access: and need to exit program, 109; one-click, 119; through Web-based training, 54

Access points, use of multiple, 115–117

Achievement, sense of, 102

Acme Incorporated case example, 138–146, 149–151

Actors and actresses, 78, 167

ADDIE (analysis, design, development, implementation, evaluation) model, 61; alternatives to, 61–62; analysis phase of, 61, 63–67; checklist for, 86; design phase of, 61, 67–70; development phase of, 73–81; evaluation phase of, 61, 83–86; implementation phase of, 61, 82–83; modified, 62–86; rapid prototype phase in, 62–63, 70–73; return on investment and, 133; steps in, 61. *See also* Systematic design process

Administration costs, estimating, 144–145

Administrators, roles and responsibilities of, 30

Adobe Acrobat, 52, 241

Adobe Illustrator, 33

Adobe Photoshop, 33, 36; in BevCo case example, 217; in Nexus case example,

256; in Virtual Oncology Center case example, 197

Adobe Premier, 32

ADSL, 51

Adult learners, 8–9, 87–105; constructivist approach to, 102–105; Gagné's events of instruction model and, 91–98; Knowles' theory of andragogy and, 89–91, 92, 93, 94; Mager's behavioral learning objectives model and, 98–100; motivating, 100–102. *See also* Learners; Learning theory

Advantages and disadvantages: of CD-ROM-based training, 45–47, 194; of technology-based training, 21–24; of Web-based training, 53–56. *See also* Benefits of technology-based training; Cost-benefit analysis; Return on investment

Aimtech IconAuthor, 33, 37, 170

Airline boarding process: introducing new, with Web-based training, 247–268; problems of, 247. *See also* Global Air Nexus

Allaire ColdFusion and Homesite, 33

Allen Communications, 32

Alpha test, 79–80

Bingham-Rodway Pharmaco (*continued*) 191–192, 205; linear tutorial in, 199, 200; log-in to, 198–199; marketing content of, 193–194; media decisions for, 194–195, 197; metaphor used in, 196–197; reference content of, 193; return on investment in, 205; technical specifications for, 194–195; technological tools used for, 197; theoretical solution of, 196; tour of, 198–204; training content of, 192–193; treatment component of, 202–203; tumor staging component of, 201–202; user interface of, 196–197; virtual diagnosis in, 200–201, 202

Bitmap graphic files, 78

Black box, 169–170

Blueprint, 67–70

.bmp extension, 78

Booker, E., 137

Bookmark feature, 70, 71, 116

Branching, tutorial, 13, 14

Brandon Hall Resources, 183, 319

Break-even analysis/point, 150–151, 152; for BevCo Office Orientation, 226; for Virtual Oncology Center, 205

British Interactive Multimedia Association (BIMA), 317

Browser-based training (BBT), 10

Bruner, J., 102

Budgeting, for outsourced projects, 153–157; factors in, 154; pricing by the hour and, 155–156, 169; pricing by the screen and, 156; pricing method and, 156–157; rules of thumb for, 154–155; tips for reducing costs and, 167–168. *See also* Cost analysis; Costs; Pricing, vendor

Bulletin boards, on-line: for collaborative learning, 245; in facilitated asynchronous training, 49

Burdened compensation for instructor, 139

Burdened costs, 136

Business case for technology-based training, 181–183

Business goals, 64. *See also* Goals of training

Business impact evaluation, 85–86

Buttons: naming of, 122; visually consistent, 122–123

Buyer's Guide, ASTD, 157

C

Cancer treatments, 189; pharmaceutical sales representative training education in, 189–190; in Virtual Oncology Center, 202–203. *See also* Bingham-Rodway Pharmaco (BRP), Virtual Oncology Center

Carey, L., 60

Case studies: of CD-ROM-based training for new hire orientation, 207–226; of CD-ROM-based training for pharmaceutical sales representatives, 189–205; sources of, 183; using, for internal marketing, 182–183; of Web-based training for management skills, 227–246; of Web-based training for work processes, 247–268. *See also* BevCo Office Orientation; Bingham-Rodway Pharmaco (BRP), Virtual Oncology Center; Global Air Nexus; RKA Management Results

CD burner, 31, 34

CD-I, 40–41

CD-ROM, accompanying *Technology-Based Training,* 3–4; folders of, 3; technical requirements for, 3–4

CD-ROM-based training, 11, 39, 44–47, 88; advantages of, 45–46, 194, 213; assessment in, 46–47; case study of, for new hire orientation, 207–226; case study of, for pharmaceutical sales representatives, 189–205; Gagné's events of instruction applied to example of, 96–98; indirect costs of, 137–138; limitations of, 46–47; multimedia training and, 11, 53; pricing rules of thumb for, 155; printed instructions for, 82, 198; production and distribution sequence of, 46, 47; questions for selection of, 57–58; rollout of, 82; technical requirements for, 44–45; updatability of, 46, 47, 55; Web-based training combined with, in Global Air Nexus case study, 253; Web-based training versus, 45, 46, 53, 55, 56–58

CD-ROM drive, 31

Certification: in Gagné's model, 96; satisfaction and, 102

Certification, automated, 23; in CD-ROM-based training, 47; in CD-ROM-based training, BevCo Office Orientation case study, 225; in CD-ROM-based training, Virtual Oncology Center case study, 204; in Web-based training, RKA Management Results case study, 234

Change, 1, 7; as driver of technology-based training, 9–10; resistance to, 175

Checklist: for cost-benefit analysis, 152; for instructional design principles, 105; for internal marketing, 185; for systematic design process, 86; for user interface design, 129; for vendor projects, 173–174

Chunking, 95, 97; in BevCo Office Orientation, 215; in Global Air Nexus, 250–251, 252

Classification of technology-based training, 12

Classroom delivery. *See* Instructor-led training (ILT), traditional

Clickable objects, 119, 122–123

Client-sponsor: attributes of, 25–26; design document sign-off of, 70; roles and responsibilities of, 25; script approval of, 77, 172; vendor relationship with, 170–172

Clip art, 167–168

Close-ups, 78

Coach simulation: in BevCo Office Orientation, 214, 215, 217–218, 222–223; in Global Air Nexus, 254–255, 257–259, 260, 266

ColdFusion, 33

Collaborative learning, technology-based, 22; in RKA Management Results case study, 231, 244–245

Commands, 109

Communication plan, 83

Compensation for instructor, 139

Complex branching structure, tutorial, 13, 14

Compression software, 40

Compressor, 31

Computer-aided instruction (CAI), as technology-based training component, 11

Computer-based education (CBE), 10

Computer-based instruction (CBI), 10, 11

Computer-based learning (CBL), 10, 11

Computer-based training (CBT), 10, 11, 88

Computer-managed instruction (CMI), as technology-based training component, 11

Computer requirements: for CD-ROM-based training, 44–45; for technology-based training project development, 30–31, 34; for Web-based training, 49. *See also* Technical requirements/specifications; Tools

Computer reseller, Web-based training value to, 135

Computer storage media company, technology-based training value to, 135

Computer-supported learning resources (CSLR), as technology-based training component, 11–12

Conditions of Learning and Theory of Instruction (Gagné), 92

Conferences, finding vendors through, 158–159

Confidence: building, in Global Air Nexus, 250; and motivation, 23, 102

Confusion, user, 109–110

Connection technology, Web. *See* Web connections

Consistency: of delivery, 23; in user interface, 120–126

Constituents, interests of, 177

Constructivism: applied in BevCo Office Orientation, 215; applied in Global Air Nexus, 254–255; applied in RKA Management Results, 231; applied in Virtual Oncology Center, 104, 195; applying, to technology-based training, 103–105; theory of, 102–103. *See also* Simulations

Consultants. *See* Vendors

Consulting firm, technology-based training value to, 135

Content: of BevCo Office Orientation, 210–212; of Global Air Nexus, 250–252; ownership of, 168–169; presentation of, 95, 97; revision of, 172; of RKA Management Results, 229–231; of Virtual Oncology Center, 192–193

Content map, 117

Content outline, 68

Control groups, for benefit analysis, 147–148

Copyeditors, as quality reviewers, 29

Copyrights, 168–169

Cost analysis, 137–146; in Acme Incorporated case example, 138–146, 149; indirect versus direct costs and, 137–138; phase five (total cost comparison) of, 145–146; phase four (administration and maintenance) of, 144–145; phase one (assumptions) of, 138–140; phase three (delivery) of, 141–143; phase two (design and development) of, 140–141

Cost-benefit analysis, 133–152; benefit measurement step in, 146–149; checklist for, 152; concepts of, 135–137; cost measurement step in, 137–146; demands for, 134; evaluating results of, 149–152; overview of, 134–137; value of, 134–135; worksheets for, 312–316

Cost-benefit ratio, 151, 152; for BevCo Office Orientation, 226; for Virtual Oncology Center, 205

Cost reduction: through technology-based training, 22, 178; through Web-based training, 54; tips for, 167–168

Cost savings: of BevCo Office Orientation, 226; calculation of, 149, 152; of Virtual Oncology Center, 205

Costs: of BevCo Office Orientation, 226; break-even analysis of, 150–151; burdened, 136; of CD-ROM reduplication, 80; determining, for outsourced projects, 153–157; direct, 137, 138; holistic approach and, 62; indirect, 137–138; instructor, 139, 141–142, 143; opportunity, 137; reduction of, tips for, 167–168; student, 142–143; of technology-based versus instructor-led training, 138–146; up-front, 23, 34; of updates, 169; of Virtual Oncology Center, 205; of Web-based training, 54. *See also* Price; Pricing, vendor

Courseware creation, cost analysis of, 140–141

Crashes, 109–110, 117

Creative themes or metaphors. *See* Metaphors and themes

Crisis management simulations, 45

Cultural change, 175

Cultural knowledge, collaborative learning and, 244–245

D

Data storage devices, portable, 40–41, 42. *See also* CD-I; CD-ROM-based training; DVD-ROM

Deadlines, 171

Debugging, programmer's responsibility for, 29

Decision grids for determining whether to use CD-ROM or Web-based training, 53, 56–57

Definition of technology-based training, 8

Delivery cost analysis, 141–143

Delivery method: CD-ROM, 11, 44–47; cost-benefit comparisons of, 136, 138, 142–146; decision grid for selection of, 56–57; questions for selection of, 57–58; selection of, 39–58; selection of, in case studies, 194, 213, 232, 252–253; technology-based training classification by, 12; Web, 47–56. *See also* CD-ROM-based training; Web-based training

Delivery phase, 173

DeMaioribus, J., 137

Demographics assessment, 65

Design document, 67–70, 160–161, 172

Design of user interface. *See* User interface

Design phase, 61, 67–70; for BevCo Office Orientation program, 210–217; content outline development in, 68; cost analysis of, 140–141; final sign-off in, 70; for

Global Air Nexus, 250–257; learning objectives determination in, 67–68; practice activities determination in, 68–69; for RKA Management Results, 229–235; user interface determination in, 69–70; for Virtual Oncology Center program, 192–197

Design process. *See* ADDIE model; Systematic design process

Designers Edge, 32, 36

Destructive messaging, 124, 125

Development cycle. *See* ADDIE model; Systematic design process

Development milestones, 172–173

Development phase, 61, 73–81; audio-video production in, 78–79; cost analysis of, 140–141, 146; formative evaluation (pilot test) step in, 80–81; graphic art creation in, 77–78; internal quality control (alpha test) step in, 79–80; programming step in, 79; script or storyboard development in, 74–77; steps in, 73; with vendors, 173

Development, project. *See* ADDIE model; Development phase; Project development; Systematic design process

Development teams. *See* Project team

DHTML, 33, 50, 67

Diagnosis, virtual, 195, 200–201, 202

Dick, W., 60

Digital Think, 320

Direct costs, 137, 138

Direct observation, 63

Director. *See* Macromedia Director

Directory structure, visual metaphor of, 114–115

Discovery-learning, 102; interface designed for, 103; in RKA Management Results, 231, 233–234, 240–241, 243; scenarios, 15, 45. *See also* Simulations

Goodbye messages, 128

Graphic art: consistency in, 120–123; creation of, 77–78; description of, in script or storyboard, 76; filenaming of, 78; types of, 77–78; use of stock art for, 167–168; in Virtual Oncology Center program, 197. *See also* User interface

Graphic art software, 32–33, 34; used in Virtual Oncology Center development, 197

Graphic artists: attributes of, 28; Macintosh computers and, 30; roles and responsibilities of, 28

Graphical user interface (GUI), 108. *See also* User interface

Guidance: providing, 95, 97; technology-based, 18–20; in user interface system, 126–128; in Virtual Oncology Center case study, 204

H

Hall, B., 23, 33, 134, 135, 136, 139, 183, 268

Hands-on approach, 91, 93

Headphones, 66

Hello messages, 128

Help button, 122

Help desk, 181

Help feature, 70, 126

History of technology-based training, 8–9, 39–44, 88–89

Holistic approach, 61–62

Hospital metaphor, 196–197. *See also* Bingham-Rodway Pharmaco (BRP), Virtual Oncology Center

Hourly pricing, 155–156, 169

HR Magazine, 134

Hyperlinks, too many, 109, 115

HyperMedia Communications, 183

Hypertext Markup Language (HTML), 29, 33, 181

I

IBM-compatible computers, 30–31

Icon-driven user interface, 235

IconAuthor. *See* Aimtech IconAuthor

Implementation phase, 61, 82–83

Index, 116

Indirect benefits, 178

Indirect costs, 137–138

Indirect observation, 63

Individualized instruction, 22

Industry-specific training conferences, 158

Information gathering: in analysis phase, 63–64; in formative evaluation step, 80–81

Information overload, 115

Information processing model, 92, 110–112

Information technology (IT) departments: concerns and language of, 179–181; pitching technology-based training to, 179–181; relationship of trainers to, 179, 180; workload of, 179

Information technology training, cost savings of, 178

Inside Technology Training, 183

Instruction, defined, 8–9

Instructional design (ID), 59, 60. *See also* Systematic design process

Instructional design software, 32, 34

Instructional design strategy: of BevCo Office Orientation, 214; checklist for, 105; constructivism and, 102–105; Gagné's events of instruction theory for, 91–98; of Global Air Nexus, 250–251, 254–255; Keller's ARCS model for, 101–102; Knowle's andragogy theory for, 89–91; Mager's behavioral learning objectives for, 98–100; motivation and, 100–102; of RKA Management Results, 231, 233; value of proven, 88–89, 96; of Virtual Oncology

Center, 195. *See also* Adult learners; Learning theory

Instructional designer: attributes of, 27; roles and responsibilities of, 27

Instructional events. *See* Events of instruction

Instructional games. *See* Games, instructional

Instructional goals, 64

Instructional modes. *See* Mode of instruction

Instructional objectives. *See* Goals of training; Learning objectives

Instructional principles. *See* Adult learners; Learning theory

Instructional systems design (ISD), 60–61; content in, 68; of RKA Management Results, 233. *See also* Systematic design process

Instructional systems design and development (ISDD), 60. *See also* Systematic design process

Instructions: navigational, 126; on-screen, 126; printed, 82, 181, 198

Instructor compensation, 139

Instructor costs, estimating, 139, 141–142

Instructor-led training (ILT), traditional: CD-ROM-based training versus, 45, 46; costs of, compared to technology-based training, 138–146, 149; indirect costs of, 137; Web-based training versus, 53–54, 55. *See also* Teachers

Instructor-led training, Web-based: in asynchronous Web-based training, 49; in synchronous Web-based training, 47, 48

Intangible benefits, 148–149

Intellectual capital, 134

Intellectual heritage of technology-based training, 8–9

Intellectual property ownership, 168–169

Interaction: reduced social and cultural, 24; between students and computers, 108–109, 128. *See also* User interface

Interactive satellite videoconferences, 11

Interactivity, 21; beneficial versus nonbeneficial, 21, 36; in CD-ROM-based training, 45; costs of, 167; description of, in script or storyboard, 77; importance of, 21, 23; simple versus complex, 167; technology-based training classification by level of, 12; in Web-based training, 54. *See also* Collaborative learning

Interactivity objects, 233, 239, 240

Interface, user. *See* User interface

Internal marketing, 82–83, 175–185; checklist for, 185; to information technology (IT) departments, 179–181; model memo for, 183–185; by presenting the business case, 181–183; project plan for, 182; to senior executives, 176–178; using case studies and research reports for, 182–183

Internal quality control, 79–80

International Data Corporation, 89, 134

International Data Group, 9

International Society for Performance Improvement (ISPI), 157; Award of Excellence for an Instructional Intervention, 205; contact information for, 318

Internet: case studies on, 183; connections to, 50, 51; history and development of, 41–43; technology-based training resources on, 3, 4, 319–320, 321

Internet-based training (IBT), 10, 43. *See also* Web-based training

Internet Explorer. *See* Microsoft Internet Explorer

Internet years, 1

Interviewing skills program: benefit analysis of, 148; in RKA Management

Learning styles, technology-based training's suitability for diverse, 21–22

Learning theory, 87–105; constructivism and, 102–105; Gagné's events of instruction model of, 91–98; importance of applying, to technology-based training, 88–89; as intellectual heritage of technology-based training, 8–9; Knowles' theory of andragogy and, 89–91, 92, 93, 94; Mager's behavioral learning objectives and, 98–100; motivation and, 100–102

Learning time: determination of, 139; estimation of, and pricing by the hour, 155–156; reduction of, 23, 139

Leverage of investment. *See* Investment leveraging

Life of training, 135–136

Life span of course, 138

Lights and backgrounds, 32

Linear structure of tutorial, 13

Local area networks (LANs), 52

Location fees, 143

Log-in screens, 118; of Global Air Nexus, 257–258, 259; of RKA Management Results, 236; of Virtual Oncology Center, 198–199

Long-term memory, 111–112

M

Macintosh computers: graphical user interface and, 108; minimum requirements for technology-based training development, 30–31; requirements for CD-ROM-based training, 44; requirements for Web-based training, 49

Macromedia Authorware, 33, 37, 52, 170; used in Global Air Nexus development, 256

Macromedia Director, 33, 52, 170, 256; used in BevCo Office Orientation development, 216–217; used in Virtual Oncology Center development, 197

Macromedia DreamWeaver, 33

Macromedia Fireworks, 33

Macromedia Flash, 33, 36, 52, 66; used in Global Air Nexus development, 257

Macromedia Shockwave, 52, 66

Mager, R., 98–100

Mager's behavioral learning objectives, 98–100

Main menu, 71, 116; organized by sequence of tasks, 112–113; in sample training program, 112–113

Maintenance costs, estimating, 144–145

Management of technology-based training projects: cost-benefit analysis for, 133–152; milestones in, 172–173; with vendors, 153–174

Management training: business impact measurement of, 86; challenges of, 227–228; in coaching skills, 230; in communication skills, 230, 233; in conflict resolution, 230; in effective meetings, 230; in financial fundamentals, 230; in interviewing skills, 230, 237–245; in leadership, 230; management skills included in, 227, 230–231; need for, 227; in performance appraisal, 230; in presentation skills, 231; in problem solving, 230; in project management, 230; Raymond Karsan Associates' Web-based program for, 227–246; in team building, 231

Manuals, cost analysis of, 143. *See also* Printed instructions

Marketing content, of Virtual Oncology Center, 193–194

Marketing, internal. *See* Internal marketing

Masie Center, 319

Materials, student, 143

McGraw Hill Online Learning, 320

Media: consistency in use of, 124–125; used in BevCo Office Orientation, 212–214, 216–217; used in Global Air Nexus, 252–253, 256–257; used in RKA Management Results, 232–233; used in Virtual Oncology Center, 194–195, 197

Media 100, 32, 36

Media Equation, The (Reeves and Nass), 128

Medical education simulations, 45, 197. *See also* Bingham-Rodway Pharmaco (BRP), Virtual Oncology Center

Medsker, K. L., 93, 102

Meetings, client-vendor, 170–171, 172

Memorandum to sell new Web-based training project, 183–186

Memory, 110–117; aids to, 110, 111–112; human processing of, 110–112; long-term, 111–112; short-term or working, 110–111; user interface design and, 110–117. *See also* Retention

Mental conditions for learning, 92–93; instructional events and, 92–96; listed, with associated instructional events, 95

Mental models, 113–115

Mentors, individualized, 207–208; simulated, in BevCo Office Orientation, 214, 215, 217–218, 222–223; simulated, in Global Air Nexus, 254–255

Menu button, 69, 77, 122

Menu items: consistency in action of, 125–126; number of, 112; organization of, 112–113, 216

Menu system, 109; behavior of, 125–126; of BevCo Office Orientation, 216; exploratory interface versus, 196, 256; of RKA Management Results, 235, 236; structure for, 112–113

Merrill, M. D., 88, 89

Messages: clear and consistent, 123–125; destructive, 124, 125; error, 127; politeness rules for, 128; status, 109–110, 117; warning, 128

Metaphors and themes: examples of, 70; of Global Air Nexus, 255–256; instructional design principles and, 88; in rapid prototype, 71; in systemic approach to development, 61–62; in user interface, 113–115; of Virtual Oncology Center, 196–197. *See also* User interface

Microphone, 31

Microsoft FrontPage, 33

Microsoft Internet Explorer, 49–50, 52, 66; visual metaphor used by, 114–115

Microsoft Office, help feature of, 15

Microsoft Word, 241

Midlevel managers, pitching technology-based training to, 177

Milestones, project, 172–173

Military branch, technology-based training value to, 135

Military simulations, 45

Mirrored or shadow server, 82

Misdiagnosis, in simulations, 195

Mixer, 31

Mode of instruction, 12–21; assessment and guidance, 18–20; combination, 20–21; electronic performance support system (EPSS), 15–18; instructional game, 18, 19; simulation, 13, 15, 103–105; technology-based training classification by, 12; training goals and, 20–21; tutorial, 12–13, 14

Modems, 50, 51

Motivation, 100–102; assessment of, 65, 101; importance of, 100–101; Keller's ARCS model for, 101–102; showing students the value of training for, 90–91

Mouse, 108, 119

Movie Cleaner Pro, 217

MPEG, 44–45, 66

Multimedia: bandwidth and, 51–52, 53, 55–56, 181; complexity of programming, 71; consistency in use of, 124–125; decision grids for, 53, 57; plug-ins for, 52, 53, 67; production of, in development phase, 78–79; for simulations, 104; storage technologies and, 40–41, 42; video shooting guidelines for, 78; in Web-based training, limits of, 55–56; in Web-based versus CD-ROM-based training, 53. *See also* Audio narration; CD-I; CD-ROM-based training; DVD-ROM; Video; Web-based training

Multimedia and Internet-Based Training Newsletter, 134, 183, 318

Multimedia artists. *See* Graphic artists

Multimedia authors, 79. *See also* Programmers

Multimedia programmers. *See* Programmers

Multimedia Review, 23

Multimedia software, 32–33

Multimedia training, 11, 45; pricing rules of thumb for, 155. *See also* CD-ROM-based training

N

Naive users, as quality reviewers, 79–80

Nass, C., 128

National HRD Executive Survey, 134

National Science Foundation, 42

National Society for Pharmaceutical Sales Trainers convention, 158

Navigation bars, 121–122

Navigation options: in BevCo Office Orientation, 216; consistency in design of, 120–126; description of, in script or storyboard, 77; examples of, 69–70. *See also* User interface

Navigational instructions, 126

Needs analysis, 160–161, 172

Netscape's Navigator, 49–50

Network connections, 50, 51

New hire orientation. *See* Orientation training

New Media, 183, 205

Next button, 69, 77

Nexus. *See* Global Air Nexus

No and yes buttons, 119

Nonlinear approach to knowledge acquisition, 104, 105

Notepad feature, 70, 71

Notes section of script, 77

O

Object-oriented exercises, types of, 242

Objectivists and objectivism, 102

Observation, 63, 80

Observation surveys, 85

Office Orientation program. *See* BevCo Office Orientation

O'Hare Airport, 111–112

On-demand availability, 23; of Web-based training, 54

On-line learning, 47. *See also* Web-based training

On-Line Learning convention, 158

On-screen text, description of, in script, 77

Oncology training, 189–190. *See also* Bingham-Rodway Pharmaco (BRP), Virtual Oncology Center

Oncology training program, student tracking system for, 19, 20

One-click access, 119

Operating system requirements: for CD-ROM-based training, 44; for Web-based training, 49

Price: of audio-visual equipment and software, 31, 32, 34; of authoring software, 34; of computer peripherals, 31, 34; of computer systems, 31, 34; of graphic design software tools, 33, 34; of instructional design software, 34; of Macintosh systems, 31; of outsourced projects, 153–157; of PC systems, 31; of technology-based training project development, summarized, 34. *See also* Cost analysis; Cost-benefit analysis; Costs

Pricing, vendor, 153–157; break out of, 163; evaluation of, 161–162; expense charges and, 169; factors that influence, 154; for future updates, 169; by the hour, 155–156, 169; method of, 156–157; negotiation of, 165; rules of thumb for, 154–155; by the screen, 156; tips for reducing costs and, 167–168

Printed instructions, 82, 181; for BevCo Office Orientation, 223; for Virtual Oncology Center, 198

Prior knowledge and experience: assessment of, 65; importance of, to adult learners, 90–91; stimulating recall of, 94, 95, 97

Producer, reliance on one, 24–25

Product launch training example, 103, 104

Profit, senior executives' interest in, 177

Programmer-ready materials (PRMs): audio-video production for, 78–79; graphic art creation for, 77–78; script development for, 74–77

Programmers: attributes of, 29; in program development step, 79–80; roles and responsibilities of, 28–29

Programming costs, 155–156, 169–170

Programming step, 79

Progress meetings, 170–171

Project budget, 153–157, 182. *See also Cost headings*

Project development: custom versus off-the-shelf, 209–210; in-house versus outsourced, 25; instructional design principles for, 87–105; milestones in, 172–173; roles and responsibilities for, 24–30; systematic design process for, 59–86; tools for, 30–34; user interface design strategies for, 107–130. *See also* ADDIE model; Development phase; Outsourced projects; Systematic design process

Project information, in script or storyboard, 74

Project kick-off, 172

Project management. *See* Management of technology-based training projects

Project manager: attributes of, 26; in client-vendor relationship, 170, 171; reference check on vendor's, 165; roles and responsibilities of, 26

Project schedules, 171

Project team: roles and responsibilities in, 24–30; total costs for equipping, 34. *See also* Roles and responsibilities

Proof of completion, automated, 23

Proposals: deadline for, 161; evaluation and selection of, 161–166, 174; request for, 160–161; sample, for Clinical Research Network Web-based training and tracking system, 273–285

Proprietary development tools, 169–170

ProTools, 32

Prototype, rapid. *See* Rapid prototype phase

Psychographics assessment, 65

Q

Quality review: internal (alpha test), 79–80; points of inspection in, 29–30

Review: of alpha version, 79–80; of pilot version, 80–81; of rapid prototype, 72–73

Revisions: based on formative evaluation, 80, 173; based on internal quality review, 79–80; complexity and costs of, 71, 80; examples of, 80; of script, 172, 173; of user interface, 171. *See also* Updates

RKA Management Results, 9, 227–246; analysis and design of, 229–235; assessment in, 231, 234, 238, 239, 241, 242–243; challenge met by, 229; collaboration in, 231, 244–245; constructivist approach in, 231; course features in, 231; course selection in, 236; curriculum content of, 229–231; electronic performance support tool from, 16–18; Gagné's events of instruction applied in, 238–239; guided tutorials in, 238–240; instructional design strategies of, 231, 233; interactivity objects in, 233, 239, 240; interviewing course of, 237–245; learning objectives for, 237; linear tutorials of, 231, 233; log-on to, 236; media decisions for, 232–233; menu system of, 235, 236; resources section of, 231, 243; simulations in, 231, 233–234, 240–241, 243; skill wizards in, 231, 234, 241, 244; student tracking in, 235, 243; target customers of, 229; technical requirements of, 232–233; theoretical solution of, 234–235; top-down design of, 235; tour of, 235–246; user benefits of, 246; user interface of, 235

Roberts, B., 134

Role-playing scenarios, 15; enhancement of, with full-motion video, 197; technical simulations for, 257

Roles and responsibilities: of administrators, 30; of audio and video producers, 29; of client-sponsor, 25–26; of graphic artist, 28; of instructional designer, 27; of programmer, 28–29; of project manager, 26; of project team, 24–30; of quality reviewers, 29–30; of subject matter expert, 26–27; of writer, 28

Rollout, 82–83; of CD-ROM-based training, 82; of Web-based training, 82

S

Safety training, cost savings of, 178

Safety training program, business impact measurement of, 86

Sales call simulation, 15, 16, 45

Sales increase, through technology-based training, 177–178

Sales training program: benefit analysis of, 147–148; business impact measurement of, 86; learner survey to evaluate, 85; main menu from, 112–113. *See also* Bingham-Rodway Pharmaco (BRP), Virtual Oncology Center

Satellite communications Web-based training program, sample script for, 336–343

Satellite connection bandwidths, 51

Satisfaction, and motivation, 102

Say What?, 242

Scanner, 31, 34

Scenarios, simulation, 15, 45. *See also* Simulations

Schedules, project, 171

Scheduling costs, 144

Scientific approach to instruction, 88–89. *See also* Learning theory

Scope creep, 71

Scorecard, vendor selection, 165–166

Scoring. *See* Assessment; Student tracking

Screen counters, 69, 74, 122, 126

Screen labels: coding of, 74; in script or storyboard, 74

Screen layout, 109; clear and logical, 120–122; principles of, 120; repetitive, 167; Z pattern of reading and, 120–121

Screen, pricing per, 156

Screen simulation, 220–221

Script writer. *See* Writer

Scripting software, 32

Scripts: defined, 74; development of, 74–77; elements of, 74, 76–77; revision of, 172; sample, 75, 337–344; vendor development of, 172–173

Scroller, 12

Seat time, 136, 139

Self Check: as object-oriented exercise, 242; on technology-based training, 34–37

Self-pacing: advantages of technology-based training and, 22, 23; in asynchronous Web-based training, 47, 48–49; page versus time measurement and, 126

Senior executives: needs and language of, 176–178; pitching benefits of technology-based training to, 176–178

Sensory storage, 110

Sensory system overload, 115

Sequence: delineation of, in content outline, 68; menu structure and, 112–113

Session number, 141

Shockwave. *See* Macromedia Shockwave

Short-term or working memory, 110–111; aids for, 110; mental models and metaphors and, 113–115

Silicon Graphics Maya, 33

Simple branching structure, tutorial, 13, 14

Simulations: in BevCo Office Orientation, 217, 220–223; CD-ROM-based, 45; constructivist approach of, 102–105, 195; examples of, 15; of expert coaches,

214, 215, 217–218, 222–223, 257–259, 260, 266; in Global Air Nexus, 252, 254–255, 257, 262, 263, 266; overview of, 13, 15; in RKA Management Results, 231, 233–234, 240–241, 243; sales call, 15, 16, 45; of situations involving failure, 195, 215, 254; types of, 15, 21; in Virtual Oncology Center, 195, 200–201, 202; as visual metaphors, 115, 116

Site map, 117

Size of audience, 136

Skill requirements, for project team members, 25–30

Skill wizards, 96, 231, 234, 241, 244

Slowdowns, status messages for, 109–110, 117

Smile sheets, 84

Socialization, in physical classrooms, 46

Society for Applied Learning Technology (SALT): conferences of, 158; contact information for, 318

Society for Insurance Trainers, 158

Socrates, 12

Software engine, 169–170

Software tools. *See* Technical requirements/specifications; Tools

Sound Forge, 32

Soundcards, 44

SoundEdit, 32

Soundproofing, 31

Source code: ownership of, 168; revision of, complexity of, 71, 80

Space exploration metaphor, 255–256. *See also* Global Air Nexus

Speakers, 66

Splash screen, 217–218, 257–258, 259

Sponsor. *See* Client-sponsor

STAR (fictitious software training program), 96–98

Status messages, 109–110, 117

Technical requirements (*continued*)
technology-based training, 30–31,
66–67; for *Technology-Based Training*
CD-ROM and Web links, 3–4; using
lowest common denominator, 232; for
Virtual Oncology Center, 194–195; for
Web-based training, 49–50

Technical support, 83; cost analysis of, 145;
information technology (IT) department and, 181

Technical training program, business impact measurement of, 86

Technological change, 1, 7, 10; in data
storage technologies, 40–41

Technology assessment, in analysis phase,
66–67

Technology-based learning (TBL), 10

Technology-based training (TBT): adult
learning theory and, 87–105; advantages of, to information technology departments, 179–181; advantages of, to
learners, 23, 176, 177; advantages of, to
organizations, 22–23, 176–185; advantages of, to trainers, 22–23, 176, 177;
branches of, 11–12; business case for,
181–183; CD-ROM delivery of, 39,
44–47; constituents of, and their interests, 177; constructivist approach to,
103–105; cost-benefit analysis for,
133–152; defined, 8; disadvantages of,
to learners, 24; disadvantages of, to organizations, 23–24, 176–178; drivers of,
9–10; growth in, 9–10, 134; historical
background of, 8–9, 39–44, 88–89; intellectual heritage of, 8–9; interactivity
in, 12, 21; internal marketing of, 82–83;
Internet resources for, 3, 4, 318–319,
320; modes of, 12–21; overview of,
7–37; selling, internally, 175–185; synonyms for, 10–11; systematic design

process for, 59–86; technologies for delivery of, 39–58; terms associated with,
10–12, 43–44; trade shows and conferences of, 158–159; transition to, barriers to, 175; types of, 12; unique features
of, 21–22; user interface design for,
107–130; Web delivery of, 10, 47–56.
See also CD-ROM-based training;
Mode of instruction; Web-based training

Technology issues: of learners, 24, 65; of
organizations, 23–24. *See also* Technical
requirement/specifications; Tools

Teleprompter, 32

10baseT, 52

Terminology, technology-based training,
10–12, 43–44

Tests, technology-based, 18–20, 119. *See
also* Assessment; Assessment, technology-based; Post-tests; Pretest; Student
tracking

Threaded discussions, 245

Title screen, 71

Toolbook, 33, 170

Tools: proprietary versus market, 169–170;
for technology-based training project
development, 30–34, 169–170; used in
BevCo Office Orientation development, 216–217; used in Virtual Oncology Center development, 197; for
Web-based training, 52. *See also* Technical requirements

Top-down designing, 235

Total cost comparison, 145–146

Total number of students, 138–139

Tournament Palace game, 264–265

Trade shows, finding vendors through,
158–159

Traditional delivery. *See* Instructor-led
training (ILT), traditional

Train-the-trainer costs, 141

Trainers: advantages of technology-based training to, 22–23; associations of, 157–158; disadvantages of technology-based training to, 23–24; Internet resources for, 318–319; marketing technology-based training to, 177; relationship between, and information technology professionals, 179, 180; trade shows and conferences of, 158–159. *See also* Vendors

Training, 7; advantages and limitations of technology-based, 21–24; investment in, 134; learning and, 10; learning theory and, 87–105; life of, 135–136; modes of, 12–21; value of, to corporations, 134

Training, 9, 89, 183, 227

Training Supersite, 319

Transfer of learning: enhancing retention and, 96, 98; evaluation of, 85; repetition and, 96

TCP/IP, 41, 44

Travel costs, 142–143

Trinity, 32

Tripods, 78

Tumor staging, 201–202

Tumor types, 192

Tutorials: complex branching structure of, 13, 14; EPSSs versus, 15; linear structure of, 13; overview of, 12–13, 14; simple branching structure of, 13, 14

U

Undo feature, 117–119

U.S. Department of Defense, 41

UOL Publishing, 320

Updatability: of CD-ROM-based training, 46, 47, 55, 56, 80; of Web-based training, 54–55, 56, 80

Updates: cost estimates of, 145, 169; timeline for, in Web-based training and CD-ROM-based training, 55. *See also* Revisions

User comments, examples of, 79–80

User evaluation form, 81, 84

User interface, 107–130; of BevCo Office Orientation, 216; checklists for, 129; consistent and logical design of, 120–126; defined, 108–109; description of, in script or storyboard, 77; design flaws in, 109–110; design of, 107–130; determination of, in design phase, 69–70; elements of, 108–109; exploratory type of, 196–197, 256; of Global Air Nexus, 255–256, 259–261; guidance and feedback mechanisms in, 126–128; human memory-based design of, 112–117; human memory processes and, 110–112; human sensory system overload and, 115; icon-driven, 235; importance of, 107, 108; items of, 69–70; keyboard support in, 119; mental models and, 113–115; menu system for, 112–113, 125–126; messages in, 109–110, 117, 123–125, 127–128; mouse support in, 119; multiple access points in, 115–117; on-screen visual objects in, 108, 109; revision of prototype, 171; of RKA Management Results, 235; sample, for discovery-learning experience, 103, 115, 116; screen layout in, 120–122; user control of, 117–119, 199; user frustrations with, 109–110; of Virtual Oncology Center, 196–197; visual cues in, 122–123; visual metaphors and, 113–115, 116

User support, 83

Utah State University, 88

V

Vendors: assumptions of, questioning, 157; checklist for working with, 173–174; company stability of, 159, 166; customer service of, 166; evaluating previous work of, 163; expense charges of, 169; experience of, 159; finding potential, 157–159; freelancer use by, 170; geographic location of, 157–158; instructional design understanding of, 159; kick-off meeting with, 172; narrowing the field of, 159; ownership issues with, 168–169; pricing of, 153–157, 161–162, 165, 166, 169; progress meetings with, 170–171; proprietary versus market tools of, 169–170; qualities to look for in, 159; quality of work of, 159, 166; reference checks of, 163–165; relationship ground rules for, 170–172; RFPs for, 160–161, 174; role setting and, 25; roles and responsibilities related to, 25, 26; sample proposal from, 273–285; scorecard of, 165–166; selection of, 161–166, 174; tricks and traps of, 168–170; working with, 153–174. *See also* Outsourced projects; Pricing, vendor; Proposals

Verbs for learning objectives, 99

Vertical slice, 71–72; flow chart of, 72

Video: in BevCo Office Orientation, 217–218; consistency in use of, 124–125; description of, in script, 76; editing of, 79; filenaming of, 78; production of, 78–79; for role-playing scenarios, 197; in Virtual Oncology Center, 197

Video equipment. *See* Audio-visual equipment and software

Video formats: assessment of, 67; for CD-ROM-based training, 44–45

Video, overuse of, 69

Video production, 78–79

Video shoots, 78, 171

Videoconferencing, 11, 55

Virtual diagnosis, 195, 200–201, 202

Virtual Oncology Center. *See* Bingham-Rodway Pharmaco (BRP), Virtual Oncology Center

Virtual reality, for simulations, 15

Visual cues, consistency in, 122–123

Visual Interdev, 33

Visual learners, 21–22

Visual metaphors, 113–115, 116. *See also* Metaphors and themes

Visual objects, in user interface, 108, 109. *See also* Graphic art

Voice-over audio, equipment for, 31–32

W

Warning messages, 128

Web-based training (WBT), 10, 47–56; advantages of, 53–55; asynchronous versus synchronous, 47–49; bandwidth issues in, 51–52, 53, 55–56, 67; case study of, for introducing new work processes, 247–268; case study of, for management training, 227–246; CD-ROM-based training combined with, in Global Air Nexus case study, 253; CD-ROM-based training versus, 45, 46, 53, 55, 56–58; cost-benefit ratio of, 151; decision tree for using multimedia in, 53; development tools for, 33; electronic performance support systems and, 16–18; growth in, 88–89; historical development of, 43–44, 88–89; indirect costs of, 138; Internet resources for, 320; limitations of, 55–56; model PowerPoint presentation of, 286–310; multimedia in, 53, 55–56; navigation bars in screens of, 121–122; plug-ins for, 52, 53, 67; questions for selection of, 58; return on investment of, 151–152; rollout of, 82; samples of, Web sites for, 320; synchronous versus asynchronous, 47–49; technical requirements for, 49–50; total expenditures on, 88–89; updatability of, 54–55

Web-Based Training Cookbook (Hall), 33

Web-Based Training Information Center, 320

Web browsers: advent of, 42–43; comparison and versions of, 49–50; as interface to Internet and Intranet education, 44; plug-ins for, 52, 53, 67; sample interface of, 50; Web-based training requirements for, 49–50

Web connections: assessment of, 67; bandwidths of various, 51; types of, 50

Web developers, 79

Web links, technology-based training, 3, 4, 183, 318–319

Web pages, 42–43; historical development of Internet, 42–43; historical development of Intranet, 43–44

Whisper Booth, 31

Wide-angle shots, 78

Windows 95, 66; for CD-ROM-based training, 44; graphical user interface and, 108; for Web-based training, 49

Wizards, 96, 231, 234, 241, 244

Work processes training program. *See* Global Air Nexus

Workplace behavior, 85

World Wide Web, history and development of, 41–43

Writer: attributes of, 28; roles and responsibilities of, 28

Writing software, 32

Y

Yes and no buttons, 119

YMCA, 89–90

Z

Z pattern of reading, 120–121

Zemke, R., 88, 89

Ziff Davis, 183

Ziff Davis University, 320

Zip disks, 40

ABOUT THE AUTHORS

KEVIN KRUSE, a principal of Raymond Karsan Associates' Performance Solutions Group, is an internationally recognized consultant, speaker, and author. His clients have included Du Pont, Johnson & Johnson, Merrill Lynch, Prudential Insurance, and SmithKline Beecham. His articles have appeared in *Corporate University Review, Multimedia & Internet-Based Training, Technical Training,* and *Training & Development.* Kruse can be reached via e-mail at kkruse@aol.com or at kkruse.raymondkarsan.com.

JASON KEIL, a graduate of Rutgers College, is an instructional designer at Raymond Karsan Associates. His technology-based training designs have been used by BASF, Delta Airlines, Liberty Mutual, and Wyeth Ayerst, among others.

ABOUT RAYMOND KARSAN ASSOCIATES

Raymond Karsan Associates, an *Inc.* 500 company, provides innovative human resource solutions that achieve measurable business results. RKA offers award-winning courseware development services, as well as off-the-shelf solutions, in a variety of delivery formats: Intranet/Internet, multimedia CD-ROM, and interactive workshops. For more information call 800–614–2211 or visit <www.raymondkarsan.com>.